ARCHAEOLOGY AT CERROS
BELIZE, CENTRAL AMERICA

David A. Freidel
Series Editor

ARCHAEOLOGY AT CERROS BELIZE, CENTRAL AMERICA

Volume I
An Interim Report

Volume Editors

Robin A. Robertson
David A. Freidel

Contributors
Helen Sorayya Carr
Maynard B. Cliff
Cathy J. Crane
David A. Freidel
James F. Garber
Sue Lewenstein
Beverly A. Mitchum
Robin A. Robertson
Vernon L. Scarborough

SOUTHERN METHODIST UNIVERSITY PRESS ● 1986

ARCHAEOLOGY AT CERROS, BELIZE, CENTRAL AMERICA
VOLUME I, AN INTERIM REPORT

Copyright © 1986 by Southern Methodist University Press
Dallas, Texas 75275
Printed in the United States of America

The paper in this book meets the standards for permanence and durability
established by the Committee on Production Guidelines for Book Longevity
of the Council on Library Resources.

Library of Congress Cataloguing-in-Publication Data

Archaeology at Cerros, Belize, Central America.

    Bibliography: v. 1 p.
    Contents: v. 1. An interim report / volume editors,
Robin A. Robertson, David A. Freidel ; contributors,
Helen Sorayya Carr . . . [et al.]
    1. Cerros Site (Belize) 1. Mayas—Antiquities.
3. Indians of Central America—Belize—Antiquities.
4. Belize—Antiquities. I. Freidel, David A.
II. Robertson, Robin A. III. Carr, Helen Sorayya.
F1435.1.C43A73   1986   972.82′1   86-3843
ISBN 0-87074-214-0 (v.1)

COVER ILLUSTRATION:

Reconstruction drawings of the modeled stucco and paint panels on the southwestern side of Structure 5C-2nd.
Drawings and interpretation by David Freidel based upon field drawings and photographs.
Inking and color formating by Karim Sadr. Stipple = red; white = cream; horizontal hatching = pink;
vertical stipple = yellow.

To Alayne — the Classic
that Cerros never revealed.

CONTENTS

PREFACE

The site of Cerros, called Cerro Maya in some early reports and variously referred to as the "bluff" and "Milagros" by local people in Corozal District, has been a lesson in humility for the archaeologists investigating it since 1974. Armed with the ideals of the New Archaeology, researchers were prepared to go into the field with problems in mind and methods in hand. We came with the methods, but the problems changed frequently in the course of work. Under the original direction of Ira R. Abrams, the archaeological research was conceived as part of a larger anthropological enterprise focusing on the modern people of Corozal District. Research at Cerros was to be carried out in conjunction with a resort to be developed around the site. As these plans faded, the archaeologists were left to investigate what appeared to be a most intriguing site.

The original research design anticipated that Cerros was a Late Classic or Postclassic community, given the strategic role of Corozal Bay in Late Postclassic commerce and examination of the site by other professionals in Belize (Hammond 1974). Our first season witnessed the completion of a topographic map of the center and some surrounding mounds, but the test pitting program aimed at establishing a preliminary chronology proved frustrating. The Postclassic was certainly there, but only in surface deposits. The Classic, both Early and Late, was surprisingly ephemeral. In fact, the only substantially represented period was the Late Preclassic, most visible along the erosion of the east main plaza, Structure 2A.

I recall exhorting the crew in some desperation to get out and find the Classic. When I complained to Ira Abrams about the lack of Classic remains in our sample, he replied, "if it looks like a duck and quacks like a duck . . ." Nothing in my training had prepared me to contemplate a hiatus right through the apogee of Maya civilization at a Maya center.

Armed with the improbable hypothesis that the major period of occupation was indeed the Late Preclassic, we set about testing the summits of the largest pyramids on the principle that if these proved to be Late Preclassic in age, there must be a major community at the site in that period. The test on Structure 3 drew a blank; the test on Structure 4 yielded a complicated and problematic deposit; but the test on Structure 6, the second largest pyramid, hit pay dirt in the form of a dedicatory offering dating to the Late Preclassic period. I do not recommend such "wildcat" sampling, for had we placed the trench 25 cm to the east, the Cerros Project would likely have ended in 1975. Systematic sampling is an ideal suited to well-funded, long-term projects. Determining whether or not a site is worth such effort, on meager funds, requires as much luck as planning.

After this first big surprise, we should have been on our guard for more surprises. The surprises continued and, in actuality, many of our discoveries are as much attributable to our ability to keep an open mind and the practical constraints of our data as to *a priori* design. The intensive investigation of function in pottery, and the equally intensive appraisal of typology in a single period, was in concert with the overwhelming size of the Late Preclassic sample relative to those from other periods. This development both demanded and allowed departure from the more usual chronological concerns of ceramicists.

The discovery of termination rituals, primary deposits on structures laid down at the time of refurbishment or abandonment, derived from the tight control on provenience demanded by our Laboratory Supervisor, and from our concern to make the most of these deposits in light of the nearly sterile construction fill and infrequent primary offerings in monuments. Because most finds of jade occurred as little broken pieces rather than as beautiful, finished artifacts, a lot of time was spent studying them. It was discovered that they could be fitted back together, showing that they had been intentionally broken rather than lost, and that they represented primary, rather than secondary, deposits. In retrospect, it is a lovely example of "Behavioral Archaeology" in action.

Mapping in the settlement zone had to be carried out in heavy secondary growth, which encouraged close examination of small undulations in the surface. This perspective, and the open mind of the surveyor, led to the discovery of the canal perimeter and eventually to the complicated hydraulic system pervading Cerros. The importance of drainage, currently poor now that the Preclassic system is mostly silted in, was impressed upon the surveyor when he tried to explore the settlement during his first summer rainy season and found himself chest deep in swamp.

The nucleated village underlying the center at Cerros began, in our perception, as a massive midden. Through pains-taking care in excavation and recording—an infinitely patient and slow pace of work I often found frustrating in my concern to cover a lot of ground with limited time and funds—the investigator in charge unraveled what is at this time the most complicated residential deposit in the Maya lowlands. This discovery that the "midden" was a village with a long and rich history of development opens up interesting prospects for other "middens" reported to underlie Maya ceremonial centers.

It was a general disappointment to me and the crew to find that every time we tested monumental architecture we found loose boulder fill, clean marl capping, and at best two construction episodes. It took some time to realize that the absence of an exquisitely complicated construction sequence did not signify a lack of data. The dramatic contrast between the village deposits and the simple monumental sequence eventually registered, and the simplicity of the monuments can be regarded as their most important empirical attribute: the ceremonial center at Cerros went up in an explosion of social energy.

The same process of discovery can be found in every aspect of research at Cerros. At every stage we discussed the significance of our information and the directions it was taking us. Gradually we learned to expect the unexpected, and, in the process, we had to divest ourselves of many ideas about what a Maya community looked like, how it developed, how Maya behaved, and how deposits were created. We generated and tested hypotheses at every step; but as often as not, the received wisdom dictating what could or could not occur as a possibility was off the mark. We learned that to discover is not to test, and that this former process requires a certain trust in perceived patterns in data, whether or not they fit the premises of hypotheses.

Some of what we know about Cerros is presented in this volume of papers. There is a great deal more information in the process of being analysed. In general, we can attest to the fact that Cerros straddles the threshhold from village agricultural life into the first great florescence of lowland Maya civilization in the Late Preclassic period. When we began research at the site, the Late Preclassic period was regarded (with notable exceptions, cf. Coe 1965) as a period of incipient complexity anticipating the Classic era.

Through current research on many sites, we know that Cerros was part of a regional society as powerful and complex in many respects as the Classic civilization which followed. More than ever, I suspect that Cerros holds typical to the regional development. To be sure, some Maya communities evince elitism and public ritual earlier than the Late Preclassic period. Yet the emergence of a social elite and central life as a regional presence with all the material concomitants of such change in material culture, settlement patterns, subsistence, and so forth, occurs in the Late Preclassic period.

If Cerros is typical, then despite centuries of earlier forays into elitism, and despite centuries of societies evincing elitism in public monuments surrounding the lowlands in a crescent of complexity, Maya civilization banged into existence in its own way and time. Considering that we have long known that the southern lowland Maya banged out of existence in a collapse, we should not be too surprised by this development. But it is unsettling. For it violates the tacit rules of diffusion and, even worse, the tacit rules of gradual evolution espoused by modern archaeology. Moreover, the notion of a society springing up in a territory ten times the size of the Basin of Mexico as a coherent totality violates the rules of spread and consolidation out of "breakthrough" areas endowed with the natural and social potential for mutation.

Finally, the Late Preclassic civilization now coming into focus differs from the Classic civilization in a fundamental way. The elite governing the Late Preclassic society is virtually anonymous, while that governing Classic Society is portrayed in every conceivable medium. The progression from one form to the other is neither logical nor necessary. The elites of many ancient civilizations were content to govern anonymously throughout their histories. No doubt there are reasons to be discovered for this transformation, but it is potentially as perplexing as the rise of Maya civilization in the first instance. Cerros, and some other known Late Preclassic centers, failed to pass over this second threshold; still others survived and flourished. In the last analysis, there is a lot to know about Maya civilization's beginnings from the work at Cerros, but the data generate more questions than answers—which of course is what one hopes for in field research.

David A. Freidel
Dallas, Texas
March 1, 1986

ACKNOWLEDGMENTS

The research at Cerros resulted from the hard work, inspiration, and encouragement of a very large number of people. The senior staff, represented in this volume, made the discoveries and gathered the data we have on the site. Ira Abrams brought the project into being. John Love paid for the critical first two seasons of research and saw to it that the site was donated to Belize. Tim Cullum and Richard Sandow sustained the Cerro Maya Foundation which provided vital support over the years. Stanley Marcus of Dallas, Texas, and the many supporters he brought to our project, underwrote an improbable dream of what Cerros might be. We are grateful for the continued support of these individuals, without whose help the publication of this volume would have been much more difficult. Additional funding for the production of this first volume in the Cerros series was provided by the Provost's Office of Southern Methodist University.

The National Science Foundation (BNS-77-07959, 78-24708; BNS-78-15905; BNS-82-17620), and, through the Foundation, our colleagues in Mesoamerican archaeology, provided the bulk of support for the project after the 1976 season. The Department of Archaeology in Belize, under the aegis of Joe Palacio, Jaime Awe, Elizabeth Graham Pendergast, and Harriot Topsey, provided encouragement and full cooperation at every stage of research. The many student members of the crew and the more than fifty men from the villages of Chunux, Copperbank, and Xaibe in Corozal District deserve special thanks for their care and devotion under difficult field conditions.

Much credit for the difficult transition from manuscript to book must go to the AnthroGraphics Laboratory of SMU and to Southern Methodist University Press. We especially appreciate the efforts of Chris Christopher and Maria Masucci (who managed to complete the composition and layout of this volume while continuing with their own graduate studies), and June Schelling, who accomplished much of the early production of galleys.

INTRODUCTION

David A. Freidel

As an interim report, this volume provides a bridge between the several articles which have already treated aspects of the research and the book-length monographs that will follow. For reasons beyond the control of the individual contributors, the book has been overlong in production. Hence, some interpretations in the chapters are more preliminary than others. On the bright side, the final result is rather more polished than originally anticipated. The timing has also engendered the confident expectation that the first volume of the Cerros monograph series will roll off the presses within a year of this publication. This work is not only interim but also introductory to the majority of authors and special fields of inquiry that will be found in the series.

THE ARCHAEOLOGIES AT CERROS

Traditionally, monograph series on long-term research in our area have included substantial introductions either as separate contributions or attached to the first major technical reports. Introductions cover such salient details as environment, history of research, field logistics, and so forth, which have been telegraphed in articles and embroidered upon in dissertations. Not to disappoint the sense of propriety or the curiosity of our readers, such material will be briefly reiterated here. My coverage will be somewhat perfunctory, however, as similar material will necessarily accompany each monograph. Furthermore, the following papers also perform the service of introducing method and data. Last, I would like to take this opportunity to consider some problems and prospects peculiar to an overview of archaeology at Cerros.

In particular, it is becoming apparent as analysis proceeds that different studies are going to yield different conclusions about key themes such as the status of Cerros as a trading community, the function of land modification in the settlement zone, and the nature of external political and religious relationships. In some cases these conclusions are likely to be contradictory; in others they will be merely perplexing. It

might be more accurate to think in terms of the archaeologies at Cerros rather than of some unitary view.

The notion of archaeologies at Cerros should not be as disturbing as some might find it at first glance. The epistemologies of different studies vary as they focus on different aspects of the data. Different kinds of past behavior created the total record. Moreover, activities at a complex community such as Cerros often must have had conflicting or competing aims. Contention and coherence were equally aspects of the dynamics of the community. Both should register in the archaeological record. Better to contemplate such abstractions further by means of the more tangible and concrete problems of the research, for the emerging patterns are also the product of the history and organization of the project.

CERROS, THE PLACE

The ruins of Cerros are situated on a narrow spit of low-lying and swampy land called Lowry's Bight (Figs. 1 and 2). The bight is sandwiched between brackish Languna Seca and the turbulent Corozal extension of Chetumal Bay. To the west and south of the site is the present mouth of the New River, and the largest mound, Structure 4, is a well-known landmark called the Bluff, which signals the approach to the river from the Bay. Presently, the central rock mass of public construction forms a small peninsula jutting out into the bay. Severe wave action has eroded the softer earthen flanks which housed the dispersed community. The government bench mark on top of Structure 4 is recorded to be at 18°21'00" north latitude, 88°21'10" west longitude.

The geology of northern Belize is ably reported by A. C. S. Wright and his colleagues (1959). The relevant details for the vicinity of Cerros are summarized in Cliff (1982) and Scarborough (1980). Generally, Cerros stands on a moderately consolidated Pliocene coral limestone bedrock of less than 5m relief. Of the soil types found on Lowry's Bight, the Louisville set (Wright et al. 1959:64–65, 211) is especially important because these black clay beds often have indurated caprock parent coral. That this caprock was the major building material for public construction at Cerros is indicated by the mines and stockpiles of such rock found abandoned a few meters east and south of the center (c.f., Scarborough 1980: Appendix A; Scarborough 1983:725). Scarborough suggests (1983) that the original setting for the community was higher well-drained terrain which was drastically lowered by quarrying for construction. This modification was in part off-set by the elaborate system of drainage developed at the site (Scarborough, this volume).

Although Wright and his colleagues (1959:63) characterize the present soils on Lowry's Bight as mediocre for agricultural purposes, Crane's work in progress (this volume) shows that the people of Cerros consumed a variety of agricultural and aboricultural products, and any observation as to what the Maya found on the Bight must await completion of her systematic palynological studies. An intriguing perplexity in the works (Crane, personal communication, 1985) is the failure of any analyzed samples from the field features bordering the main canal to yield economic pollen. Whether this is a sampling problem, a disputation of the function of these features as agricultural plots, or an indication that the fields were never finished (like some other features at the site), remains to be seen.

While the Maya at Cerros no doubt practiced agriculture and hunted wild game, a key feature of the place was its location at or near the mouth of the New River on Chetumal Bay. Carr's work in progress (this volume) shows that the inhabitants were fishermen exploiting not only the local riverine, estuary, and bay environments, but also in all likelihood the cays bordering coastal Belize. Although the proportion of the diet provided by seafood remains to be determined, it was no doubt substantial.

Fishermen use boats, and the Maya used dug-out canoes. In addition to the fact that Belize is famous for its logging industry, and northern Belize was no exception, Lewenstein's work on the function of stone tools (this volume) suggests extensive wood-working at Cerros. It is likely, then, that there were stocks of suitable wood in the near vicinity of the community for the production of canoes and other common artifacts. Crane's analyses of wood charcoal will help elucidate which species were favored at Cerros. Plant inven-

tories are given in Crane's chapter for the contemporary setting.

As discussed by Wright and others (1959) and summarized by Cliff (1982:180–183), the area of Cerros is relatively dry compared with the rest of Belize. Less than 152 cm of rain falls annually. In this "dry tropical environment," four months a year average less than 5.08 cm of rainfall, producing delightful working conditions for field archaeology in the Maya lowlands. Nevertheless, the place also has some spectacular downpours. Three months of the year average more than 15 cm of rain each. For modern inhabitants such as ourselves, this means serious swamp conditions are created in the immediate vicinity, giving rise to a population of mosquitoes rivalling any in Maya country. The ancient inhabitants must have had similar problems. Scarborough (1983) suggests that while the elaborate system of artificial drainage built at Cerros would have helped, the potential volume of a June storm could quite exceed the estimated capacity of the system as mapped. Either the people at Cerros got their feet wet in the rainy season or there was more to the system than we observed. Only further investigation can decide the matter. Surely the hydraulic system helped to even out the comparatively extreme fluctuation in available fresh water as experienced by our expedition.

Our paleoecological studies show that the ancient inhabitants of Cerros effectively exploited their environment and, indeed, showed considerable ingenuity and effort in doing so. In addition to the system of fields and canals within the community, there are fields less than a kilometer from the center in the direction of the New River's mouth (Scarborough, this volume). In contrast to the fields directly associated with the center, which are oriented to the cardinal points, these others are oriented to the present coastline of the bay directly northward. Although some Early Classic material was found in the vicinity, we have no clear and substantive dating for these latter fields. An Early Classic construction of fields so close to Cerros would be quite perplexing. People continued to live at the site through the Early Classic period, but all evidence points to an occupation by a squatter population which did not even bother to refurbish the masonry platforms before occupying them. In addition, Scarborough's work on the hydraulic system within the community strongly suggests that it rapidly deteriorated following the Late Preclassic collapse of Cerros as a political capital (Scarborough, this volume, Scarborough 1983, Freidel

1983). It is hard to imagine such a group launching a major construction program near the mouth of the river. On the other hand, the orientation of those fields to the river and bay suggests that here, as elsewhere in Classic period northern Belize (B. L. Turner II, 1983), the fields were designed for flow relative to a body of fresh water. Such a system is different in principle from that seen inside the community (Scarborough 1983). Doubtless the Preclassic Maya were familiar with more than one way to juxtapose water and land, but the dating issue remains unresolved with respect to these riverine fields. In any case, the swampy environs of the site could have been significantly upgraded through such intensive techniques.

The matter of fresh water fronting Lowry's Bight raises a final unresolved issue concerning Cerros the place. Was the Preclassic community founded on an open bay such as presently exists, or was it on a calmer lagoon behind the mouth of the river such as can be found directly upstream of the present mouth of the New River? Unfortunately, the project was unable to bring in the appropriate geological experts to settle the matter unequivocally. Cliff (1982) regards the open bay hypothesis as most parsimonious since it requires no drastic change in the coastline between the Preclassic and the present. On the other hand, the substantial exploitation of freshwater welk (Carr, this volume, and A. Andrews, personal communication), the raised fields fronting the present bay near the mouth of the river, and the dearth of jars appropriate to water transport in the earliest phase of occupation which is right next to the water (Robertson-Freidel 1981:281), all point to the lagoon hypothesis. In either case, it is documented by Cliff (this volume) that the original community was founded directly next to a body of water, and this location at the mouth of the New River was clearly strategic with regard to a culturally defined resource: transportation and communication.

The extent to which the people of Cerros took advantage of this location is a matter of continuing evaluation and analysis. It was definitely a factor in the development of the SMU research project at the site, originally designed to mitigate the impact of a tourist resort to be built on Lowry's Bight.

THE CERROS PROJECT: A BRIEF HISTORY

The site of Cerros was briefly discussed and placed on the map of northern Belize by Hammond (1973) in his regional survey. Before that, Gann (1900:686) makes a vague allusion to "lookout" mounds along the coast, a category which probably included Structure 4 at the site. A number of professional archaeologists had visited Cerros, including Raymond Sidrys and Bruce Dahlins, and Mary Nievens of the University of the Americas was initiating research at the site when it was bought by Metroplex Corporation of Dallas. Metroplex hired SMU to carry out work there, and Nievens proceeded to investigate the substantial site of El Posito to the south of Orange Walk Town. Metroplex intended to build a tourist resort surrounding a restored ceremonial center. While these plans did not work out, the owners deeded over the property to the Belizean government, facilitating continued research there.

Although it was clear to observers that Cerros was a major center by Belizean standards, the extent and age of the site were not known when the SMU investigations began. Raymond Sidrys (personal communication, 1985) says that he showed some beach sherds to Leroy Joesink-Mandeville, who immediately recognized them as Chicanel in age, but this is the only hint that anyone anticipated the site's antiquity. We worked on the assumption that the site was late, probably Postclassic (although it looked nothing like the East Coast sites dating to that era). Our first summer season in 1974 was devoted to mapping the center and testing the plaza areas for architectural stratigraphy and ceramic chronology. By the end of that season, it was clear that the site had a major Preclassic component. In a second brief season in the spring of 1975, we tested the hypothesis that the major construction of mounds took place in the Preclassic. After some spectacular corroboration of that idea in the form of a Late Preclassic dedicatory offering cached at the summit of the second largest mound, Structure 6, our attention focused on doing as much as we could with a Preclassic community.

Despite originally grandiose plans for research at Cerros under the auspices of Metroplex, the first three seasons at the site were small scale. Assuming that every season was the last one, we aimed at maximizing our information. We did not have the luxury of long-term planning until the National Science Foundation funded the fourth and fifth seasons. Even then, it was not until well into the fifth season that a resubmission to NSF was planned for further work. Several factors mitigated the potentially disastrous effects of such a hand-to-mouth existence. First, the project was blessed from the start with some very well-organized key personnel, Robertson and Cliff; and it acquired a core of highly dedicated and skilled staff who stayed with the project throughout its duration. These loyalists are represented in this volume and the following series of monographs. Robertson and Freidel established the field nomenclature, and Robertson, drawing on extensive previous laboratory experience, established the laboratory recording system. Despite some hitches, these rather unwieldy systems served us well and continue to do so. James Webb, the original surveyor, contributed a professional-quality base map of the center before leaving the project.

The allocation of final responsibility for segments of the research accumulated with the longevity of the project and our increasingly ambitious goals in the field. From the outset, Robertson planned to study the ceramics for her dissertation at Harvard. Cliff and Webb were slated for dissertation research as well. Webb, as surveyor, logically was assigned the settlement patterns at the site. Maynard Cliff was given the deposits underlying Feature 2A because they were clearly rich in data and he is a particularly adept and patient field observer. This decision subsequently guided our field priorities toward more extensive and intensive exposure of the nucleated village. At the time, this followed rationally from the high information content of the context. In retrospect, the striking contrast in spatial organization evinced by the nucleated village and the later dispersed community set the stage for a theoretical focus on the transformation of Cerros from a simple village into a complex political center.

The monumental architecture was also a focus from the beginning of the project. Over the years of the project, the public buildings remained a focus because their early date in Maya civilization made them an object of special interest. The buildings, with their elaborate decoration, have required me to embark on a long-term study of Maya iconography and epigraphy to arrive at functional interpretations of the construction, use, and destruction of these ritual places.

At the end of our second season the future of the project still remained uncertain despite success in documenting major Late Preclassic construction at Cerros. The intervening period was spent devising means of maximizing data for the committed students and in raising funds for a third season. That third season was funded by members of the Dallas and Fort Worth communities, primarily through the efforts of Stanley Marcus, T. Tim Cullum, and Richard Sandow. In the summer of 1976, I hoped to garner enough information

to substantiate the hypothesis that Cerros was a Late Preclassic community.

Despite the replacement of our surveyor, Jim Webb, with Vernon Scarborough during this summer season, torrential rains in June forced us to sharply curtail settlement pattern survey in favor of excavation. Working, as I exhorted the staff, from the known to the unknown, we opened up extensive exposures in the nucleated village and on Structures 4 and 6. The former work documented the fact that the deposits underlying the eastern plaza were indeed remains of a settlement dating exclusively to the Late Preclassic period. The latter work confirmed the presence of decorated architecture dating to the Late Preclassic at Cerros— although the facades on Structure 6B were not in a good state of preservation. The surprising discovery of polychrome painted decoration on some well-preserved elements, the clear use of outset stairways (a Classic period convention contrasting with the partially inset stairways of Late Preclassic Tikal and Uaxactun), and the overall sophistication of the decoration encouraged the notion that Cerros in particular, and northern Belize in general, actively participated in the establishment of Maya civilization in the lowlands and were not passive recipients of high culture from the Peten in Guatemala.

By the end of three brief field seasons we had established that Cerros had major public architecture dating to the Late Preclassic period containing rich exotic offerings and decorated with sophisticated symbolism. We also knew that there was a complex residential zone underlying the east plaza, Feature 2, and extensive occupation of the surrounding area which also dated to Late Preclassic times. It was in light of these findings that I devised the hypothesis that Cerros participated in a regional interaction sphere responsible for the simultaneous emergence of hierarchical society in many natural settings across the lowlands. This idea, and the corollary that Cerros was a trading community, formed the framework for the NSF-funded fourth and fifth seasons. In general, the broad principle of regional emergence has received growing support both at Cerros and elsewhere in the lowlands. That Cerros was a major trading port and that political and economic centrality were necessarily congruent in Maya society remain more problematic propositions.

In our proposal to the NSF, I included James Garber along with Robertson, Cliff, and Scarborough. Following success with that proposal, I also invited

Beverly Mitchum and Sue Lewenstein to join the project staff. Numerous other graduate and undergraduate students worked hard in the field, but these particular individuals sustained long-term commitment and are represented in this volume. Subsequent years saw Sorayya Carr and Cathy Crane join the project. Although it progressed in piecemeal fashion, the allocation of data and the establishment of research topics at Cerros followed the traditional divisions in Maya archaeology: major contexts, settlement patterns, monuments, and artifacts by material. These imposed divisions facilitate comparison of the Cerros results with findings from other projects and will necessarily condition the views we construct of ancient Maya behavior at the site. But while fragmenting the total can distort, we hope that it might also clarify by isolating the pervasive patterns generated by the Cerros inhabitants themselves—patterns such as the termination rituals discussed below. The fruits of comparative analysis within the project, however, usually followed the field experience. While we worked the site, compelling discoveries often guided our evolving research strategy.

Important discoveries made during the 1977 and 1978 seasons included the extraordinarily decorated Structures 5C-2nd and 29, Structure 2A-Sub.2, a large and low platform next to the water associated with the original nucleated village which could have functioned as a docking facility, and a massive artificial canal designed as a perimeter of the dispersed settlement zone and draining the low-lying area around the center. Our data suggested that all of these features were part of the Late Preclassic community and served to confirm the magnitude of Cerros in that period. The docking facility, along with retrieval of imported ceramics and far-flung stylistic affinities in that medium, reinforced the notion of Cerros as a trading community. The canal indicated the extent of the labor force available to the community and showed that we were dealing with a virtually intact totality rather than just a fragment of a Late Preclassic society. Further, the discovery of elaborate decoration on Structure 29, a large building out in the dispersed settlement zone, showed that public space was embedded in this final Late Preclassic community. This evidence shifted our attention from documenting the existence of an early complex community to discerning its internal organization in space.

By the end of an over-long and exhausting season in the spring and summer of 1978, it was clear to me that we needed substantially more data from Cerros to do justice to its preservation. The empirical desirability of acquiring more information on the dispersed and nucleated settlement zones combined with a discovery in the field and one in the laboratory to yield a revised framework for a new proposal to NSF. In the field, a large trench through the basal substructure of Structure 4 failed to produce the intricate layering of gradual modifications we had expected. Instead, the evidence pointed to a single massive effort over a much smaller and unreachable initial phase of construction. In the lab, Robertson's ceramic analysis showed that both the nucleated village underlying the center and the later complicated and dispersed community associated with the center dated to the Late Preclassic period, with clear typological continuities linking them. In other words, the people who built the closely packed residences and small public platforms of the nucleated village were the immediate ancestors of the people who built the massive pyramids and lived in dispersed households. It seemed that Cerros had undergone a dramatic transformation from an egalitarian fishing and trading community to the cosmopolitan political capital of a hierarchical society in the course of the Late Preclassic period. This notion of a rapid "jump" into the status of civilized at Cerros has stood the test of further fieldwork and analysis.

The field testing of direct concomitants, such as evidence for elite residences and for changes in economic organization, proved perplexing and surprising. For example, although excavation of Structure 11B in 1977 supported the idea of a residential elite in the dispersed settlement zone, excavation in other elaborate multi-building groups during the 1979 season did not substantiate a pattern of large elite household compounds. Instead, the groups we dug in 1979 turned out to be ballcourts—demonstrating an even more complicated pattern of public space in the dispersed settlement zone than previously envisioned. To add to the confusion, Lewenstein (1984) has recently argued that one of the two end court buildings associated with the largest ballcourt, the Structure 50 group, is indeed residential in function based upon trash deposits. If she is correct, then the tandem plan "range structure" or "palace" of the Classic period may have its antecedents at Cerros. If Structure 50D is a "range structure," this would also point to complicated combinations of dwellings and public buildings at the outset of Maya civilization—a pattern also seen in the subsequent periods of Maya history. It is possible that the homes of the Cerros elite were embedded in public places which, in turn, were embedded in the larger residential community. Unfortunately, excavation of the elaborate hydraulic system (Scarborough 1983), was a priority in the settlement zone that necessitated curtailing extensive horizontal exposure of many of the structure groups needed to adequately explore this possibility during the final 1979 and 1981 seasons.

On the other hand, the complex residential deposit of the nucleated village revealed a trend of increasingly elaborate domestic architecture concomitant with indicators of more wealth and status in the community. Cliff (in press, 1982) has cogently argued that increased investment of labor and wealth in housing began as a means of obscuring differences in status. People built artificial platforms for dwellings that replicated the natural mounding of more established house sites in the community. The dynamics of social change in the several centuries of occupation of that nucleated village will be treated in Cliff's monograph. Suffice it to say here that the general proposition that the social structure was changing is fully corroborated. In the end, the village district underlying the east plaza was evidently restricted to elite residences and associated public buildings. One of the public buildings discovered in 1979, Structure 2A-Sub.4-1st, proved both a link and a punctuation between the village phase and the temple town phase at Cerros.

SOCIAL CHANGE AND CULTURAL PERCEPTION AT CERROS

Structure 2A-Sub.4-1st is a small pyramid that displayed the basic accoutrements of Maya public architecture: apron moldings, inset panels, basal moldings, outset stairways, red-painted stucco. More importantly, its orientation was closely duplicated in the massive acropolis Structure 4 directly west of it. Since Structure 4 is the only major pyramid at Cerros to face in this direction, it seems highly likely that it was designed to replicate and replace the smaller building— if not immediately, then through the mediation of an intervening smaller structure deeply buried within it. Structure 2A-Sub.4-1st documents conclusively that temple architecture was initially built as a component of the nucleated community before the center-dispersed settlement pattern was established. Further,

the design and orientation of that structure provide a clear link to the later center.

Excavation of Structure 2A-Sub.4-1st revealed not only architectural continuity, but clear evidence of ritual continuity between the earlier and later community as well. Termination ritual activity on public architecture represents a genuine emic pattern identified first through distinctive ceramic types associated with heavy marl deposits on the outer surfaces of buildings, then further confirmed and corroborated through other associated artifact types (Robertson-Freidel 1980; Garber 1981). The implications of having primary, single-event deposits on the outer and unsealed surfaces of buildings could be far-reaching in Maya archaeology. Fortunately for us, by the time we excavated Structure 2A-Sub.4-1st we knew that such deposits existed at Cerros. Hence the quantities of smashed pottery, burned areas, layered marl, and other artifacts were very carefully recorded in space (Cliff, this volume). Subsequently, Robertson and her students discovered fits between pottery fragments that suggested a sustained ritual event beginning with the official termination of Structure 2A-Sub4-1st and ending with its burial (Robertson 1983:112). Extensive connections beyond the immediate area of the pyramid into the east plaza Feature 2A were indicated as well. The notion that the residential area of the nucleated community was also terminated ritually received further independent support from Garber's discovery of smashed jade in the final deposits on the surface of the village (Garber 1983). Finally, Cliff's excavations in the nucleated village (Cliff 1982) determined that the main east plaza Feature 2A was designed just to cover and bury the easternmost dwellings in the community; the eastern edge of this plaza is clearly not oriented to the cardinal directions but rather is angled in a manner consistent with this objective.

In brief, the elaborate termination of Structure 2A-Sub.4-1st was not only a singular and deliberate ritual event, it was apparently also a component in a much larger singular event: the ritual termination of the nucleated community as such (Cliff, this volume). No doubt the act was symbolic of social change rather than a reflection of political collapse or demographic abandonment. The later community flourished. The termination of the village documents the hypothesized transformation at Cerros. It shows a self-conscious, deliberate change from one social and spatial organization to another. What did this spectacular punctuation mean to the Maya who acknowledged it? In my opinion, this question is as answerable as the traditional archaeological questions of material cause behind such change.

In the final, 1981, field season at Cerros we managed to anchor the core sequence of central public architecture into the nucleated village. What we discovered was that the spectacular termination of the eastern district of the village was paralleled by an equally spectacular inauguration of a new ritual—and by inference, political—order at Cerros. Structure 5C-2nd and its low fronting plaza Structure 5A-Sub 1 were constructed directly upon remains of perishable buildings in the nucleated community. Structure 5C-2nd established a north and south center line for the entire larger dispersed community at Cerros, an axis forming the spatial armature for all further public construction there. Further, Structure 5C-2nd displayed a complete cosmogram (Freidel and Schele, in press) with the ancestral sun and Venus Hero Twins arrayed hierarchically and flanked by the symbols of power and sacrifice wielded by Lowland monarchs for the next thousand years. Whatever the economic organization of Cerros after this, there can be no doubt that it was a political capital of a society recognizing a nobility and a rudimentary form of monarchy.

It would be only logical to suppose that such a masterpiece as Structure 5C-2nd represents arcane knowledge and technology introduced to Cerros from elsewhere in the Maya world. Actually, it is impossible to identify a singular antecedent in the lowlands or highlands. The other known decorated Late Preclassic buildings in the lowlands show the same general cosmology, but all fall within the same final phase of the Late Preclassic period ceramically and by radiocarbon assay. The symbolism shows clear antecedents in Olmec and Epi-Olmec art but employs architecture rather than stone as the primary medium. As I have suggested elsewhere (Freidel and Schele, in press, Freidel 1981, 1979), the evidence shows a simultaneous emergence of a new political order throughout the lowlands in this period.

From a theoretical vantage point it is important to recognize that such momentous change did not just happen to the Maya of Cerros but was an intentional reordering of reality. Somehow, archaeologists generally have persuaded themselves that only historically known peoples have had self-conscious politicians and revolutions. Fortunately, in the Maya case their Classic politicians are rapidly finding their tongues through text translation. Their immediate

ancestors left few texts, but a wealth of symbols registers materially their machinations. Archaeologists have long recognized rituals of inauguration in the Maya record through dedicatory offerings buried in buildings and we are now beginning to see termination events as well (Robertson 1983, Garber 1983). We have yet to appreciate that these behaviors imply a cultural model for change and continuity broadly registering in the archaeological record. Such a model, I would suggest, informed the change at Cerros and probably similarly abrupt changes at other Maya centers.

Methodologically, the Cerros research suggests that ritual activity is not just cerebral contemplation by a detached elite. Architectural design shows that the buildings spatially embedded in the residential community, were designed as theaters for massed audiences. The use of construction pens suggests standardized units of labor contribution by factions of the Cerros polity. Garber's (1983) identification of humble offerings of prosaic stone tools in the fill of these construction pens underscores the idea that work on public places was in itself ritual activity. Was there, indeed, such a thing as profane space and activity uninformed by the visions celebrated in the public places? Homes in both the nucleated village and the later community had offerings placed in them. There is overlap in the ceramics accompanying home burials and offerings in public places (Robertson 1983, this volume). The stacking of images on the pyramids—sun emerging from earth surmounted by Venus; human emerging from jaguar or dragon—is replicated in the stacking of offering vessels on top of cylindrical effigy stands (M. Masucci, n.d.). In the last analysis, what we might term ritual was, to the Maya of Cerros, merely the most overt expression of a shared social reality. Our hope is that the patterns of ritual action linking public and private domains in a consensus of hierarchical social order will take on increasing definition as analysis proceeds.

But the Maya of Cerros did not live by ritual alone, and much of our effort in the final two seasons at the site was aimed at elucidating certain practical dimensions of life in the community. It was during the 1981 season that Carr made most of her comparative faunal collections, Crane initiated the first of two seasons' work on palaeobotany, and Lewenstein carried out her replicative experiments with stone tools. The primary focus of the final season was the hydraulic system of canals and ditches (Scarborough 1983). As noted in the foregoing pages, these and other analyses reveal a complex and perhaps contradictory view of the economy at the site. Lewenstein's (1984) lithic analyses, for example, do not register any particular craft specialization within the community. Garber's (1981) study of small finds suggests that any trade attending the Late Preclassic heyday of the community was focused primarily on light-bulk commodities normally termed exotic luxuries. And yet Cerros has a center which is clearly larger and more cosmopolitan than the contemporary site of Colha (Shaffer, 1976) with its extraordinary craft specialization and stone tool production. Either the economic functions of Cerros commensurate with such centrality are not registering effectively in our admittedly limited sample, or political and economic centrality here, as in some other Mesoamerican instances (Blanton, 1978), are not congruent. The location of Cerros still favors the former position. Trade and exchange are notoriously difficult functions to substantiate archaeologically.

Finally, a very substantial portion of our effort in the last season was devoted to rebuilding construction pens, stairways, and back-filling our excavations of the previous seasons.

CERROS IN LARGER CONTEXT

The Cerros research is admittedly and manifestly site-centric, and there has been a lot of criticism leveled against students of the Maya for emphasizing such work over regional survey (Blanton et al., 1981, for example). Undoubtedly, the vicinity of Cerros deserves a comprehensive survey within the context of the eastern bank of the New River (Fig. 2). We know, for example, that there is a promising satellite community at Saltillo less than 10 km south of the center, and other occupation at Ramonale, near the village of Chinux. In general, however, northern Belize enjoys fairly substantive control over the spatial distribution of sites due to the long-term survey effort of Norman Hammond, Ray Sidrys, Arlen Chase and Diane Chase, Peter Harrison and Bill Turner II, Tom Hester and Harry Shafer, and R. S. MacNeish. Indeed, northern Belize enjoys the highest density of archaeologists in the Maya area at the moment. We very much appreciated the opportunities for collegial interaction supplied by these scholars and also felt that their work eased the pressure to extend our resources beyond the community itself.

I personally believe that site-centric research in the Maya area is vital to any useful understanding of the civilization and indeed is vital to understanding the other civilizations of Mesoamerica. It is becoming painfully clear that while we know much of the spatial order of such great hearths as the Basin of Mexico and Oaxaca Valley, we know almost nothing of their political organizations or religious institutions compared to what we know about their Maya contemporaries. This is in part due to the literacy of the Maya, but it is also due to the wealth of information Mayanists have compiled on central places with their central institutions, activities, and people. Surely a balance must be sought in research objectives, and the Maya area needs more survey; but the evolution of complex society requires a full investigation of elitism as practiced primarily out of such sites as Cerros.

I have hinted in previous pages that the empirical record at Cerros, conjoined with data from other Maya centers, will provide the basis for a new theory of the evolution of Maya civilization. Although this theory is detailed in another forthcoming work (Freidel and Schele, in press), it is perhaps worth outlining here as an illustration of how I believe site-centric research can contribute directly to the clarification of such general problems.

Stated briefly, Preclassic Maya society evolved as a vast segmentary network of lateral social, economic, and cultural alliances (c.f. Blanton, et al. 1981 for a recent affirmation of this traditional view) which suddenly redefined itself as a mosaic of centralized polities in the first century B.C. The iconography of the Late Preclassic breakthrough period can be effectively tied to the iconography of the ensuing Classic period wherein it is annotated by accompanying hieroglyphic texts. Controlling for such structural changes as inversion, substitution, and conflation between the Preclassic corpus and the Classic one, it is possible to hypothesize in a testable way that the Preclassic Maya were celebrating heirarchy as a concept of brotherhood (the ancestral hero twins) which doubled as a concept of descent (parent/child, father/son). Linda Schele and I argue that the pre-breakthrough Maya already held in common the concept of ancestral hero twins, Venus and the sun, and that their cycles of myths and sacrificial ritual were the lateral means of social and economic integration of lowlanders—analogous as Blanton (1981) and his colleagues have pointed out for such vast societies as the Tiv of West Africa. In the context of such successful integration, the Preclassic

Maya experienced significant increase in the quantity and quality of exchange, increasingly elaborate material definition of social status, and increasingly complicated social relations of production, i.e., differential productivity engendering differential access to productive resources. In simple terms, the amalgamation of the lowlands into a vast segmentary society—likely aimed at avoiding acculturative pressure from neighboring hierarchical societies (Freidel 1981)—created the conditions of social inequality among them. The social conditions stood in conflict with a broadly shared ethos of equality based in the brotherhood of the ancestral twins, an ethos we suggest was responsible for the very sparse representation of elitist material symbols among the pre-breakthrough Maya communities. In the context of a crisis produced by the contradictions of an egalitarian ethos and actual social inequality, the Maya reinvented the hero twin mythology and structurally transformed it into a charter for hierarchical order. In the context of such a transformation, the lowland Maya passed over a threshold to publicly affirmed and celebrated hierarchical order.

Clearly this interpretive framework is anchored in the Cerros research. The iconographic material is not treated in this volume but provides substantial empirical support for the identification of the hero twin mythology and its hierarchical organization in this Late Preclassic breakthrough period. The rest of the archaeological record at this site shows a clear pattern of dramatic social and ideological disjunction in the context of sustained cultural continuities which show that the transformation is taking place *in situ*. Although the framework is germane to Cerros, it is testable as a general model for the evolution of lowland Maya society because of the wealth of site-centric, and more specifically center-centric, work in the region. Research in progress (Fig. 1) at Lamanai (Pendergast 1981), and El Mirador (Morley, Brainerd and Sharer 1983), and earlier work at Tikal (Coe 1965) and Uaxactun (Ricketson and Ricketson 1937) provide the empirical foundation for testing the idea of rapid social change in the Late Preclassic and its concomitants in ideological transformation. In particular, the sudden appearance of monumental architecture, or the sudden shift in scale from small to large public buildings, with the advent of cosmological decoration, seems to be a pattern throughout this record. Detailed descriptions of

accompanying changes in settlement patterns, production/consumption habits, and other dimensions of the record remain to be reported for most of these cases, but they surely will clarify the situation further.

The model devised by Linda Schele and myself would not have been possible without the equally intensive site-centric work carried out by Schele and her colleagues at the site of Palenque. This epigraphic work, reported in many places but most especially in the Mesa Redonda volumes edited by Merle Greene Robertson, provided the Classic period basis in art and ancient writings for the decoding of the Late Preclassic period theological program. The model postulates a series of subsequent transformations following the Late Preclassic period; particularly notable are the Proto-Classic redefinition of kingship, the Middle Classic incorporation of international ritual, and the Terminal Classic demise of divine kingship in the great Collapse. These proposed dynamics in the material symbols and cultural realities of the Maya are in keeping with a long-standing tradition in Maya studies to study the intellectual achievements of these people in tandem with the evidence of their daily lives. The challenge to the current generation of students is to integrate the various sources of independent data from the social sciences and humanities (linguistics, art history, etc.) with those from the "hard" sciences (faunal analysis, palynology, geomorphology) into coherent interpretations of the archaeological record. I feel that we are at least attempting to do this at Cerros, within the constraints of our opportunities.

FUTURE PLANS

With this inaugural offering I look forward to the speedy production of the book-length monographs to follow and to a terminal effort which, I know, will include new views on the site. I would hope that in the not-to-distant future further work could be carried out at this pristine early "civilized" Maya community and in the communities surrounding it. To be sure, there is a need for more reconnaissance and regional survey in the Maya lowlands. For the Maya, however, the heart of their existence lay in the complex communities which they worked so hard to build and maintain. I know I speak for my staff when I say how pleased and privileged we were to reveal that heart at Cerros.

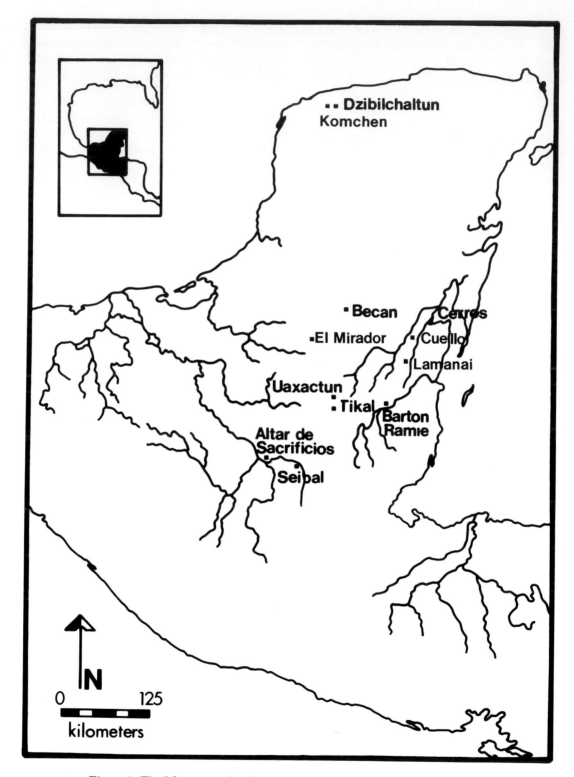

Figure 1. The Maya area showing major sites of the Late Preclassic Period.

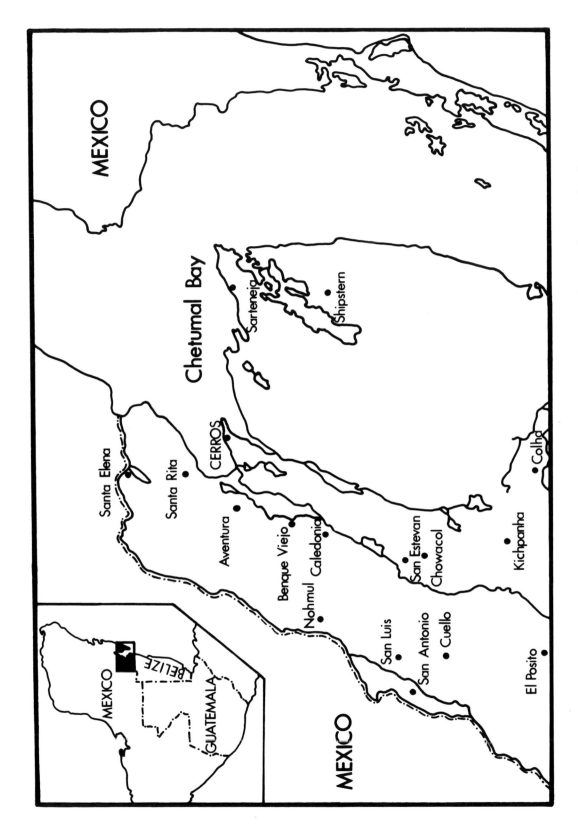

Figure 2. Northern Belize showing Cerros in relation to other ancient settlements in the area.

THE MONUMENTAL ARCHITECTURE

David A. Freidel

The term monumental architecture as used at Cerros specifically refers to the five large pyramidal structures at the site and the plazas or smaller structures associated with them. Four of these structures, together with their plazas, comprise some 5.5 ha of continuous areal coverage at the site center (Fig. 1.1). A fifth structure complex, Group 29, is located to the southeast of the center within the canal perimeter of the community (Fig. 1.2). On the one hand, the overall design of Cerros makes it clear that these structures are indeed major foci of public activity. On the other hand, other smaller structures in the settlement zone such as the two ballcourts were also foci of such activity (cf. Scarborough et al. 1982). This chapter deals with the larger and more elaborate public buildings.

The alphanumeric nomenclature used for structures at Cerros, a modification of that used by the Tikal Project (Shook and Coe 1961), was designed to be flexible and rational. Although commitment to permanent designation prior to excavation inevitably leads to inconsistencies in usage, it has the advantage of clarity in recording. In principle, the lowermost primary substructure is labeled with a number and the letter A. A secondary substructure resting on the primary one is labeled B and so on. Inconsistencies in this system of numbering will be pointed out as the structures are described.

The center of Cerros consists of four major complexes: one at the northern edge and three others radiating star-fashion around this cluster to the east, south and southwest. The Structure 5 complex is to the north. Structure 5A refers to the plaza, edged by Structures 5C through E. To the south and east of this complex is Structure 4, the largest building at Cerros. Structure 4A has one major secondary substructure, 4B, and there are traces of small secondary substructures along its eastern margin, Structures 4C and D. Structure 4A borders a large, low plaza termed Structure 2A. Structure 2A, in turn, supports Structures 2B and C.

To the south of Structure 4 is a complex focusing on Structure 3A, the third largest pyramid at Cerros. Structure 3A supports Structures 3B through D.

Fronting Structure 3A on the south is a low plaza termed Structure 8A, which is bordered by secondary substructures 8B through D. Southeast of the Structure 5 complex is the most elaborate architectural group in the center. The focus of this complex is Structure 6A, the second largest pyramid at Cerros. Structure 6A rests on 6A-Sub 1 and supports Structures 6B through E on its summit. It faces onto, and partially rests on, a plaza to the south termed Structure 7A. Structure 7A supports two secondary substructures along its southern margin, Structures 7B and C. Structure 7A and Structure 6A-Sub are probably one and the same architectural unit, although this was not documented through excavation. The Structure 7A plaza in turn opens onto a lower broad plaza area to the south termed Structure 9A. Structure 9A is formally closed at its southern margin by Structure 9B, although it continues as a pavement beyond this (Scarborough, this volume).

The Structure 29 complex lies roughly 300 m to the south of the center at Cerros. Structure 29A is a massive low plaza bordered on the east by Structure 29B. The Structure 29 complex is the only major monument to face westward at Cerros. The western edge of Structure 29A is close to the main north-south axis of the community which terminates in the north at Structure 5C. Structure 29B is nearly equidistant from the two ballcourts resting on this primary axis. Finally, Structure 29 complements Structure 4A, which has its back to the north-south axis and faces east. This overall pattern shows that Structure 29 is a formal extension of the center.

The structures described comprise the major monuments of the Tulix, or final, phase (cf. Robertson, this volume) of the Late Preclassic community at Cerros. Their dimensions are given in Table 1.1. The incipient phase of public construction associated with the nucleated village (Cliff, this volume) is poorly known because most of the village is buried under the later center. As will be elaborated in the course of discussion, there are good grounds to believe that the transformation of the nucleated village into a center was accomplished in the span of a few generations.

TABLE 1.1

Structure Dimensions for Public Architecture at Cerros

Structure	Height	Length[1]	Width	Stairway (width×length)
2A	2.5	80 (n) 60 (s)	104 (w) 88 (e)	
3A	5	27	44	9.5 × 15
3B	2	6	22	
4A	7	68	58	10 × 15
4B	12	36	38	7 × 16
5A	1.75	30+	32	
5A-Sub 1	1.5	21.4	20+	2.4 × 8
5C-2nd	4.5	15	17	4.5 × 11.5
5C-1st	6	24	21.5	5.5 × 13
5E	1.75	7.4	22+	
6A	7	54	54	
6A-Sub 1	1.7	100+	64+	
6B	4.6	15	20	5 × 12
7A	3	43	105	39 × 4.5
7B		14	30	
7C		14	30	
8A	1.7	45	90	
9A	1	120	125	
9B	2.14	24	66	
29A	1.5	100	90	
29B	10	25	40	11.5 × 14
29C	1.55	7	7	1.75 × 1.5
29D	2.15	8	8.5	3 × 3
29E	?*	?*	7.5	2 × ?*

*Unknown factor
[1]Primary axis of orientation

OPERATIONS IN THE
STRUCTURE 5 COMPLEX

With the exception of Structure 2A-Sub 4 (Cliff, this volume), the initial construction of pyramids at Cerros is documented in the Structure 5 complex (Table 1.2 and 1.3). Major excavations in this complex included a stratigraphic trench linking Structure 5C to the corners of Structures 6A and 4A across the plaza (Structure 5A), and horizontal exposure of Structure 5C. These are Ops 39 and 35, respectively.

Op 39 (Fig. 1.3) revealed that the earliest occupation at this locus consisted of the perishable remains of small residences with their associated trash lenses and activity areas. In every respect these deposits compare with the nucleated village described by Cliff elsewhere in this volume and constitute a westward extension of that village. Like Structure 2A-Sub 4, the first public construction in the Structure 5 complex was built directly over residences of the village.

The first construction here consists of a small acropolis formed by Structure 5C-2nd and a plaza (Structure 5A-Sub 1) fronting it to the south. Trenching at the summit of Structure 5C-2nd and at the juncture of its stairway with the plaza (Fig. 1.4) showed that these structures were built in a single construction effort. The original plaza floor of Structure 5A-Sub 1 terminates in a marl construction pause under the basal treds of Structure 5C-2nd. The core of Structure 5C-2nd was penetrated to within a meter of the elevation of this plaza floor without encountering buried construction.

While we have no hard evidence on the presence or absence of public structures in the loci of the two major pyramids in the center (Structures 4 and 6) that is contemporaneous with the construction of the acropolis formed by Structures 5C-2nd and 5A-Sub 1, circumstantial evidence suggests that this acropolis forms the nucleus of the Tulix phase center. Firstly, the other known substantial public building footed directly on residential deposits, Structure 2A-Sub 4, remained open and in association with the village for some time before that entire sector of the village was buried by the broad plaza, Structure 2A. In principle, the initial public buildings at Cerros were incorporated into the surrounding village. Secondly, this acropolis defines the north-south axis maintained in the final design of Tulix phase Cerros. Finally, a layer of midden trash was found at the foot of the stairway giving access to Structure 5A-Sub 1 from ground level (Fig. 1.5). This midden was sandwiched between a plaster floor defining

the plaza at ground level to the south of Structure 5A-Sub 1, and a layer of white marl constituting a probable reflooring. The use of midden trash in construction of the center is elsewhere only associated with buildings in the nucleated village. In this context, it shows that there were still residences in the immediate vicinity of Structure 5A-Sub 1 following its erection.

While Structure 5C-2nd was open and still in use, the inhabitants of Cerros undertook a major expansion of the center. Our stratigraphic exposure of this event is confined to Op 39 (Fig. 1.5), but it shows that the original low Plaza of the 5A acropolis was buried under a new plaza level that was 25 cm higher. This new plaza level extended southward toward the location of Structures 6 and 4. At 9.4 m south and 0.8 m west of the southern margin of Structure 5A-Sub 1, Structure 5A banks up against the retaining wall of Structure 6A-Sub 1, a buried substructure supporting the Structure 6A acropolis.

A single plaster floor runs across the top of Structure 6A-Sub 1 and terminates in construction fill at the corner walls of Structure 6A. In turn, the plaza level Structure 5A (Fig. 1.6) terminates at the retaining wall of Structure 6A-Sub 1. It is clear, then, that the construction of the plaza level burying the original low plaza of the acropolis in the Structure 5 locus was carried out in conjunction with the raising of Structure 6A-Sub 1 and the massive acropolis it supported, Structure 6A. In short, the southward extension of the plaza (Structure 5A) fronting Structure 5C was part of a massive modification in the size and design of the center involving the replication of the northern terminus of the north-south axis in Structure 6A and its associated support substructure, Structure 6A-Sub 1.

It is likely that monumental structures were built in the locus of Structure 4 in conjunction with this revision of the center, because the plaza level of Structure 5A continues southward under the corner of Structure 4A. Here, as elsewhere at Cerros, tunneling after buried buildings was precluded by the loose boulder fill regularly used in construction.

The surface of Structure 5A was repaved and raised slightly twice at the juncture of Structure 6A-Sub 1. At the foot of Structure 5C, this plaza was repaved three times, but the initial repaving was carried out in conjunction with the careful burial of Structure 5C-2nd under Structure 5C-1st. For a time, then, Structure 5C-2nd remained open after the modification involving Structures 5A, 6A-Sub 1, and 6A. The two major repavings detected at the retaining wall of Structure

TABLE 1.2

The Core Stratigraphic Sequence for Monumental Construction
in the Center at Cerros*

Phase VII	Structure 4B			
Phase VI	Structure 4B-Sub.1		Structure 4A	
Phase V			Structure 2A	Structure 5E
Phase IV	Structure 5C-1st.			
Phase III		Structure 5A	Structure 6A-Sub.1	Structure 6A-E
Phase II	Structure 5C-2nd		Structure 5A-Sub.1	
Phase I	Feature 1A (residential midden of the nucleated village)			

*as documented in Operation 39

TABLE 1.3

General Sequence of Monumental Construction at Cerros*

Phase VIII	Structure 29A-E	Structure 50		Structure 61
Phase VII	Structure 4B	Structure 3A-D		Structure 8A-D
Phase VI	Structure 4B-Sub.1	Structure 4A		
Phase V		Structure 2A		Structure 5E
Phase IV	Structure 5C-1st			Structures 5B and D (?)
Phase III	Structure 5A Structure 6A-Sub.1		Structure 6A-E	Structure 7A-C/Str. 9A
Phase II	Structure 5C-2nd	Structure 5A-Sub.1		Structure 2A-Sub.4
	Feature 1A (residential midden of the nucleated village)			

*Based upon the following: Op39 (cf. Table 1.2); the internal stratigraphy of Operations in Structures 7, 9, 3, 8, and 29; the relative footing of Structures 5C-2nd, 5A-Sub.1, and 2A-Sub.4 on residential remains of the nucleated community; and the accretionary design of the center suggesting the construction of Structures 3, 8, 29, 50, and 61 subsequent to the raising of the core Structures 4, 5, and 6 in the center.

6A-Sub 1, however, are associated with the burial of Structure 5C-2nd under 5C-1st. This modification occurs before the raising of Structure 4A, for these repavings run under that structure.

The final construction on Structure 5A was carried out in association with the raising of Structure 4A. The southern margin of 5A was closed off by a long, low platform, Structure 5E, which constituted a new raised plaza level connecting Structures 6A and 4A at the same elevation. In actuality, Structure 5E is as much an extension of Structure 6A-Sub 1 to provide a continuous substructure supporting Structures 6A and 4A, as it is a means of demarcating the southern edge of the Structure 5 Group. Not only did Structure E demarcate the Structure 5 Group from the now major foci of the center, it also gave the plaza fronting Structure 5C a sunken design. The builders of Structure 5E apparently still knew the dimensions of the original acropolis at the Structure 5 locus, for the retaining wall of 5E rested directly above the southern margin of Structure 5A-Sub 1. As a result, Structure 5E redefined the original plaza fronting Structure 5C.

We have no information on when Structures 5B and 5D were added to the group. In terms of design, it is plausible that they were added when Structure 6A was established as the main north-south focus in order to elaborate this now obscured earlier focus for the community.

To recapitulate the sequence found in Operation 39, the original public complex was a low acropolis and associated temple with a primary orientation to the south. This acropolis displaced the ground level residential architecture. Subsequently, the north-south axis was reiterated in a much more massive complex immediately to the south and west of the original public focus. The area to the south and east of the original focus was also paved and probably supported smaller public structures. Finally, the area to the south and east provided a third major focus for public life in the form of Structure 4A and its associated plaza, Structure 2A. This final construction in the core sequence involved the deliberate burial of nucleated residence on the eastern side of the community.

As revealed in Op 35 (Fig. 1.7), Structure 5C-2nd is basically an elaborate building platform supporting a multi-roomed masonry superstructure. As is typical at Cerros, the original 4.5 m high building platform was constructed using an internal lattice of rough stone pens. These square blocks of fill were sometimes built up with walls tailed into construction and sometimes as free-standing pens to be filled up. The layers of fill graded from loose large boulders at the base through smaller and smaller fill, often punctuated by tamped layers of marl for increased vertical stability. This technique was well understood at the beginning of public construction at Cerros and is used subsequently in all major structures.

The finished "back" or northern face of Structure 5C-2nd comprised an elaborate arrangement of apron moldings and in-set panels. The masonry technique used here is the same found, with few exceptions, throughout the center. Small, loaf-shaped blocks with rounded edges were set with their long-axes perpendicular to the surface in a heavy marl grout. The two exceptions to this technique are the monolithic stones used on Structure 7A and the faced stones found on Structure 50.

The masonry superstructure at the summit of Structure 5C-2nd is the only example of such a building at Cerros. Generally, the summits of pyramids appear to have been open. The side and back walls of the superstructure have been lost through erosion and stone-robbing. Estimates for room size are thus based upon the basal dimensions of the building platform, to which the superstructure closely conformed. The superstructure walls are 50-60 cm thick and were found preserved to a maximum height of 1.4 m. Inner walls were painted pink in the front room and carried a basal molding in plaster. The floors and basal moldings were painted red. The back room was reached by at least one doorway, preserved at the western edge of the medial wall, and stepped up 25 cm from the front room. The front room was divided into compartments by a wall just to the east of the doorway. The narrow walls preclude the possibility of masonry vaults, and the interior space, 109.6 m² in all, is substantial by later Maya standards.

The south sides of the building platform and lower terraces flanking the out-set stairway are decorated with remarkably well preserved panels. At the center of each panel is a large mask. Flanking the masks are smaller panels containing ear-plug assemblages and profile polymorphs. The panels are completed by top and side panels decorated with J-scroll and bracket motifs and profile polymorphs respectively (cf. Freidel 1978, 1979, 1982). At the base, there are plain moldings which are painted red except where depending elements intrude onto them.

It is noteworthy that Structure 5C-2nd on its primary east-west dimension is only 1 m wider than

Structure 2A-Sub 4 on its primary north-south dimension. What distinguishes these two earliest public pyramids at Cerros, then, is not size or basic design so much as the fully articulated symbol system on Structure 5C-2nd. This suggests that the principle of decorating pyramids at Cerros was introduced or innovated suddenly and in conjunction with the establishment of the public center which rapidly buried the village surrounding it. All the subsequent structures of the center were so decorated, although the preservation elsewhere is not as good as on Structure 5C-2nd.

The preservation on Structure 5C-2nd is due to its careful burial under Structure 5C-1st. While the panels were partially defaced, for the most part they were left in place and efforts were made to keep them there. Two offerings on the centerline of the structure were deposited in association with the construction of Structure 5C-1st. Both contained pottery vessels dating to the Tulix phase.

The lower terraces of Structure 5C-1st carried modeled stucco and polychrome painted panels, but this decoration had been defaced and ruined by exposure by the time of excavation. Block masonry armatures show that the practice of displaying large central masks was maintained on this structure. The overall design, however, is simpler than Structure 5C-2nd. The summit was either open or supported a perishable building, and the building platform was decorated with a plain set of step-like terraces flanking the stairway. The decreased elaboration of the structure is commensurate with the replacement of Structure 5C by Structure 6A as the main focus of public life at Cerros.

OPERATIONS IN THE STRUCTURE 6 COMPLEX

In contrast to the original acropolis in the Structure 5 locus, the acropolis which replaced it on the Structure 6 locus was designed with a visually inaccessible upper court approximately 7 m above the level of its support substructure. This upper court, in turn, was hedged by four secondary substructures with a primary focus on Structure 6B along the northern margin. At the same time, the lower plazas, Structures 7A and 9A, provided extensive gathering space from which to view events occurring on the main southern stairway of Structure 6A. In this way, the inaccessible upper court replicates the interior space of the superstructure on Structure 5C-2nd, while the southern side of Structure 6A

reiterates on grand scale the visually accessible space on the southern face of Structure 5C-2nd.

Excavations on Structure 6 were confined to limited test exposures: Op 8, a 2 × 2 m test in the upper court; Op 19, a 2 × 2 m test on Structure 6C on the eastern margin of the court; Op 17, a 2 × 3 m test on the summit of Structure 6B; and Op 18, a 77 m² exposure of the southeastern side of Structure 6B.

The excavations on Structure 6 confirm the evidence (see above) that Structure 6 was raised in a single major effort. Op 8 revealed a humic surface on the court underlain by marl and rubble construction layers. The operation was terminated in large, loose boulder construction core at a depth of 2.2 m. A section through the main stairway of Structure 6B, part of Op 18, revealed that the single plaster surface on the court graded into marl under the basal treds and that the construction fill of Structure 6A was continuous with that of Structure 6B. Under these basal treds were the articulated remains of roughly one third of a large Tulix Phase plate. Supporting the construction of 6A and 6B as a single episode, Op 17 at the summit of Structure 6B penetrated 2 m of the 4.7 m height of the structure without encountering any earlier construction. The northern side of Structure 6B is flush with that of Structure 6A, and the northern basal wall of Structure 6A was exposed in Op 39. As noted previously, this corner on Structure 6A was built in conjunction with Structure 6A-Sub 1. Structure 6B, then, was built once Structure 6A had achieved its final dimensions, which the evidence from Op 39 suggests were its original dimensions. Finally, Op 19 showed that Structure 6C was built in a single effort and that its fill is continuous with that of Structure 6A. It is entirely possible that a much smaller comples lies deeply buried under Structures 6A and 6a-Sub 1 but, even so, Structure 6A represents a massive redefinition of public space at this locus.

Op 17 at the summit of Structure 6B exposed fragmentary remains of a single plaster surface. Under the gravel underflooring was a rough pavement of flat boulders. This pavement covered a dedicatory offering of seven Tulix phase vessels located 1.15 to 1.51 cm below the surface (Freidel 1979). This offering was placed in a construction pen built on a tamped marl construction pause. The marl of this construction pause, upon which the offering also was placed, was tinged pink with ochre. There is reason to believe, then, that the offering was built into Structure 6B during the final period of construction and was not placed in a pit dug down into it subsequently.

The 77 m² exposure of Op 18 revealed a section of the main stairway on the southern side of Structure 6B and preserved fragments of the badly deteriorated upper and lower flanking terraces (Fig. 1.8). In basic design, Structure 6B is quite similar to Structure 5C-2nd, although the masonry superstructure was not included. The structure features two main terraces, the upper set well back from the lower, each decorated with centrally placed monumental masks flanked by ear-plug assemblages. There is a single outset stairway providing access to the summit. If the main masks were centrally placed relative to flanking decoration, as on Structures 5C-2nd, 5C-1st, and 29B at Cerros, then the estimated basal width of the lower terraces is 7.5 m and the total basal width, including a 5 m wide stairway, is 20 m, or only slightly larger than Structure 5C-2nd.

Because the upper portions of the terrace panels were destroyed, their elevations can only be estimated by projecting the dimensions of fragmentary elements, particularly ear-flares, against the zone of marl and rock underlying the decoration. The lower panel sloped between 1.8 and 2.2 m wide and was 1.2 m high. The upper panel sloped roughly 2 m from base to top and was 1.5 m high. Above the upper panel, there were fragmentary remains of a stairway set back from the main out-set stairway, as in the design of Structure 5C-1st. In all, Structure 6B stood about 4.5 m above the court of Structure 6A.

Termination ritual activity and natural erosion severely damaged the stuccoed and painted panels of Structure 6B. Nevertheless, the over-all composition is sufficiently preserved to document that it is a general replication of the design found on Structure 5C-2nd. The lower main mask (Fig. 1.8) is a composite form as seen in the lower main masks of Structure 5C-2nd (Fig. 1.7). The Structure 6B mask shows diagnostic remains only of the lower polymorph from which the upper polymorph can be seen emerging on Structure 5C-2nd. The preserved motifs include the cheek and flame brow on the inner or western side. The upper, emerging, mask on the lower panel of Structure 6B was destroyed down to the masonry armature. On the upper panel of Structure 6B, the main mask is clearly a singular, non-composite, form with a modeled stucco chin curving down onto the horizontal surface of the terrace. The upper masks on Structure 5C-2nd are likewise singular. Although the principle of vertical stacking of masks is general and pervasive in Maya iconography, this particular combination of composite below and singular above is presently documented only on these

two buildings in the Late Preclassic period (cf. Freidel 1981, Freidel and Schele, in press). Other diagnostic motifs linking Structure 5C-2nd and 6B include the use of downward facing side panel polymorphs, and elaborate ear-plug assemblages. In sum, the iconography of these structures provides independent support for the stratigraphic argument that the massive Structure 6 acropolis replaces the Structure 5 acropolis as the central ritual focus at Cerros.

OPERATIONS IN STRUCTURES 7 AND 9

Structure 7, the raised plaza fronting Structure 6A to the south, is at the same elevation roughly as the surface of Structure 6A-Sub 1 at the northwest corner of this acropolis. It is likely, then, that these are one and the same and that Structure 7A was extended south of Structure 6A-Sub 1 to provide a lower plaza on the main axis of the acropolis. This plaza extends 43 m south of Structure 6A before dropping down to Structure 9A. Structures 7B and C, on the southern margin of Structure 7A, block visual access to activities immediately in front of Structure 6A from the lower plaza of Structure 9A except those taking place on the main axis. Together these structures provide only 24 m of visual and physical access on the main axis of the overall complex.

Four test excavations, encompassed by Op 37, were carried out along the juncture of Structures 7A and 9A. The original 2 × 8 m trench, Op 37, was laid out against the slope of Structure 7A close to the medial axis of Structure 7C. The trench came down directly on the western edge of the stairway connecting Structures 7A and 9A (Fig. 1.9), showing that this grand access extended about 5 m beyond the inner edges of the structures on top of Structure 7A.

This final stairway was at least 39 m wide (the eastern side was destroyed by the growth of a large tree) and the upper two Structure 9A Plaza floors were each associated with a stairway construction episode. Unfortunately, one problem remains. Underlying the upper two stairways and their floors, there was rubble construction fill instead of the anticipated third stairway associated with the original construction of Structure 7A (Fig. 1.10). Either the original stairway contacted in Op 37 on the west was not continuous across the length of the final stairway, or the raising of the plaza level of Structure 9A and the construction of an associated new stairway involved the removal and reuse of the tred stones from the original stairway and their replacement with construction fill. While the history of the stairway remains problematic, it is clear that the final stairway, some 180 m² of stepped space, anticipates the grand stairways used as reviewing stands in the Classic period centers of the Maya.

Op 37 also showed that the retaining wall of Structure 7A and the west wall of the stairway were preserved to a height of 1.1 m above the final floor on Structure 9A (Fig. 1.9). The continuing slope of debris above this level suggests that the stairway continued for another meter to the level of Structure 7A. Immediately under this final floor was an earlier plaza level. The side wall of the stairway continued downward below this plaza for another meter until excavation was terminated 25 cm below the present water table. A basal molding on the retaining wall of Structure 7A was encountered 25 cm below the upper two floors. Outset 65 cm from the upper wall, this molding continued down at least 85 cm below the upper wall.

Based on the Op 37 exposure, the original level of Structure 9A lay minimally 3 m below the upper surface of Structure 7A. This is roughly twice the height of the retainer of Structure 6A-Sub 1 above Structure 5A-Sub 1, but about the same as the combined heights of these structures above the ground surface exposed in Op 39. Although water impeded further exposure, it seems highly likely that Structure 7A was originally footed on ground level, and that the original plaza fronting it to the south, Structure 9A, was at that level. This evidence increases the probability that Structures 6A-Sub 1 and 7A are one and the same.

All of the diagnostic material found in construction fill or at the western edge of the stairway dated to the Late Preclassic period. Although dating must remain problematic in the absence of primary deposits the probability that Structure 7A is the same as Structure 6A-Sub 1, and the design of this accessway in association with firmly dated Structure 6A, suggest that this stairway also dates to the Late Preclassic period.

Two test excavations, Ops 10 and 13, were carried out on Structure 9B at the southern margin of the broad plaza Structure 9A. Operation 10, a 2 × 2 m test on the summit at the center of the mound, revealed continuous construction fill of rubble and tamped marl construction pauses layered to a depth of 2.3 m, or 15 cm below the base of the mound. A concentration of over 500 sherds was found in one of these construction layers and all diagnostics dated to the Late Preclassic period. The surface of Structure 9A was littered with Late Postclassic trash, and remains of two perishable superstructures associated with this trash were found at the ends of the mound.

Op 13 was a 20 m² exposure of the northwestern side of Structure 9A. Above a partially collapsed masonry retaining wall a rich Late Postclassic midden had been deposited. At the eastern end of this trench, close to the medial axis, there was a round protrusion faced with vertical slabs. This might have been an armature for a mask, but no stucco was recovered. Soft marl flooring banked against the basal molding of the retaining wall. Approximately 20 cm below the level of the molding, a hard plaster floor was discovered which ran under the structure.

It is clear from the disposition of the midden that Structure 9B was already in ruin by the time of the Postclassic reoccupation. Sherds in construction fill suggest a Late Preclassic date for this structure. The fact that at least one paving of Structure 9A runs under the structure shows that the plaza was in place before being closed off by Structure 9B. Indeed, other excavations in the western sector of the settlement zone suggest extensive paving beyond the formal boundaries of Structure 9A.

OPERATIONS IN STRUCTURE 4

Structure 4 is both the largest acropolis at Cerros and also the one public building showing extensive reuse after the Late Preclassic demise of the center. The major operations on this acropolis were Op 20, a horizontal exposure of the summit of Structure 4B; Op 22, a clearing of the upper eastern slope of Structure 4B; and Op 25, an axial trench through the base of Structure 4B, along the upper court of Structure 4A, and through the main eastern stairway on Structure 4A.

Op 25h, 3.5 × 26 m, revealed that Structure 4A probably was raised to its final dimensions in a single construction episode (Fig. 1.11). The trench exposed a rough inner core platform resting on a finished plaster floor which continued eastward over Structure 2A, the east plaza. Structure 2A, then, was in place before Structure 4A was raised. It is likely that the Structure 4 locus supported a smaller proto-type for the later acropolis buried by this core platform. The 2.6 m high core platform consisted of roughly coursed, unshaped blocks in heavy marl grout.

Over the core platform the builders raised two layers of construction pens, thus forming a lattice of internal buttressing. As exposed in the trench, these pens were about 4 × 4 × 2 m. At the eastern edge of Structure 4A, the pen walls were sloped back inward to provide increased stability. This sloping suggests that the bulk of Structure 4A was constructed first and then the formal stairway was built against it.

The first of the two main stairways oriented to the east was constructed with the pen technique and was outset 7 m from the core platform. Subsequently, a second stairway was built over the first. It was outset an additional 3.5 m to the east. We do not know if this second stairway involved modification of the flanking side walls of Structure 4A. However, its close conformity with the underlying stairway suggests that, if this is the case, it was a thin encapsulation of the original walls like that on Structure 29B discussed below. Fragments of a Late Preclassic vessel were found smashed under the treds of the final stairway. Construction fill yielded pure samples of Late Preclassic ceramics below the disturbed and unsealed surface of the upper court.

The trench across the upper court of Structure 4A, connecting Op 25h with Ops 25a-g, showed that the medial axis of this structure had been intensively used in the Late Postclassic period. Beyond the foot of Structure 4B, the plaster paving was completely destroyed. Late Postclassic people built a small square altar in the middle of the court and deposited a series of offerings between this altar and the base of Structure 4B, including censerware, redwares, obsidian, and human remains. Between the altar and Structure 4B, these people dug down into the construction fill (leaving a clear pit outline) and deposited a very rich cache of copper, gold and tumbaga ornaments, effigy vessels, chert bifaces, jade, shell and turquoise beads. Finally, they built a rough slab stairway over the ruins of the original stairway in order to get to the summit, where they built a perishable superstructure on a masonry foundation. The intense Late Postclassic reuse of Structure 4 hampered attempts to date the original construction. Sherd material below the surface of the court, however, dated exclusively to the Late Preclassic period.

Operation 25a-g exposed the base of the stairway on Structure 4B and also exposed the southern side of the stairway and a portion of the flanking wall. Excavation showed two preserved stepped terraces and fragments of a third on this flanking wall. The first and second terraces are 2.12 and 2.25 m high respectively. If the wall was terraced to the small, step-like stairs

encircling the summit, then there were probably four of them all together, each about 2.2 m high.

Banked against the base of the lowermost terrace were abundant fragments of modeled and painted stucco decoration fallen or torn from the walls. Interspersed with these fragments were large quantities of smashed pottery including worked sherd lids. The deposit yielded charcoal, fragments of chert tools and bone. Since several of the vessels are partially restorable, it is likely that this deposit represents a termination ritual for Structure 4B, comparable to rituals found on other buildings at Cerros (cf. Garber, this volume). If this is such a primary deposit, then Structure 4B can be assigned to the terminal Late Preclassic occupation at Cerros on the basis of the recovered sherds.

Excavation of the stairway on Structure 4B revealed a buried second stairway footed 2.3 m underneath the upper one. In contrast to the first stairway, which runs steeply up the slope to the summit, this second stairway levels off after two steps and disappears under the bulk of Structure 4B. Whether this second stairway, associated with Structure 4B-Sub 1, permits access to a substantially smaller structure or merely has a broad step before rising steeply could not be determined. It is certain, however, that Structure 4B involved a major modification of the design of Structure 4-Sub 1. This contrasts with the rebuilding of the stairway on Structure 4A which represented a minor modification of the original stairway.

Exposure of the eastern face of the Structure 4B at the summit, Op 22, showed that the final design was either an open platform or one supporting a perishable superstructure surmounting at least three broad steps running along the eastern face. An offering was found on the second step from the summit, north of the medial axis of the structure. This offering combines whole Late Preclassic vessels with partial vessels dating to the Postclassic period. Evidently Postclassic people had encountered a Late Preclassic offering somewhere on the mound and had redeposited it with some of their own vessels.

At the summit, Op 20 showed that the Late Postclassic perishable superstructure overlay the collapsed remains of a vaulted subterranean chamber. This chamber, originally 2.6 m wide and at least 9.4 m long, had two faced inner walls on the eastern side. Attempts to discover a doorway in the original wall were unsuccessful and it appears that the chamber was designed to be sub-surface. The second wall seemingly was added to narrow the span over which the vault had to be sprung. Excavation through the floor of the chamber yielded a substantial sample of Late Pre-classic sherds used as ballast. The dating of the chamber is complicated, however, by intensive use following construction. Overlying the floor and a raised bench area at the northern end was a thick deposit of marl, charcoal, copal, smashed vessels, jade fragments, obsidian lancets and other materials. The many layers in the deposit indicate either a sustained ritual with many pauses, or repeated ritual use. A cache pit dug down into the surface of the bench area contained a single vessel. The earth surrounding the vessel had minute fragments of smashed jade and quantities of sherds broken during the ritual. Along the northern edge of the bench was a stack of vessels including a large cylinder which originally rested on a drum stand and fragments of similar vessels. One of these assemblages had been smashed in place by collapse of the vault. The diagnostics in these ritual events all point to a Tzakol 1 date. It is clear that these activities post-date construction of the chamber and do not pertain to its intended function as a tomb. It seems that the room, though intended to be a tomb, never was so used.

The southern end of the chamber was virtually empty. No remains of tomb furniture or fragments of human bone were found. In fact, there is no evidence that the northern and southern end walls of the chamber were ever finished, which would have left the chamber open and accessible after abandonment. The termination deposits at the base of Structure 4B suggest a terminal Late Preclassic date for abandonment of construction on the acropolis. The ritual activities in the summit chamber, however, indicate that Structure 4B remained a focus for the residual Early Classic community in the settlement zone prior to the collapse of the vault.

In summary, Structure 4A was raised in a single construction effort over the probable remains of a smaller proto-type designed in conjunction with the raising of Structure 2A. The stairway on Structure 4A was rebuilt once. Structure 4B shows two construction episodes, 4B-Sub 1, a deeply buried structure raised in conjunction with the original construction of 4A, and Structure 4B, a substantial modification crowned by a sub-surface vaulted chamber.

OPERATIONS IN STRUCTURES 3 AND 8

Investigations on Structure 3, the third largest acropolis at Cerros, consisted of four excavations: Op 4, a 2 × 2 m test on the upper court of Structure 3A; Op 21, a 2 × 3 m trench on the medial axis and summit of Structure 3B; Op 14, a 1.5 × 8.5 m trench into the southeast face of Structure 3A east of the main stairway; and Op 36, a 53 m² exposure on the stairway and medial axis of Structure 3A, with an extension on to the plaza.

Operations on Structure 3 indicate that this acropolis was raised in a single episode. However, the possibility of much smaller and deeply buried buildings cannot be precluded. Op 21 at the summit of Structure 3B revealed continuous construction fill to a depth of 2.8 m below the surface, or roughly 50 cm below the level of the upper court, indicating that it was built in conjunction with Structure 3A. No diagnostic artifacts were found in this operation. Op 4, on the upper court of Structure 3A, exposed continuous construction fill of gravel, tamped marl and rock down into a loose large boulder core 2 m below the surface. Op 36 revealed a single main stairway approximately 9.5 m wide on the southern face of Structure 3A. Excavation of a 2 m wide trench on the medial axis through the stairway at its juncture with the lower plaza, Structure 8A, re-vealed that the lower plaza was built in a single episode on top of paleosol sparsely littered with Late Preclassic trash. The first of two floorings on this plaza terminates under the basal treds of the stairway on Structure 3A (Fig. 1.12), while the second involved minor modification of the basal treds of the stairway on Structure 3A but no complete rebuilding. No evidence of an earlier stairway or construction episode was found in the axial trench for a distance of 5 m behind the basal treds of the stairway. It is clear, then, that the single stairway on Structure 3A was raised in conjunction with the laying down of the plaza south of it, Structure 8A. Since this is the only stairway associated with Structure 3A, it is likely that the acropolis was built in conjunction with the plaza. Structure 3B was raised in conjunction with Structure 3A. While the possibility of small ground level public buildings at this locus cannot be precluded, Structures 3 and 8 were designed and raised as a unit.

Op 14 exposed the basal wall of Structure 3A to the east of the stairway. This wall was made of the same loaf-shaped masonry used throughout the center at Cerros. The wall was decorated with an apron molding and inset panel which was plastered and painted red. At the base of this wall, there was a thick layer of marl containing fragments of painted plaster from the wall. This deposit also had all the characteristics of a termination ritual dating to the end of the Tulix phase.

In terms of design, Structure 3A and its plaza reiterate the main north-south axis of the Tulix phase community directly south of the eastward facing Structure 4 acropolis. It is perhaps significant that Structure 8A is the only plaza in the center to evince a closed off design with substructures bordering its margins. This is a design which becomes popular in the Early Classic period.

OPERATIONS IN STRUCTURE 29

Excavations in the Structure 29 Complex, collectively designated Op 111, included extensive exposure of the final architectural episode on Structure 29B and probes into the adjacent plaza area of Structure 29A at the juncture of these structures. Excavations cleared 107 m² at the summit of Structure 29B, while a 91 m² exposure was opened up at the base of this structure on its western side facing onto the plaza.

A trench on the medial axis at the juncture of Structures 29A and 29B showed that the plaza in this area had been raised in a single construction effort. In contrast to construction elsewhere at Cerros, the fill of this plaza consisted of marl and earth with little rock. This fill is comparable to the material underlying caprock at the site and may have been excavated from nearby canal channels (Scarborough 1980). The original plaster surface of Structure 29A terminates in continuous construction fill under the basal treds of the out-set stairway on Structure 29B and no earlier stairways were found. Hence Structure 29A was raised in conjunction with the construction of Structure 29B.

Structure 29B was modified along the basal terraces flanking the 11.5 m wide stairway. This encasing of the original terrace walls was not accompanied by refurbishment of the stairway and served to shorten the out-set from 5.5 m to 4.5 m. No decoration was found in association with these terrace walls and no evidence of termination rituals was forth-coming.

Excavation at the summit of Structure 29B revealed the presence of three platforms, hereafter designated Structures 29C-E. A summit trench on Structure 29D, the central platform, showed that it was raised in a single effort on a prepared plaster surface covering the top of Structure 29B. Since there is no evidence that an earlier platform stood on the summit of Structure 29B, it is certain that this summit surface either served as open space for a time, or was intentionally designed to support these three platforms. As the expanse of the

summit of Structure 29B is very broad compared to the summits of other public buildings at Cerros, the latter possibility seems more likely. Penetration 1.5 m below the summit surface of Structure 29B failed to reveal earlier construction. While it remains possible that Structure 29B encased a smaller building built on ground level, the plaza, pyramid and platforms form a design unit and show evidence of having been raised as such.

Although the triple platform design on Structure 29B is unique at Cerros (Fig. 1.13), it has been found on the Late Preclassic Structure N10-54 Lamanai, farther up the New River (Pendergast 1981). At Cerros the central platform, Structure 29D, faces west onto the plaza below. An outset stairway, 3 m wide and 3 m long, is flanked by decorated panels featuring jaguars in modeled and painted stucco with humanoid heads emerging above them (Freidel 1981). These masks are flanked by ear-plug assemblages as in the case of other panels at Cerros. In addition to these panels, Structure 29D had a vertical frieze of modeled and painted plaster running around the edge of its summit. Excavation of this summit revealed remains of a Late Postclassic superstructure, the northern wall of which lay over the alleyway between Structures 29C and 29D.

Structures 29C and 29E face inward toward Structure 29D. This very awkward arrangement made both visual and physical access to these flanking structures difficult. Evidently the ritual importance of the arrangement overrode such practical considerations. Like Structure 29D, Structures 29C and E have outset stairways flanked by panels decorated with monumental masks. The preserved stucco on Structure 29C shows that these masks consisted of long-lipped polymorphs with humanoid heads emerging above. The masonry armatures on Structure 29E indicate that these panels also had long-lipped polymorphs on them. Structures 29C and E are so close to Structure 29D at their eastern ends that the alleyways between the structures are effectively closed off by the snouts of the long-lipped masks merging with the heavy apron moldings decorating the side walls of Structure 29D. Apron moldings also decorated the side walls of Structures 29C. Structure 29E was destroyed to below the level of such moldings. The masks on Structures 29C-E display more realistic zoomorphs and anthropomorphs than other preserved panels at Cerros on Structure 5C-2nd.

Structure 29 was abandoned with a substantial termination ritual, best preserved in the alleyway between Structures 29C and 29D. Fires were banked up against the masks, scorching the plaster and leaving abundant charcoal. Quantities of pottery vessels were smashed and intermixed with plaster torn off the upper frieze and the panels. All the pottery dates to the Tulix phase and a radiocarbon date on the charcoal provides a date of 25 B.C. ± 50 (Freidel and Scarborough 1982). Structure 29, like the other major public structures at Cerros, was constructed rapidly and abandoned in the Late Preclassic period.

CONCLUSIONS

Excavations in public architecture at Cerros, while admittedly limited in extent, are consistent in the evidence they provide for a sudden and rapid transformation of the nucleated village into a ceremonial center of impressive proportions for its era (see Table 1.3). Structure 5C-2nd is not only the most elaborately decorated structure preserved at the site, it is also the earliest known decorated structure there. It would be only reasonable to postulate the introduction of the principle of ceremonial center construction and its accompanying iconography from elsewhere in the Maya region. However, current research on the Late Preclassic occupation of other centers in the lowlands (e.g., Matheny 1980, Pendergast 1981) has so far yielded analogous results to those found at Cerros. The introduction of decoration and large formal structures are coeval in this period. While future research may show that somewhere in the lowlands there is a gradual development leading up to this hallmark of florescence, it may well turn out that the advent of civilization in the southern Maya lowlands is as sudden and precipitous an episode as its downfall nearly a millennium later.

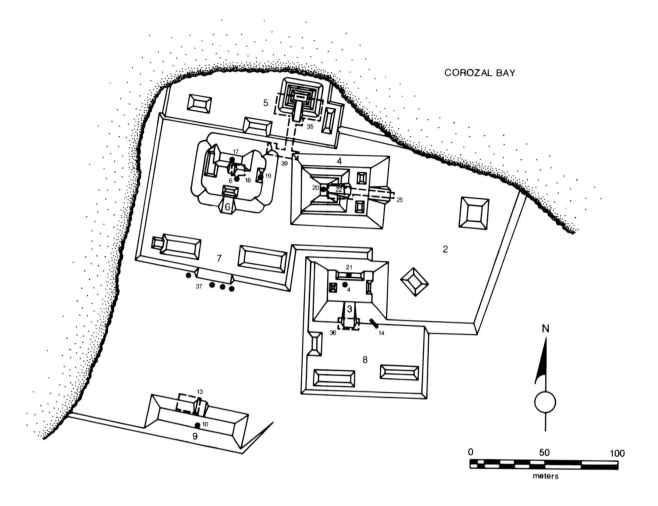

Figure 1.1. The center at Cerros, showing the locations of major operations and test excavations described in the text. Deviations from Maler conventions are based on excavated detail.

Key: Dashed lines show major exposures; dots show limited exposures; large numbers designate Structures; small numbers identify Operations.

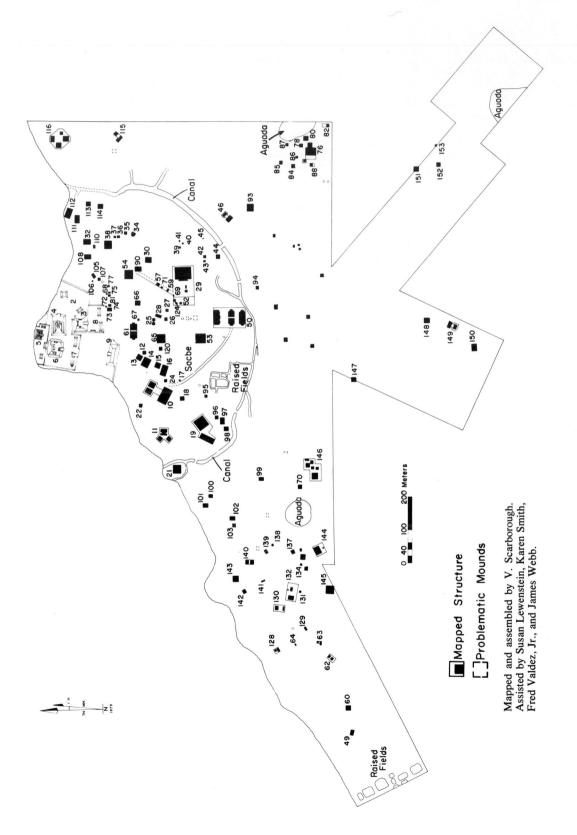

Figure 1.2. The settlement at Cerros. Mapped small structures in the dispersed settlement zone are conventionally oriented to the cardinal directions unless true orientation is known through excavation. Public buildings such as the ballcourts show true orientation.

Figure 1.3. The stairway of Structure 5A-Sub.1 looking north in Operation 39. The wall behind the stairway is a mason's wall inside the construction fill of Structure 5A-Sub.1.

Figure 1.4. The basal treds of Structure 5C-2nd at the juncture with the plaza of Structure 5A-Sub.1 showing continuous marl underflooring and construction pause conjoining the raising of these buildings.

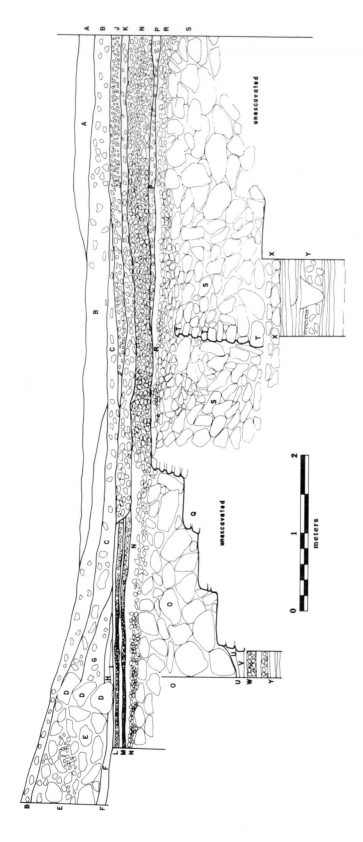

Figure 1.5. The western profile of Operation 39 in the plaza of Structure 5, showing sections of Structures 5A–Sub.1, 5A, and 5E.

Key: a, backdirt from Operation 35; b, dark brown humus and angular small rock; c, greyish brown loam; d, retaining wall of Structure 5E; e, large angular rubble in marl matrix, fill of Structure 5E behind retainer; f, tan, sandy loam; g, grey loam; h, light greyish brown loam; i, plaster surfacing patch on Structure 5A, associated with Structure 5E; j, gravel floor ballast in greyish brown loam; k, smaller gravel in grey powdery loam, decomposed flooring; l, Plaza Floor 3 of Structure 5A; m, Plaza Floor 2 of Structure 5A; n, Plaza Floor 1 of Structure 5A; o, construction fill of Structure 5A, dry-laid, large angular rubble; p, gravel in greyish tan dirt; q, stair treds of Structure 5A–Sub.1; r, plaster flooring of Structure 5A–Sub.1; s, large angular rubble construction fill of Structure 5A–Sub.1; t, mason's wall behind finished wall of Structure 5A–Sub.1; u, soft plaster or marl; v, black midden lens; w, plaster surface and ballast of flooring at foot of Structure 5A–Sub.1 stairway; x, flat-laid rubble pavement foundation of Structure 5A–Sub.1 stairway, underflooring at foot of the Structure 5A–Sub.1 stairway; y, ballast in beach sand underflooring at foot of the Structure 5A–Sub.1 stairway, tierra quemada flooring, in this locality. midden lenses; post-hole residential debris associated with the nucleated village occupation, Feature 1, in this locality.

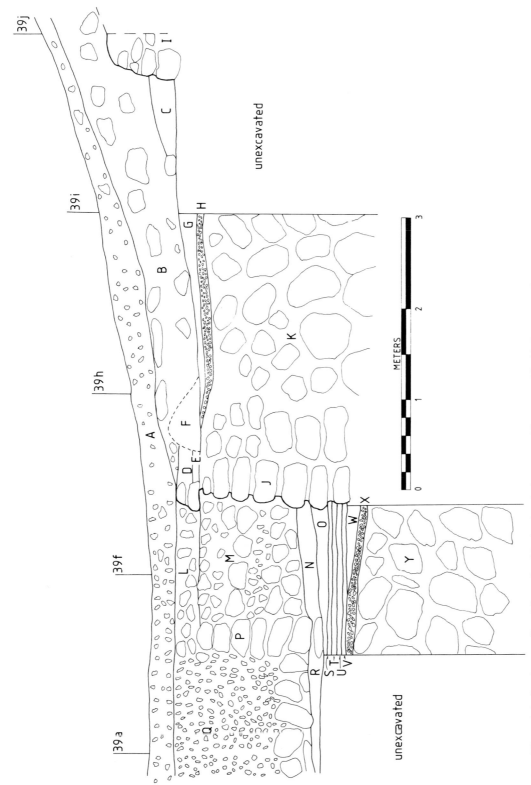

Figure 1.6. Southern profile of Operation 39, showing the junctures of Structures 5A, 6A-Sub.1, and 6A. Key: A, humus at surface; B, grey loam with rubble inclusions, fall from Structure 6A; C, packed grey marl; D, grey marl; E, white marl; F, tree disturbance; G, grey over white marl; H, gravel ballast; I, basal molding of Structure 6A; J, retaining wall of Structure 6A-Sub.1; K, rubble hearting of Structure 6A-Sub.1; L, Small angular rock in grey marl; M, small angular rock, large rubble, in tan dirt; N, tan sandy loam; O, dark grey marl; P, mason's wall; Q, dry gravel; R, tan sandy loam; S, plaza floor 3 of Structure 5A, plaster surface; T, plaza floor 3 of Structure 5A, gravel ballast; U, plaza floor 2 of Structure 5A; V, plaza floor 1 of Structure 5A, plaster surface; W, plaza floor 1 of Structure 5A, marl underflooring; X, plaza floor 1 of structure 5A, gravel ballast; Y, rubble construction hearting of Structure 5A.

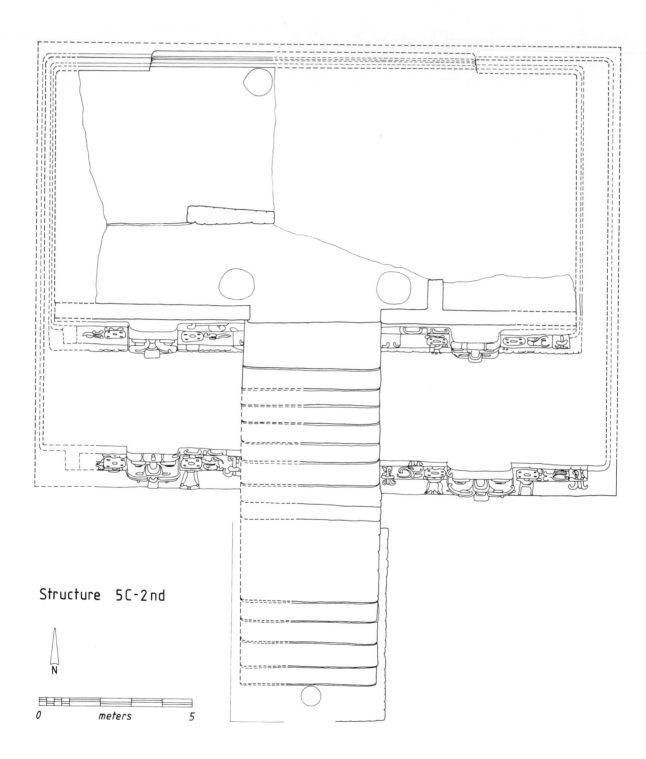

Structure   5C-2nd

N

0   meters   5

Figure 1.7. The plan of Structure 5C-2nd. Solid lines show exposure in Operation 34, dotted lines are extrapolation. Holes at the summit are part of original construction, hole at the foot of the stairs is a dedicatory, cached offering.

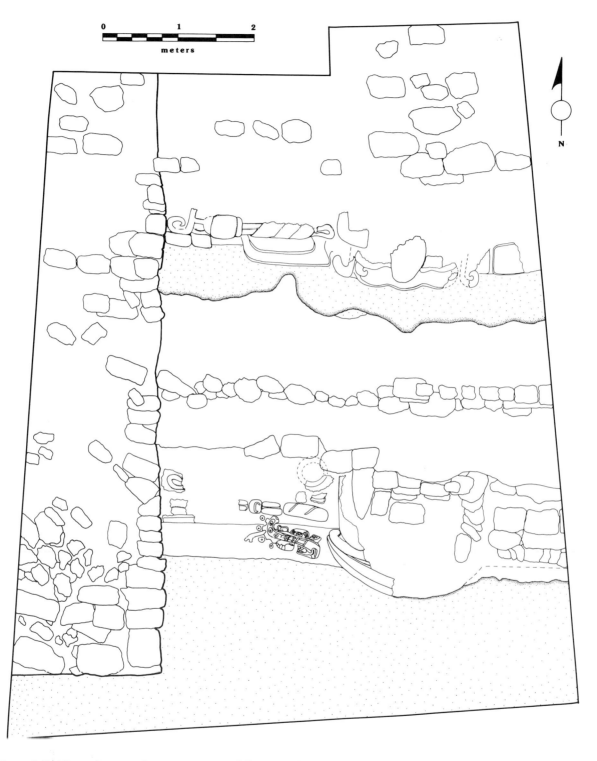

Figure 1.8. The stairway and eastern terrace of Structure 6B as exposed in Operation 18. Fragmentary remains of stucco decorated panels featuring large masks are shown.

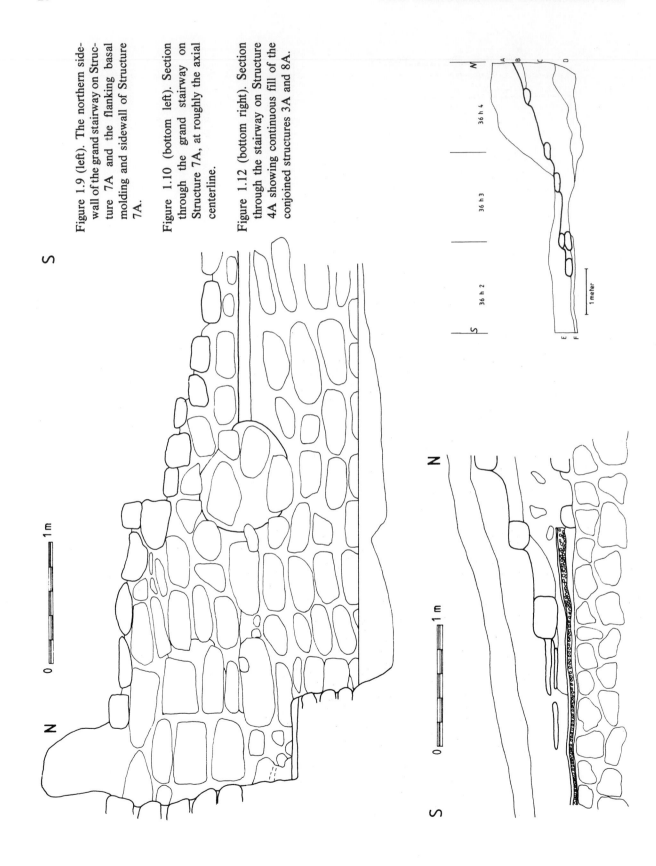

Figure 1.9 (left). The northern sidewall of the grand stairway on Structure 7A and the flanking basal molding and sidewall of Structure 7A.

Figure 1.10 (bottom left). Section through the grand stairway on Structure 7A, at roughly the axial centerline.

Figure 1.12 (bottom right). Section through the stairway on Structure 4A showing continuous fill of the conjoined structures 3A and 8A.

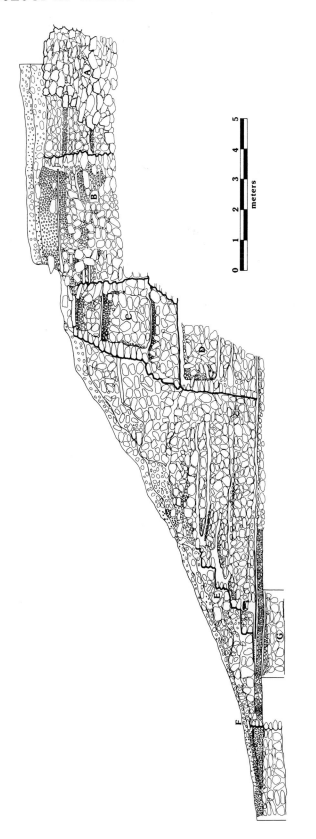

Figure 1.11. Section through the stairway and primary substructure of 4A in Operation 25 H, showing construction techniques.

Key: A, Face of a mason's wall on the uppermost layer of construction pens, Structure 4A; B, A construction pen in the uppermost layer of pens; C, A smaller construction pen at the edge of the structure; D, The core construction of the structure; E, Stairway 1; F, Stairway 2; G, Hearting of Structure 2A underlying Structure 4A stairway.

Figure 1.13. Structure 29B after excavation, looking east.

THE DISPERSED SETTLEMENT

Vernon L. Scarborough

An intensive field survey program in 1977 recorded features within a three-quarter square kilometer survey area surrounding the central precinct (Freidel, this volume). In 1978 and 1979 the mounds in an additional 75 ha around the center were cleared and mapped. To date all mounded features within a twenty-minute walk of the main plaza have been mapped (Fig. 1.1). This survey coupled with an extensive test excavation program will provide a means of comprehensively examining a 1.5 km² area immediately surrounding the central precinct.

Survey operations at Cerros began in 1974 with an A-line closed traverse using a theodolite and were designed to expedite the accurate location of features and excavations within a 9 ha unit that included the central precinct. More recent and extensive survey operations have been carried out using a transit and 50 m chain in addition to a plane table and alidade for the detailed recording of mounded features. A systematic quadrat survey design incorporating a 100 m *brechia* interval has been found most efficient in the thick secondary regrowth at Cerros.

A topographic map using a 0.5 m contour interval as well as the definition of extant microenvironments has been reproduced for the entire survey area (Fig. 2.1). Because no standing architecture has been identified in the settlement, this interval has proved to be particularly useful in defining the range of features present. Moreover, the flat natural relief at Cerros has facilitated the use of such a small contour interval over a large area. Figure 1.1 reflects the rectification of the contoured mounds following the conventions of the Tikal mapping project (Carr and Hazard 1961). It should be noted that the major mounds in the central precinct have been rendered using the Maler convention because more is known about this area as a result of intensive excavation programs.

From a theoretical point of view, the focus of the survey has been on the question of spatial variability within and between mound groups relative to the central precinct. In order to deal with this variability, a working morphological typology of mounded features using form, size and groupings was devised for the settlement zone in 1977. Table 2.1 presents this preliminary classification which was developed, in part, because of the absence of masonry architecture in the settlement. It deals only with the data collected during the 1974–1978 seasons and is limited to mounds within the 75 ha immediately surrounding the center. Table 2.2 presents the length, width and height data from the mounds described below as well as the potential summit floor space and absolute volume for each mound.

This typology was used to stratify the known sample of mounds around the center and to provide the basis for selecting particular mounds for excavation. It was argued that the size of these mounds (reflected by their respective volumes) would be correlated with the status of the occupants. Even if the resident was not directly responsible for the initial construction of the mound, his ability to elevate himself above another in terms of occupying a larger or more complicated mound grouping would indicate his rank in the community. Intra-site distance relationships were also expected to reflect elements of the social organization related to the clustering of mound groups (cf. Kurjack 1974, 1976).

Underlying this typology is the implicit assumption that the majority of mounds served a residential function. Information collected during the 1978 and 1979 seasons, however, showed that there are public structures in this zone. Although the functional justification for stratifying the mound excavation sample must be reassessed, the typology still stands on formal grounds. The basic strength of the typology all along was that it allowed the stratification of our basic unit of analysis, mounded features.

The excavation program has involved a series of test excavations geographically dispersed throughout the settlement. Mound groups were selected for excavation from a stratified judgmental sample. A minimum of a 30% sample was taken from each of the formal typological divisions in the mound typology (Table 2.1). However, a larger sample percentage was used when sample sizes within the typological divisions

23

TABLE 2.1

Structure Types, Frequency, and Exposure in the Systematically
Surveyed and Excavated Settlement Area

Type	Description	Frequency	Percent Tested	Total Exposure/ Stratum
1	Four or more building platforms on a shared substructure	2	100	451 m²
2	Three building platforms on a shared substructure	4	100	269 m²
3	Two building platforms on a shared substructure	4	75	101 m²
4	Substructure greater than 150 m², and more than 1 m high	18	72	82 m²*
5	Substructure greater than 150 m², and less than or equal to 1 m high	28	21	73 m²
6	Substructure less than 150 m² and less than or equal to 1 m high	34	21	26 m²

*Excludes extensive exposure on Structure 29B

were small. Specific mound selection was determined by (1) the biased maintenance of dispersed geographical representation and (2) fortuitous trash exposures revealed by natural agents (windfalls, shoreline erosional profiles, etc.). Elaborate statistical equations were not employed in our sampling decision because of the low probability of statistical meaningfulness given the size and complexity of the site. Our judgmental sample was developed to take advantage of known and meaningful surface indicators in order to obtain maximum data retrieval at a minimum cost in labor. Although the sample was not statistically controlled geographically, great effort was made to test in every environmental and spatial sector of the community. A more rigid statistical selection would have provided a less useful data set.

Excavation and recovery techniques involved the excavation and screening of naturally defined levels. Our initial excavation exposures reflected a period of experimentation in terms of the precise size and location of our test units. However, our experience in the initial testing phase of the settlement showed that midden debris and architectural detail were identified through the exposure of 2 × 2 m units located on the flanks of the structures. Extensive lateral exposure was carried out on four of the six formal structure types in the settlement. Structure Types 2 and 4 include two Late Preclassic ballcourts and have been discussed elsewhere (Scarborough et al. 1982).

STRUCTURE 10 GROUP

Group 10, composed of Structures 10B, 10C and 10D (Fig. 2.2a) represents the largest mound cluster in the settlement. This Type 2 structure group rests on the southern flank of the low-lying plaza (Structure 9A) south of Structure 9B within a *huamil* setting. It is located near the northern terminus of the western *sacbe* (Feature 126) with both its southern and western margins near the depressed *zacatal* setting. The mound group appears to be oriented toward the central precinct in a manner not unlike Structures 13, 14, 15, and 16, which are all structures in the immediate vicinity of the Structure 10 Group. Although the structure itself has been assigned an Early Classic date, the underlying sub-plaza Structure 9A was constructed during Tulix times. The imposing size and complexity of this structure group suggests that it served a nonresidential or elite function. Given the general paucity of Classic architecture at the site, the Structure 10 Group was likely one of the major foci of Classic period civic activity following the reoccupation of the center. The surface collection showed evidence of some Postclassic occupation.

Structure 10B

This structure is the largest and southeastern-most mound in the group. In addition, an apparent *chultun*

TABLE 2.2

Dimensions of Structures in the Dispersed Settlement

Structure Number	Length (m)	Width (m)	Height (m)	Potential Floor Summit Space (m²)	Absolute Volume (m³)
10B	45	27	5.0	270	3,713
10C	28	25	5.0	80	1,950
11B	25	20	3.5	130	1,103
11C	25	22	1.5	192	557
11D	20	15	1.5	140	330
9B	70	24	3.5	480	3,948
34A	16	14	1.0	36	130
76B	34	33	4.0	320	2,884
76D	20	12	1.8	64	274
84A	15	12	0.5	18	50
38A	28	24	1.3	100	502
66A	24	17	1.5	80	366
65A	31	23	1.5	108	616
53A	32	30	3.0	72	1,548
116B	23	22	2.2	120	689
115B	19	14	1.2	100	220
46C	25	16	1.1	80	264
94A	17	11	0.4	187	75
77A	8	7	1.0	9	33
26A	12	12	0.5	24	42
24A	11	10	0.5	16	32
112A	32	18	1.6	98	539
54A	29	24	3.5	80	1,358
57A	13	9	1.0*	16	67
13A	26	22	2.5	25	746
14A	33	22	4.5	40	1,724
19C	45	34	3.5	1,280	4,918
16A	23	11	0.5	48	75
15A	42	39	1.2	96	1,040
21A	32	25	5.0	70	2,175
22A	12	9	0.5	16	31
18A	15	12	0.8	80	130
102A	20	14	0.5	36	79
98A	24	19	1.5	160	462

*Includes underlying *sacbe*

was located 10 m south of Structure 10B and outside the plazuela group. It seems to have been cut into the limestone bedrock. Only a small constricted orifice is visible from the surface.

A 6.75 m by 1.5 m trench (Op 12) was put into the southwestern edge of the mound in hopes of uncovering trash deposits and/or a retaining wall during the initial field season. Unfortunately, neither a retaining wall nor a plaster melt was encountered. Mound layering, however, was evident, with the bulk of the mound consisting of dry rubble fill underlain by a lens of larger rubble within a light grey loam. If a retaining wall existed, it was composed of uncut rubble that has long since been destroyed. The small artifact inventory contained a mixture of Late Preclassic and Late Postclassic material.

Op 110, a 16 m² exposure, was opened at the summit of Structure 10B during the 1977 field season. These excavations were conducted along the medial axis of the mound immediately above what appeared to be an outset stairway section. Anticipating a range structure, given the size and elongated shape of the outset mound and its similarity to Structure 11B (another Type 2 plazuela group structure discussed below), we predicted the presence of masonry walls and plaster floors. This prediction was plainly disconfirmed. Instead, we defined a 30 m thick lens of hearting gravel underlain by boulder size fill. Although Late Preclassic ceramic diagnostics were identified, the most recent debris from within the unsealed hearting was Classic utility ware.

Structure 10C

Structure 10C is one of two conical mounds approximately 22 m north of Structure 10B. Op 109 was excavated during the 1977 field season in anticipation of architectural features and trash concentrations. Part of this operation consisted of a 2 × 10 m proximation trench excavated to a depth of 1.4 m that extended from the plaza up to the edge of a crude platform. Unfortunately, this sub-operation provided only minimal information. The absence of any indications of a masonry stairway on the medial axis of the mound, however, suggests that there never was one.

A more productive sub-operation in which 43 m² were excavated to a depth of 1.7 m was conducted on the summit of the mound. Artifactual debris was recovered in low frequencies and no primary features were located. However, one concentration of utility ware ceramics of Classic period date was recovered approximately 20 cm above the remains of the platform mentioned above.

The platform appears to be D-shaped in plan with its straight face oriented into the plaza. The front exposure is four courses high and composed of crude undressed stones set in a marl grout. The backside of the platform is defined by a poorly preserved curvilinear single course alignment. The platform appears to have projected above the frontal slope of the mound. Willey and others (1965:97) indicate a similar pattern on BR123 during Period 3. The tendency of the Maya in all periods to level previous mound occupations to make way for subsequent structures may suggest that another occupation, as yet unrevealed, underlies this platform. The apparent use of only a portion of the total mound

surface area available to the platform builders might suggest this to be the case here as well.

Five ill-defined, "clean" marl lenses sandwiched between layers of rubble fill within one meter of vertical exposure indicate that the interior of the structure was artificially raised above the lower retaining wall, probably in the Classic period. It should be noted that the nearly clean white marl and rubble fill of Structure 10C contrasts sharply with the trash laden fill of Structure 11B (below) as well as with the tan topsoil overlying the rubble core of Structure 10B. This difference relates Structure 10C to the conventions of construction found in the monumental public architecture of the central precinct where clean fill is strongly preferred (Freidel 1977:30). Although it is difficult to estimate the floor space provided by the platform, the exposed western side of the retaining wall enclosed an area of 12 m². Symmetry would suggest a similar platform wing area to the east in an area which has yet to be excavated.

The age of the above platform is puzzling. Although there is a meter of overburden capping the site which is thought to be Classic in date, there is no clear weathering horizon suggesting that the platform may be Classic as well, particularly since the group as a whole dates to the Classic.

Our inability to obtain a firm date for this platform necessitated a revision in our sampling technique. Limited postholing on the back and lateral sides of this and other poorly dated mounds was carried out in an attempt to locate associated midden deposits (after Fry 1969). However, the limited number of sherds collected from the preliminary postholing program, even after controlled test pitting operations, forced us to return to sealed construction fill contextual dating (cf. Rice and Rice 1980 for discussion of these techniques).

STRUCTURE 11 GROUP

Group 11 is composed of three structures on a raised plaza labeled Structures 11B, 11C and 11D (Fig. 2.2b). This Type 2 structure group rests within a *huamil* setting flanked on three sides by depressed *zacatal* and thornscrub savanna. The present shoreline is less than 40 m to the northwest. The largest mound, Structure 11B, is oriented to the west and the two other structures appear to be directed toward this better preserved structure. The structure group has been assigned to the Tulix phase although there are indications of an Early Classic period use of this structure. There is also evidence for Late Postclassic period reoccupation here. This structure group is thought to represent an elite residence (cf. Lewenstein, this volume).

Structure 11A

Structure 11A is the raised plaza area supporting the three associated substructures. Op 102 was excavated during the 1976 season in order to obtain midden debris while documenting the constructional history of the plazuela group. The 1 × 5 m trench was located on the backside of Structure 11D. Assuming the prevailing winds had not changed over time, the location of the trench downwind and behind the plaza area was thought to be ideal for trash deposition. Unfortunately, primary deposition trash was not located.

The trench was also extended into the raised plaza area. The data indicate that the plaza may have been paved in the Tulix period with a dark soil matrix. An overlying Late Postclassic period humus was underlain by this Late Preclassic pavement, which was in turn supported by a loosely packed limestone rubble core. The plaza construction fill appeared to be less tightly packed than that of the mounds themselves.

Structure 11B

Structure 11B is approximately 2 m higher and east of the adjacent mounds in the Structure 11 Group. The plan of Structure 11B (Fig. 2.3a) is not unlike a scaled down version of Structures 29, 30 and 31 on the North Acropolis of Tikal (Coe 1974). Each of these structures is oriented to the west and perhaps dates to the Early Classic period in final forms.

During the 1974 field season a 1 × 3 m unit was excavated to a depth of 2.15 m at the summit of the mound. This exposure provided a degree of stratigraphic control for subsequent work on the mound. During 1977 the mound was excavated horizontally in an attempt to expose architectural and artifactual associations. More than 125 m² or nearly all of the northwestern half of the platform was exposed and mapped to a maximum depth of 2.3 m. A 2 × 2 m arbitrary grid control was maintained during the course of excavations to insure accurate horizontal as well as vertical provenience for anticipated activity area relationships.

The earliest construction activity is represented by a lens of friable reddish brown clay underlain by trash, soil and gravel ballast. This deposit appears to represent the leveling of an earlier occupation in preparation for the next construction episode. Because this lens is at the same elevation both inside and outside the overlying building, the entire mound surface was evidently prepared by the builders responsible for the subsequent building. Ceramic diagnostics from the trash deposit underlying the lens date to the Tulix phase.

The elaborate building platform overlying this leveling event is Tulix in date as well, although no primary caches or burials were found. The building platform is composite in plan. A large rectangular west room fronting the plaza is connected to an eastern rear room by a constricted accessway. The masonry is more substantial than many other architectural contexts in the settlement zone. The chinked walls are composed of rectangular stones that were covered by a thick coat of red and white plaster. The backside of the platform may have been curvilinear in plan, a building convention similar to that revealed in Structure 10C. Unfortunately, the rear portion of the platform was badly deteriorated, preventing the testing of this hypothesis.

Near the southwestern corner of the platform, a recessed wall niche (1 × 1 m) was exposed. It appears to have been adorned by a relief panel of plaster, molded on dressed stone and painted red, buff, black and white. This polychrome molded stucco facade was probably supported by four tenoned and grooved stones projecting from an upper course in the niche which has since collapsed. Excavation of the niche also produced an interior south wall behind the wall supporting the relief, indicating that the building platform was originally constricted an additional 80 cm.

Although the front of the building platform was only briefly examined, a stairway probably ascended from the plaza to the building. A plaster floor extended over the building platform on the front, or plaza side of the niche, creating an enclosed rectangular space separated from the main building and stairway by wall stub alignments. Three plaster floors were accounted for on this veranda-like frontal room, one immediately overlying another. The main, or rear, superstructural room was not as well preserved, but two temporally separated plaster floors were discernible. The stones defining the front and side walls of the main room appeared to be well dressed loaf-shaped blocks similar to those found in the center and dating to the Late Preclassic period. Although the rear wall was not discovered, the main room must have been over 4 m wide by 6 m in length. In addition, the veranda-like frontal room was 3 m wide by at least 8 m in length. The southern third of the mound was not excavated, due to the presence of a modern water tower, hence the exact dimensions for these rooms were not discovered.

Associated evidence indicates that the two rooms were originally at the same elevation. They were defined by stone foundation walls with perishable upper walls. No postholes, post molds or post impressed briquettes were recovered. The rooms were connected by two or more entrance ways. At a later time the main eastern room was raised and the doorways were modified with the addition of steps. The Preclassic date accepted for these events was derived from diagnostic ceramics taken from sealed floors in the front and back rooms, from sealed wall fill representing sequential modifications of the building plan and from construction fill incorporated into the building platform.

An Early Classic occupation of the mound is suggested by the appearance of Tzakol basal flange bowl fragments in extremely low frequencies. These five sherds would appear to suggest the presence of an ephemeral reuse of the site by an Early Classic group, not unlike that found in contexts within the central precinct. The proximity of Classic materials to the final Preclassic construction phase, coupled with the absence of any subsequent construction datable to the Classic period suggests that the building platform was still largely visible and reused by Classic period occupants.

The most recent pre-Columbian occupants of this site appear to have been Late Postclassic groups, represented by a poorly defined rectilinear wall stub and patches of poorly preserved plaster flooring. This structure and hypothesized perishable room extensions may have covered most of the level mound surface. The occupants appear to have constructed their foundation on top of the earlier Preclassic wall stub foundation. The floor within the wall alignment seems to have been underlain by large flat laid limestone ballast. This type flooring may be similar to Wauchope's (1938:15) description of *embutido*, in which large flat stones were irregularly placed in a matrix of lime and marl. A threshold area was located along the medial axis of the structure. A small Postclassic dedicatory cache was discovered immediately outside the structural wall alignment to the west.

A trash deposit on the southeastern slope of the mound contained a high frequency of lithic debris. A concentration of sherds, apparently from a single pot, was found strewn over the northwestern wall foundation, suggesting post-occupational reuse. A chlorite schist ax was also collected from this context.

The dry laid rubble defining the northeastern portion of the mound suggests that the occupants may have purposely buried the underlying retaining wall or platform (cf. Willey *et al*. 1965:69; Bullard 1973:236). The wall alignment overlying this disturbance indicates that between the Late Preclassic/Early Classic and Postclassic periods, a large portion of the Preclassic component was destroyed and subsequently overlain by a large amount of rubble fill.

Even though Structure 11B lacks diagnostic household features (Haviland 1970), its form and size, coupled with its relationship to the ancillary plazuela Structures 11C and Structure 11D, resemble other domestic structures in the Maya area. The elaborate nature of Preclassic period architecture on Structure 11B suggests a strong social linkage to the central precinct approximately 460 m to the northeast. Although the differential consumption of luxury ceramics, lithics, and exotic materials must await analysis, the evidence at hand supports the notion of occupation in this group.

Structure 11C

Structure 11C lies approximately 15 m northwest of Structure 11B. During the 1977 season a 24 m² exposure was excavated to a depth of 1.2 m (Op 108). Instead of employing a proximation trench, a contiguous horizontal exposure was opened at the summit of the mound. The low, flat appearance of Structure 11C and the absence of raised masonry retaining walls associated with other small mounds in the settlement made this type of excavation preferable. Although smaller in size than the other structures, Structure 11C was excavated in an attempt to elucidate variability within the plazuela group.

The building platform was composed of light grey marl intruded by cobble size and larger stones. The excavation produced a sizeable sample of Postclassic lithic debris (see Rovner 1975) as well as Late Preclassic and Late Postclassic ceramic diagnostics. Unfortunately, architectural features were not defined for any period. No ceramics were found in primary deposits, although Late Preclassic debris was encountered approximately 50 cm below the surface.

Structure 11D

Structure 11D is located approximately 15 m southwest of Structure 11B. During the 1974 field season a 2 × 2 m test unit was excavated to a depth of 2 m at the summit of the mound (Op 16), to establish a stratigraphic column.

The mound was constructed of dry laid rubble overlying a deposit of dark brown clay (5-10 cm thick) containing Tulix phase ceramics at 1.4 m below the summit of the structure. The depth of this lens corresponds to the same absolute elevation at which trash and dark soil were recovered from Structure 11B. This suggests an extensive, though poorly preserved, occupation or deposition of materials before the plazuela mounding occurred. This stratum corresponds to the earliest leveling event described for Structure 11B. A thin marl lens underlies this deposit and appears to be a preparatory surface overlying the sterile paleosol.

STRUCTURE 9

Structure 9A is a large plaza area on the southeast margin of the central precinct. Structure 9B is a Type 4 structure located in this *huamil* setting. It is oriented toward the central precinct, lying 180 m south of Structure 6B. The paved plaza Structure 9A extends north to the foot of plaza Structure 7A and as far south as the Structure 10 Group. The more elevated northern half of the plaza is further defined by the present shoreline and the western margin of plaza Structure 8A. The southwestern limits of the plaza are less distinct, though the western shoreline is again suggested (a portion of it may have been removed recently for rock fill). Its southeastern edge is defined by Structures 13, 14 and 15 which rest upon it. Plaza Structure 9A covers approximately 26,400 m².

Structures 9A and 9B have been assigned a Tulix phase date, although there is a Late Postclassic reoccupation. Structure 9B served a civic/ritual function based on its imposing size, proximity to the center and the ceramic inventory recovered.

Structure 9A/Feature 33A

Feature 33A represents a flat test excavation approximately 90 m southwest of Structure 9B (Fig. 2.3b). An uprooted coconut tree revealed the location of this feature within plaza Structure 9A. Op 107 was excavated during the 1976 field season in anticipation of midden debris. A 2 × 4 m unit was exposed to a maximum depth of 1.0 m. The long axis of the unit was oriented to magnetic north.

Six naturally defined and two arbitrarily defined levels were divided into nine lots. The surface level consisted of a loose, grey humus loam intruded by boulder size rubble fill. This 40 cm thick surface rubble deposit represents plaza Structure 9A and it contains Tulix phase ceramics. No flooring was preserved due to the exposed nature of the plaza.

Levels 3 and 4 were arbitrary lots consisting of a loose, moist, dark grey clay intruded by angular limestone gravel underlying the plaza. This deposit was excavated in 10 cm vertical units due to the abundance of midden debris collected. Sherds, charcoal, ash, bone and shell were present in high frequencies. A high percentage of ceramic diagnostics, together with thermoluminescence dating, indicate that the midden was probably deposited as the plaza was extended a short time after the midden accumulated in Op 1. This trash has been assigned a firm C'oh Phase date.

Level 5 consisted of a compact, moist 5-10 cm thick *sascab* floor mottled by the overlying grey clay trash deposit. Predictably, the trash inventory decreased substantially on the house floor. Level 6 was defined as a compact, moist, well sorted beige clay underlying the floor. It was intruded by a discontinuous band of severely eroded pebble to cobble size hearting stones. A posthole was located in the southeastern portion of the unit apparently associated with the *sascab* floor. In section, it was found to be 14 cm in diameter and to extend approximately 20 cm below the *sascab* floor surface. The *sascab* floor appeared to feather out on two of the four sides of the unit. Although the perimeter of the structure could not be traced, evidence suggests that our test unit may have straddled the edge of the structure. Artifact densities inside and outside the structure were not revealing.

Level 7 consisted of a compact, moist, well sorted blue clay gumbo. The water table was contacted at 80 cm BSD. This matrix contained a few unidentifiable sherds and appears to be a riverine clay deposit associated with the earliest occupation at the site (Cliff, this volume). Level 8 was a decomposing yellow granular caprock deposit.

Feature 33 has produced a significant information base. The underlying C'oh phase midden deposit and ground level structure as well as the underlying clays further support the hypothesis that Cerros developed out of an Ixtabai/C'oh phase village adapted to a riverine economy. The presence of the Tulix phase plaza Structure 9A corresponds with a major sociopolitical change at Cerros. By the Tulix phase the intra-site area as defined by the canal had taken on a civic character unlike earlier occupations.

Structure 9B

Op 10 was excavated during the 1974 field season. A test pit was placed near the center of the mound between two slightly elevated superstructural platforms at either end of the east-west oriented mount. This 4 m² exposure was excavated to a depth of 2.3 m in an attempt to date the mound by means of a primary associated cache. Although no dedicatory offerings were located, a stratigraphic sequence was discernible.

A scattered Postclassic component was located within the humus horizon in Op 10, and this was underlain by white marl and rubble fill. A brown sandy matrix was encountered approximately 90 cm BSD. Rubble fill severely intruded into this matrix. Three additional marl lenses, also intruded by rubble fill, were noted before terminating the exposure. These marl concentrations were ephemeral and mixed with a sandy matrix making them difficult to isolate. This suggests that the fill for the mound was thrown together rather than deposited in clean fine lenses.

At approximately 1.05 m BSD one of the marl layers in Op 10 was continuous across the horizontal exposure. It was 2 cm thick and contained burned limestone chunks. There were few artifactual diagnostics in this lens, which lay at approximately the same depth as the marl lens reported in Op 101 (a test on the eastern end of Structure 9B). Unfortunately we cannot yet confirm this lens as being so continuous. Finally, an abrupt increase in sherd fill was noted at 1.5-1.9 m BSD. This appears to be a Late Preclassic component, but the limited exposure in construction fill did not allow primary contextual control for a firm date.

Op 13 was excavated during the 1974 field season. It was a trenching operation located on the northwestern slope of the mound. The 3 × 8 m exposure was excavated parallel to the long axis of the mound on its upper slope. An additional 1.25 m × 1.5 m exposure extended below and perpendicular to this trench. This T-trench was excavated in anticipation of architectural features and the surface suggested trash deposits. Upon removing the fall overlying the structure, a crude riser was exposed. It was defined by five uncut limestone slabs placed vertically as a retaining wall for the cobble size rubble and marl fill composing the mound. The sherd inventory overlying this feature contained a high percentage of Postclassic censer ware as well as chert flakes and a low frequency of obsidian blade fragments. Fish and sea turtle bone in addition to numerous ceramic fish net weights (cf. Eaton 1976) were also found in this context.

The Op 13 T-trench further exposed a cut stone wall 1.7 m BSD behind and to the west of the riser. The cut stone wall consisted of a four to five course chinked wall exposure with a basal moulding. Each cobble size stone was rectilinear in form. Bits of plaster and *sascab* suggest that the surface was covered to prevent the exposure of the irregular arrangement of stone coursing. The height of the wall was 80 cm at its best preserved location. The basal moulding consisted of horizontally bedded cut stones extending out from the wall. The lateral extent of the moulding and the underlying floor could not be determined. The sherds collected behind and under these features date to the Tulix period exclusively (see also Freidel, this volume, for further discussion of this structure).

Structure 9C

Structure 9C is a slight superstructural feature at the top eastern side of Structure 9B. The superstructure is poorly defined by a rectilinear single course arrangement of limestone blocks approximately 2 m east-west by 4 m north-south. It appears to be associated with a Late Postclassic occupation of the site.

Op 101 was excavated during the 1975 field season. It was a restricted 1 × 2 m exposure excavated in an attempt to date the feature. A marl matrix intruded with large limestone blocks was located upon penetration of the mound. It was in turn underlain by large dry laid rubble fill. The marl deposition may be an occupational event, but little associated debris was collected. Some evidence of construction pauses within the fill of the mound is suggested by the appearance of a sandy soil sandwiched between the rubble fill at 1.5 m BSD.

STRUCTURE 34

This Type 5 structure (Fig. 2.4) rests in a well-drained *huamil* setting in the scoured and pitted caprock relief associated with the northeastern intrasite area. The southern margin of the mound is flanked by an apparent run-off channel issuing into the main canal. Structure 34 is oriented N45°W of magnetic north so that its primary axis is directed toward the central precinct. The structure has been assigned a Late Tulix phase date. Although the construction appears to have been initiated during the Late Tulix phase, significant modifications occurred during the Terminal Preclassic period. The structure was reused in Early Classic times and Postclassic debris was collected on the surface. The structure is interpreted as a housemound.

During the 1978 field season a 2 × 2 m unit was placed on the northern flank of Structure 34 (Op 118). It was excavated to a maximum depth of 1.4 m (Fig. 2.4c). Upon exposure of two retaining wall features and an exterior plaster floor, Structure 34 was selected for further lateral exposure. The horizontal exposure revealed 53 m² on the northern half of the structure to a maximum depth of 1.7 m. A 2 × 2 m arbitrary grid control was maintained to insure accurate horizontal and vertical provenience for anticipated activity area relationships. These data were to be compared and contrasted with Structure 11B and other less extensive excavations.

The earliest component at this site locus is a Tulix phase ground level occupation. Architecturally it is not well documented, though ceramically the inventory included large sherds and other trash debris in and overlying the sterile black gumbo paleosol. A discontinuous 5-10 m thick lens of gravel size hearting stone capped the paleosol and probably represents the remains of the original flooring of the structure. The overlying small boulder size rubble coring together with a thick concentration of *sascab* may represent the razed remains of this former dwelling.

The next component has been defined as a simple rectangular Late Tulix phase platform. It was approximately 6.95 m long by 5.70 m wide and attained a maximum preserved height of 90 cm (6-8 courses in elevation). The chinked retaining wall was composed of rectangular stones set in a thick marl grout. The construction fill consisted of a dry laid small boulder size rubble overlain by a cobble size ballast encased in an intruding humus fill. No flooring was associated with the platform surface. It apparently was stripped away during the subsequent modification of the mound. There was a hard plaster floor at the base of the platform along the northern side.

The major construction phase on Structure 34 was a two-step terminal Preclassic platform with an outset staircase or ramp. It was approximately 7.75 m long, 6.60 m wide and attained a maximum height of 90 cm. The outset staircase was 3.75 m long and 3.20 m wide. The treads and risers were severely damaged. The structure incorporated the Tulix phase platform by adding an additional retaining wall to the entire structure. This outer wall was placed 30-50 cm from the inner wall running parallel to its N45°W orientation. It was constructed with the same rectangular stones set in

a marl grout as identified for the inner wall. The fill between the two walls consisted of cobble size coring packed in a white marl matrix. The outer wall was one to two courses lower than the inner wall, giving a stepped appearance to the structure. Excavation revealed no preserved plaster on the platform. A plaster floor was found preserved within the inset corner areas of the outset staircase as well as at the eastern corner of the structure. Traces of flooring were also noted along the northeastern side of the structure suggesting that the area immediately outside the structure generally had been plastered. Hearting stones 5-7 cm thick were found to underlie the better preserved portions of this floor.

The outset staircase was hung on the northwest side of the outer platform wall. It was composed of the same rectangular stone masonry as found in the other two walls. At the juncture of the outer platform wall and the outset, the staircase attained a height of six courses (60 cm). The fill within the outset was the same cobble size ballast found between the platform walls, but it contained a large percentage of *sascab* as well.

A substantial Early Classic reuse of the structure was evinced by a continuous clean marl cap or lens (5-10 cm thick) covering most of the summit of the platform. One possible posthole, similar to those defined on Structure 50D (cf. Scarborough, *et al.* 1982) was located between the two platform walls and approximately 1.0 m northeast of the southwest inset. It was 10 cm in diameter. A Tzakol basal flange bowl at a shallow depth was found along the medial axis of the mound and 50 cm southeast of the inner wall. It was badly crushed and does not seem to have contained any additional offering.

Size and place indicate that Structure 34 was a dwelling. Its orientation and location on a plastered plaza suggest that it may have been an elite residence during the Late and Terminal Preclassic times. Unfortunately the sherd inventory was too small to confirm this interpretation.

STRUCTURE 76 GROUP

This structure group represents the focus for a complex of eight separate mounds within 100 m of Aguada 1 (Feature 79). Structure 76 can be classified as a Type 2 mound group (Fig. 2.5), although its form and orientation are unlike that defined elsewhere in the settlement. It lies within the *monte alto* setting. A Tulix phase construction date has been assigned, and ephemeral Classic and Postclassic occupation have been noted. Aguada 1 appears to be a Tulix phase man-made reservoir formed as a consequence of the fill necessary for constructing Structure 76. The clustering of the mounds around Structure 76 as well as their proximity to Aguada 1 may suggest a degree of water management at the southern margin of the *hulub bajo* setting.

Although our sample from the Structure 76 Group is small, the absence of household midden debris indicates a non-residential function for this group. Surely the size and relative dominance of Structure 76 when compared to the adjacent structures would argue for a different function. Moreover, the pottery suggests a civic or ritual orientation.

Structure 76B

This site was selected for excavation because of its imposing size and its distance from the central precinct. During the 1978 field season a 2 × 4 m trench was positioned on the sloping western margin of this acropolis-like platform which rests on an elevated substructure (Structure 76A). The excavation is believed to have intersected the medial axis of the structure. The long axis of the unit was oriented N10°W. The trench was excavated to a maximum depth of 2.4 m, with the southern half of the unit being terminated at 1.15 m.

Our excavations suggest that the northern and western portions of the unit supported a ramp or stairway connecting Structure 76D (to the northwest) with the raised substructure (Structure 76A), given the thickness of the hearting within the trench. Although no evidence for plaster surfacing was recovered, a thick, dense ballast would be expected in this location. The large rubble fill near the surface in the southern portion of the unit may indicate that less traffic was directed across this surface. Although erosional agents may account for some of the missing hearting, the slope angle at this location is not critical and would not seem to be greatly affected by wasting. The profiles further suggest that the acropolis, or Structure 76B, was not a later addition to the structure but was part of the initial form of the structure.

Structure 76D

This structure lies to the immediate northwest of Structure 76B. Although our summit trench (Op 113)

provided an unmixed late C'oh phase date for the structure group, the sherd sample collected was from an unsealed context. During 1977 we located a 2 × 5 m trench between the northwest margin of Structure 76A and the southeast edge of Structure 76D in anticipation of sealed construction fill as well as architectural detail. The long axis of the unit was oriented to magnetic north. The trench was excavated to a maximum depth of 2.0 m. This location was selected because slope wash and wasting from above had apparently settled in the trough between the two structures quite early on. This overburden was believed to have lessened the surface deterioration of the original structure unlike the unprotected summit exposure. In addition, a portion of the hypothesized ramp or stairway between the two structures, suggested by our summit trench, was anticipated at this location.

A poorly preserved four course high retaining wall (Wall 1) was contacted in cross-section in the southern excavation wall. To the southwest, a thick, dense deposit of *sascab* melt containing sizable chunks of plaster was isolated in front (west) of this retaining wall. A second crudely faced retaining wall (Wall 2), three courses high, located in the western profile defined the northern-most extent of the plaster melt. The two retaining walls are interpreted to have joined in forming an inset corner between Structures 76A and 76D. The plaster melt outside the poorly preserved walls is argued to represent the razing of a superstructure or facade from the summit of Structure 76D. The hard plaster floor appears to have formerly overlain and defined the edges of the retaining walls.

STRUCTURE 84

This Type 6 structure represents one of eight isolated structures surrounding the Structure 76 Group. It was selected for excavation because of its diminutive size in relation to Structure 76 Group and because there was a greater sherd scatter on the surface than there was on the other small Type 6 mounds in the vicinity. The mound rests in proximity to a *huanal* setting, although *monte alto* defines the immediate surrounding. The structure has been assigned an Early Classic period date, although Postclassic reoccupation is suggested. It has been tentatively identified as a house locus.

STRUCTURE 38

This structure rests within a well drained *huamil* setting. The ground is generally elevated but riddled with pits and shallow quarry scars. It appears to have undergone limited quarrying activity, perhaps as a consequence of the exhaustion of other nearby caprock locations. Structures 37 and 105, both within 10 m of Structure 38, appear to be stockpiles of limestone construction fill rather than occupation facilities. Two poorly defined, well-like features occur immediately southwest of Structure 38 in addition to an amorphous depression speculated to have been *sascabero*. Structure 38 is one of the larger structures in this location, but unlike other mounds of this size, it appears to be constructed primarily of earthen fill.

The mound has been assigned a Late C'oh phase date, which suggests that extensive quarrying of the caprock was seldom undertaken in this phase, perhaps reflecting the absence of social mechanisms necessary to prevent damage to the fragile drainage system at the site. Earth fill is obtainable by simply scraping the surface of the decomposing caprock over a rather extensive area. However, this practice would eventually force the occupants to quarry for new mound fill as the earth fill would be exhausted relatively quickly. A Tulix occupation as well as an ephemeral Classic and Postclassic reoccupation of the mound was demonstrated. Judging from the Late C'oh trash lens, this Type 5 mound is identified as a house locus.

Although Structure 38 was not completely composed of earth fill, the bulk of the mound is suggested to have been light grey marl. This matrix would have been easily obtained from the adjacent ground surface without a concentrated quarrying effort, suggesting there were constraints on monumental architecture during this phase.

STRUCTURE 66

This structure rests on an elevated island of well-drained *huamil* flanked by broad run-off thornscrub depressions. This raised ground is suggested to have been surrounded by the drainage depressions channeling the central precinct run-off. The mound was test excavated because of its isolated position with respect to the number of large mound clusters in this vicinity. Structure 66 is a Type 5 mound. The mound is argued to be a Tulix phase construction with a very ephemeral Classic and Postclassic reoccupation. Judging from the

amount of debris and its nature the mound has been tentatively identified as an elite house.

Although little can be made of the exposed architecture relative to the surface contours of the mound, the position and orientation of a wall fragment is not unlike the patio wings or extensions revealed on Structure 11B. The wall fragments may be the interior inset behind and blow a western facing veranda.

STRUCTURE 65

Structure 65 rests on an elevated *huamil* setting shared with Structure 120. This area is surrounded by thornscrub with an eliptical catchment basin defining the southern margin of the elevated *huamil*. In plan, the mound bears a northern orientational relationship to Structure 29 and ballcourt Structure 61 Group similar to that of the more southern Structure 53 to Structure 29 and ballcourt Structure 50 Group. This Type 5 mound was selected for study because of its position in the settlement.

Although no midden debris was isolated, sealed construction fill has provided a Late C'oh construction date. A Classic and Postclassic reoccupation of the mound is evidenced.

Structure 65 is postulated to have functioned as a non-residential facility. This identification is based on very slim evidence, but is suggested on grounds of the spatial relationship it manifests with the structures mentioned above. Although a hard plaster floor, unassociated with domestic trash, can be argued to represent sampling error, it is predicted that little midden debris will be collected from this mound if further exposure is undertaken. The ceramic sample was too small to clarify the situation.

STRUCTURE 53

This structure is a Type 4 structure located in the same relationship (to the south) to Structure 29 and the ballcourt Structure 50 Group as Structure 65 is to Structure 29 and the ballcourt Structure 61 Group (to the north). The structure is nearly surrounded by depressed *zacatal* and thornscrub savanna. Except for a strip of elevated ground to the south, the structure can be viewed as an island. The large size and isolated location of the structure suggest that it was not a residential locus but a civic facility. Ceramics taken from construction fill indicate a Late C'oh construction date with later Tulix phase modifications. Ephemeral Classic and Postclassic occupations are indicated as well. The excavation did not identify the function of the structure. However, size and isolation suggest a public building.

STRUCTURE 116 GROUP

This Type 1 structure group rests within the *hulub bajo* outside and northeast of the main canal. The four structures in this group appear to be oriented to the cardinal directions (or toward the central precinct) and rest on a low platform. Judging from our test unit the elevated platform is perhaps best seen as the original ground surface with the surrounding matrix having been culturally or naturally removed. The group was tested because of its architectural complexity and position outside the canal within the poorly drained *hulubol*. Its proximity to the coast was considered important as well, given the trade network postulated for Cerros. The group is argued to have functioned as a residential plazuela, perhaps monitoring raised field agriculture outside the canal. A Tulix phase date has been assigned to the group, though the sherd inventory collected was small. An ephemeral Postclassic occupation is evident.

The structure did not reveal a dense midden deposit or clear architectural detail. However, given its distance from the center and by analogy to other plazuela groups in the lowlands, it is thought to have functioned as a residential cluster. The structure group's position within the *bajo* strongly suggests its role in raised field agriculture. The size and formal complexity of the group may suggest that a managerial elite resided at this location. Even allowing for subsidence and erosion of the shoreline, the proximity of the coast would have permitted possible petty riverine exchange.

STRUCTURE 115 GROUP

This group of three structures lies 150 m south of the Structure 116 Group, resting east and outside the main canal segment. The plazuela group is located on an elevated *monte alto* setting and surrounded by *hulubol*. The group orientation may be toward the central precinct. The group is tentatively defined as a residential facility analogous to the Structure 116 group. Immediately to the west of the plazuela is a problematic mound which may be the remains of an ancient raised

field platform. It was entirely circumscribed by linear depressions. A Tulix phase date has been assigned to the construction of this group, though an ephemeral Classic and Postclassic occupation is apparent.

This mound group is postulated to have functioned as a residential area. Despite the small size of the plazuela and the poor quality of architecture, elite ceramic material is present. The proximity of the adjacent bajo suggests that the occupants secured a living from the bajo setting. The high ground on which the Structure 115 Group rests is argued to represent the eastern-most extent of quarry and canal maintenance at the site. It is unlikely that the managerial elite at Cerros would have allowed the upper middle class service population characterized by the Structure 115 Group to occupy this elevated *monte alto* setting if this area were at a premium for additional fill or drainage.

STRUCTURE 46

This Type 3 plazuela group of two mounds lies approximately 50 m to the southeast and is outside the canal. It is 70 m east of a causeway or check dam bridging the canal. The group rests in a *monte alto* setting, but it is flanked on three sides by *huanal*. The structures face one another northeast-southwest and rest on a raised platform. This orientation runs parallel to the nearby canal axis. Although Tulix phase ceramics were well represented in the excavation, a clear Early Classic date has been obtained for this group from a sealed construction fill context. An ephemeral Postclassic occupation is also apparent. Although this plazuela was constructed in the Early Classic, the amount of Late Preclassic debris suggests the presence of a Tulix phase construction in this vicinity.

Two construction/occupation events are documented at this structure. The earliest is associated with the midden debris. Whether or not it is a primary or secondary context deposit, it implies that the immediate vicinity was lived on by Early Classic residents prior to the construction of the plaza and Structure 46C. The later construction reflects a continuous occupation of the area culminating in exposed architecture. The preparatory surface suggests an affinity to the Late Preclassic practice of spreading this white marl across a site before the onset of construction.

The Early Classic occupation of the settlement is not well defined and is usually quite ephemeral. However, the presence of the Structure 46 Group may suggest a continuity in tradition from the Preclassic florescence at Cerros. If smaller Early Classic populations maintained small, well-drained plots that were perhaps directed by a few managerial families, then the Structure 46 Group may represent a "rural elite" residence.

STRUCTURE 94

This Type 6 mound lies within the *huanal* approximately 40 m south and outside of the canal. The diminutive size and isolated position of the mound coupled with the presence of Postclassic debris suggest that Structure 94 was a farmstead constructed during the Late Postclassic.

STRUCTURE 77

This Type 6 structure rests 60 m east-southeast of plaza Structure 8A in a well-drained *huamil* setting. The mound occurs in an area of disturbed relief probably due to high winds and uprooted trees. A portion of the main plaza run-off depression passes to the immediate west. The water table appears to rise in this vicinity as evidenced by the mottled gleilike condition of the soils and the graham cracker consistency of the ceramics retrieved. This is further supported by the presence of a recently abandoned well site to the immediate west. This unusual feature may have provided suitable drinking water for a segment of the prehistoric population. The mound was dug as much to increase our Type 6 count as to test the prospect that some of these very small mounds were not the result of human energies. The majority of sherds collected from the mound date to the Postclassic period.

This mound is identified as a Postclassic domestic facility at the foot of the main plaza. Although the high water table may have posed some problems for the occupants, the proximity of a potentially potable water source may have outweighed any disadvantage.

STRUCTURE 26

This Type 6 mound is located in a *huamil* setting in close proximity to Structures 25, 26 and 28. The caprock in this area is exposed in some locations. However, the soil overlying it is quite moist apparently due to the drainage depressions surrounding the area. The mound is interpreted as a domestic dwelling

constructed during the Tulix phase. It appears to have been reoccupied during the Postclassic period. The mound has been disturbed by post-depositional agents. Our test unit was placed away from the most obvious disturbances to the south. The mound was selected for excavation because of its formal and spatial affinity to the other mounds in proximity.

Structure 26 appears to represent a non-elite residential facility. It appears to reflect the centrifugal force pulling the C'oh phase occupants away from the Ixtabai phase nucleated village.

STRUCTURE 24

This structure rests at the northern end of the *sacbe* (Feature 126) at the margin of the depressed *zacatal*. It lies in a well-drained *huamil* setting at the southern reaches of plaza 9A. Structure 24 is interpreted as a Late C'oh Phase construction reoccupied in Tulix as well as in Classic and Postclassic times. The function of the mound is equivocal, but its small size and association with Structures 13, 14, 15 and 16 at the edge of the plaza 9A may suggest an outbuilding or service population residence.

This structure was excavated because of its size and proximity to the relatively larger mounds of this zone. The absence of a paleosol suggests the deliberate removal of the topsoil prior to construction. Again, it may suggest the premium placed on the soil itself, perhaps for agricultural fields. The C'oh phase occupation of this mound appears to be at ground level.

STRUCTURE 112

This structure lies on the edge of the present bay approximately 200 m east of the main plaza. It rests on a well-drained *huamil* setting, and it is flanked on three sides by *hulub*. An apparent run-off channel passes south of the structure and may drain into the main canal. The structure was selected for excavation because it was uniquely located on the shoreline, suggesting direct involvement in maritime exchange. The structure dates to the Tulix phase, though a Postclassic reoccupation is indicated. In addition to the mound, our excavations demonstrated the presence of ground level occupation during the Tulix phase, sealed by the overlying structure.

Structure 112 presents a rapid developmental sequence involving four constructional events occurring within the Tulix phase. Although the precise function of the mound is not well understood, a docking facility hypothesis cannot be discounted. The ceramics indicate a civic/ritual function for the mound. The underlying three floors and an associated burial best describe a ground level residential locus early in the phase. Most researchers suggest that burials in small structures indicate a household function for the mound. Analysis suggests in this and other contexts that C'oh and early Tulix phase ground level dwellings later had mounded structures built over them. This practice would appear to be a comment on kin spatial continuity through time. The mounds in these cases represent the establishment and assertion of greater family authority within the community.

STRUCTURE 54

This Type 4 structure rests at the north end of the eastern *sacbe* or plaza edge (Feature 51). The structure lies in an elevated *huamil* setting, although thornscrub lies in the immediate vicinity. The structure was tested because of its imposing size as well as its location at the end of the *sacbe*. It is hypothesized to be public architecture. The mound was constructed during the Tulix phase. This date accords well with Structure 29 at the south end of the *sacbe* (or plaza edge) and provides a tentative date for the *sacbe* itself.

Although Structure 54 is believed to be a Tulix phase civic structure, the date is equivocal due to the presence of Early Classic debris in low frequencies on the upper reaches of the mound. However, these sherds are argued to be a consequence of vertical migration due to the decomposed nature of the upper tred surfaces. Only Tulix ceramics were taken from the lower 2.2 m of fill.

STRUCTURE 57

This Type 6 structure lies near the center of the *sacbe* or plaza edge defined in the eastern intra-site area (Feature 51). The mound lies in a *huamil* setting at the edge of a thornscrub environ. The structure was excavated to augment our Type 6 sample as well as to provide a cross-section of the underlying *sacbe* on which it rests. The structure is understood to be a non-residential facility on the grounds of its diminutive size and its central position on the *sacbe*. Our sherd inventory from unsealed construction fill suggests that

the mound dates to the Tulix phase, as does the underlying *sacbe*. Classic and Postclassic reuse of this facility is also indicated.

This structure is posited to be a shrine or outbuilding of unknown function resting on the *sacbe* or plaza edge. The surface of the *sacbe* is ill-defined except for the appearance of the flat laid cobbles.

STRUCTURE 13

This Type 5 structure rests on the eastern flank of the low-lying plaza Structure 9A south of Structure 9B within a *huamil* setting. The mound appears to be oriented toward the central precinct, as are the neighboring Structures 14, 15, 16 and the 10 group. The structure lies on the western flank of a shallow run-off channel draining the southwestern central precinct plaza. Our excavation has revealed three distinct construction phases on this mound, the most recent being a meter thick mantle dating to the Classic and/or Postclassic. The earlier events are associated with clear Tulix phase construction activity.

Structure 13 shows four events, including the underlying midden deposit which is thought to be associated with an early Tulix phase ground level occupation. The ballast supporting and including a *sascab*/plaster floor (F1) is understood to represent the southeastern portion of subplaza Structure 9A. This feature underlies most of the structures in this quadrat. A retaining wall is a feature associated with the initial construction of Structure 13. The most recent construction event was a later occupation associated with the Classic and Postclassic reoccupation of the site. The Tulix phase retaining wall was razed except for the extant four courses and, correspondingly, the adjacent area outside the wall was raised. This appears to have occurred sometime after Tulix phase abandonment as evidenced by the truncated tree root disturbance. The overlying fill was poorly consolidated.

STRUCTURE 14

This Type 4 structure rests on the eastern margin of subplaza Structure 9A within a *huamil* setting. The mound shares the same orientation toward the central precinct as the adjacent Structures 13, 15, 16 and the 10 Group. A shallow, poorly defined run-off channel draining the main plaza lies to the east. The imposing size, limited summit space and spatial disposition to other mounds suggest that it is not a residential locus. Unfortunately the ceramic inventory was too small to be of any use. It should be noted that the southwest side of the mound appears to be terraced. The structure has been assigned a Tulix phase date, though an ephemeral Classic and Postclassic occupation are evident. A C'oh phase ground level structure may be suggested as well.

Structure 14 is understood to be a Tulix phase non-residential structure mantled by a Classic and Postclassic reoccupation. A smaller platform resting upon the underlying subplaza Structure 9A is suggested. This latter structure was stratigraphically constructed in the early Tulix phase. The plaza appears to be contemporaneous with the smaller platform. The earliest evidence for occupation of this locus is from the paleosol surface underlying the plaza and dating to the C'oh phase.

STRUCTURE 19

This Type 3 structure group rests in a well-drained *huamil* setting near the western margin of the intra-site area. A depressed *zacatal* setting lies in proximity. The structure group was selected for excavation because of its imposing size and unique form. This structure group has been more severely damaged than any other structure in the settlement. Bulldozer action in the 1960's has removed the southern third of range Structure 19C and perhaps disturbed the adjacent southern portion of plaza Structure 19A. Informants participating in this damage relate that the fill removed from Structure 19C was used to infill a portion of the western segment of the main canal. The size and elaborate form of the group suggest that this mound was a non-residential facility. The large platform area of Structure 19B may indicate a storage facility of some kind. Our excavations demonstrate a Tulix phase date from sealed construction fill, though a Classic and Postclassic reoccupation are indicated. The Structure 19 Group is understood to be a non-residential facility, although there is some evidence for a domestic occupation prior to the plaza construction during early Tulix times.

STRUCTURE 16

This Type 5 structure rests at the southeast margin of the subplaza Structure 9A within a *huamil* setting but immediately north of the depressed *zacatal* near

the center of the intra-site area. This relatively small range structure is oriented toward the center in the manner similar to that noted in Structures 13, 14, 15 and the Structure 10 Group, all of which are nearby. The mound and underlying ground-level floors date to the Late C'oh phase. Although no features were exposed, this structure is hypothesized to be a domestic facility because of its size and the suggestion that the underlying domestic occupation resulted in a later mounded residence. Tulix phase occupation is suggested and Postclassic diagnostics indicate a substantial reoccupation. The underlying ground level structure would appear to be contemporaneous with the Feature 33 exposure (Op 107) underlying subplaza Structure 9A and only slightly earlier than the postulated Tulix phase ground level occupations under Structures 13 and 14. It should be noted that the floors exposed under Structure 16 appear identical to those defined under subplaza Structure 2A of the central precinct which in part date to the C'oh phase.

STRUCTURE 15

This Type 5 structure rests to the immediate northeast of Structure 16 within a well-drained *huamil* setting. The mound lies at the immediate southeast margin of subplaza Structure 9A. The major intrasite *zacatal* depression lies to the south. The mound is oriented toward the central precinct in keeping with the other mounds resting on subplaza Structure 9A. The structure dates to the Late C'oh and is underlain by the same type of midden debris exposed under Structure 16. The mound is believed to be an elite residence because of its size and ceramic inventory. The underlying midden deposit further argues for functional continuity through time and space. Tulix phase occupation is indicated, but later Classic and Postclassic reoccupation appears more substantial.

Structure 15 is viewed as C'oh phase housemound associated with Structure 16. They antedate subplaza Structure 9A, though Tulix phase occupation is suggested. The underlying midden deposit is similar to that identified under Structure 16. It is postulated to be associated with a ground level occupation similar to Feature 33 (Op 107) and to that underlying Structure 16. It should be noted that the ground level occupation underlying subplaza Structure 9A appears to be more dispersed than the nucleated village defined under subplaza Structure 2A.

STRUCTURE 21

This Type 4 structure rests in a fork of the main canal at the northwest edge of the intrasite area, 30 m south of the bay. It is surrounded by *zacatal* and *hulub*, but occupies an island of well-drained caprock. A Tulix phase date has been assigned to this structure, though the ceramic inventory was very small. Given the imposing size and position of this mound at the entrance of the canal system, this structure is suggested to have functioned as a civic facility.

Structure 21 provided little architectural or functional evidence from our limited test excavations. The Tulix phase date is derived from a construction fill context.

STRUCTURE 22

This Type 5 mound structure is located 40 m south of the present bay in the northwest portion of the intra-site area. The mound is located in well-drained *huamil*, but flanked to the west by *zacatal*. The structure has been assigned a Tulix construction date and probably functioned as a small non-elite domestic unit. The entire stratigraphic exposure was mottled by vertical intrusions, making the dating of the structure suspect. The ceramic inventory consisted of a Postclassic/Preclassic mix.

STRUCTURE 18

The Type 5 structure rests in the western portion of the intra-site area. It lies in the northwestern margin of the largely depressed thornbush and *zacatal* zone at the center of the site. This structure is positioned in a less well-drained *huamil* setting. The mound has been assigned a Tulix date. The structure appears to be a small but elite residential locus, given the recovered ceramic inventory.

STRUCTURE 102

This Type 6 structure lies in the western portion of the site 180 m outside the main canal and 90 m south of the bay. The setting is a well-drained *huamil*. The mound was selected for excavation to increase our structure sample from the western portion of the site. A Late Tulix date has been assigned to this apparent domestic facility.

STRUCTURE 98

This Type 5 structure rests in a *huamil* setting in the southwestern margin of the intrasite area. It lies 10 m north of the main canal. The structure was selected for investigation because of its small size and commanding position on the bank of the canal. The structure has been assigned a Tulix phase date and appears to be an elite residential facility.

Structure 98 is a Tulix phase mound. Given its proximity to the canal and the nature of its fill, it is argued that it was constructed from a dredging event in the canal's prehistory. Some of the larger limestone rubble may have been removed from the banks of the canal in an effort to widen or deepen it.

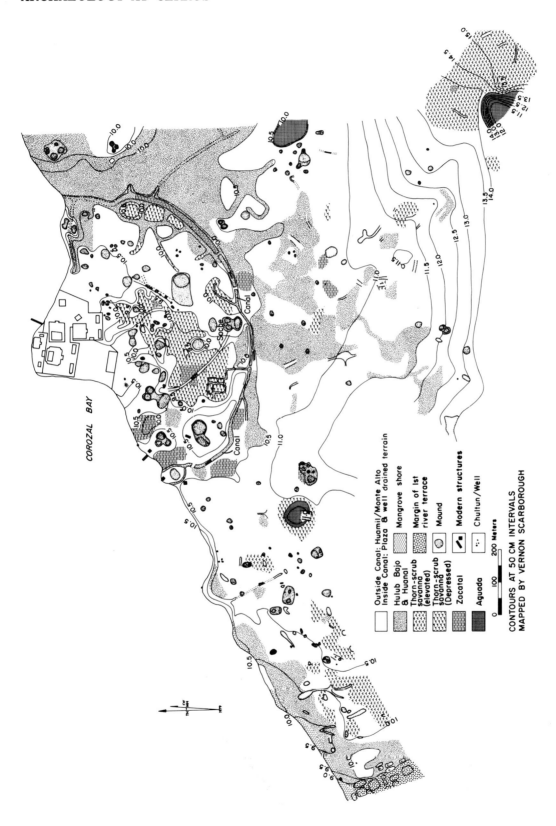

Figure 2.1. Contour map of the environs of the site.

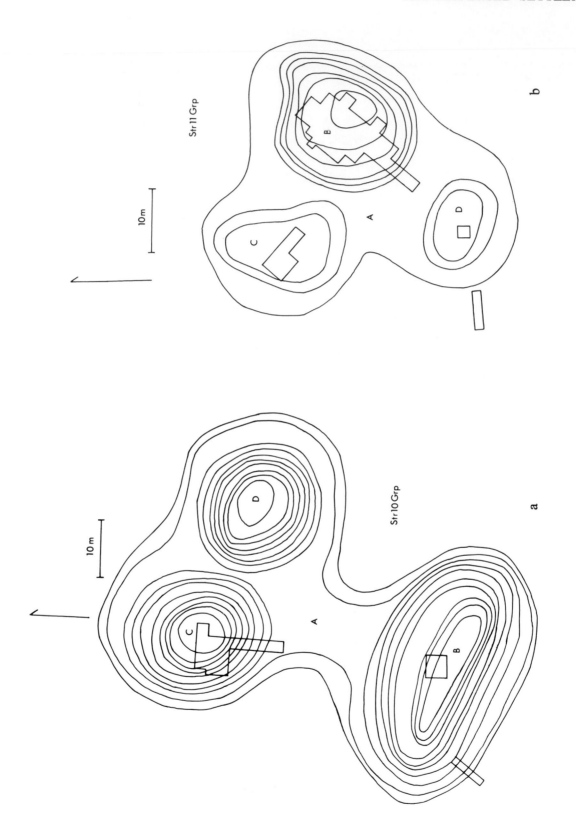

Figure 2.2. Structure Groups 10 and 11. a, contour map of Group 10; b, contour map of Group 11.

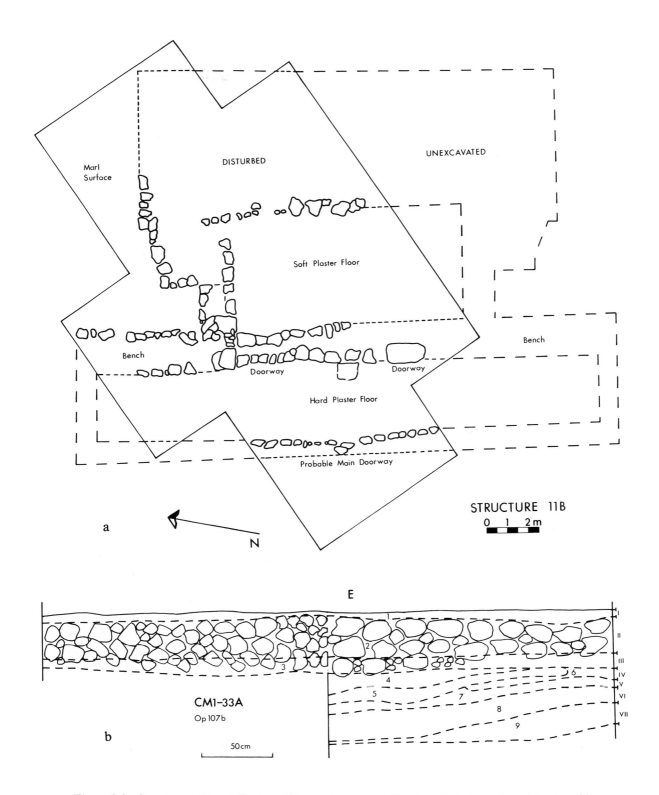

Figure 2.3. Structure 11B and Feature 33A. a, plan map of Structure 11B; b, profile of Feature 33a.

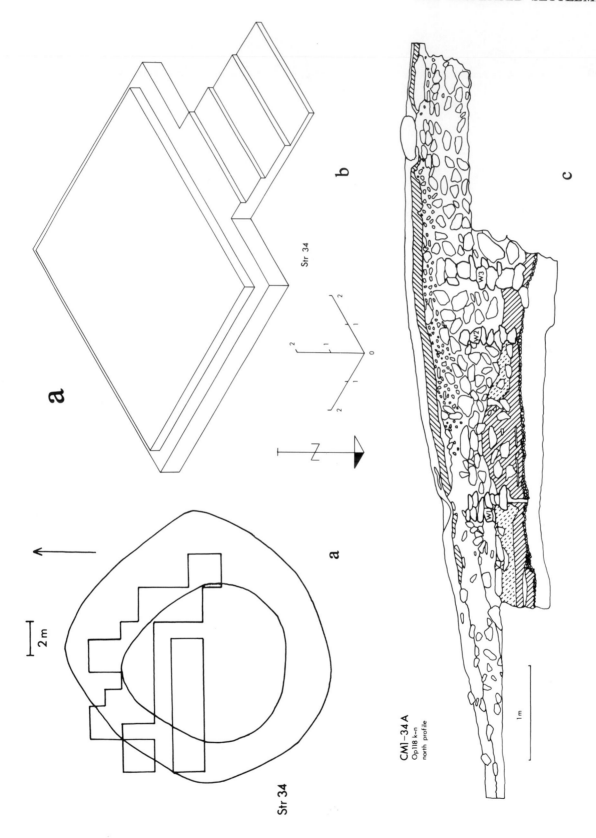

CMl–34 A
Op 118 k–n
north profile

Str 34

Str 34

Figure 2.4. Structure 34. a, contour map; b, isometric map; c, north profile of Op 118 into Structure 34.

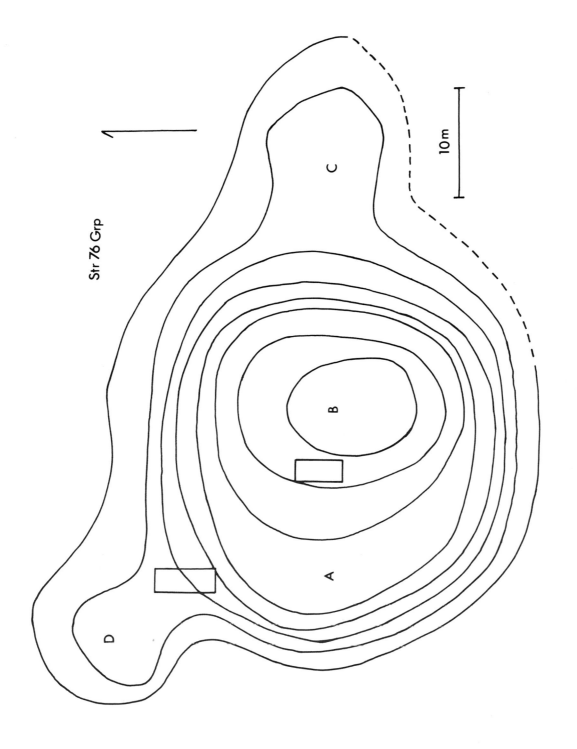

Figure 2.5. Contour map of Group 76.

EXCAVATIONS IN THE LATE PRECLASSIC NUCLEATED VILLAGE

Maynard B. Cliff

Among the goals of the archaeological investigations at Cerros has been the excavation of an extremely rich cultural deposit which underlies a large portion of the main plaza (Structure 2A) of the central ceremonial precinct (cf. Freidel 1979)[1]. The northern margin of this deposit (as well as that of the main plaza) has been eroded away for an indeterminate distance by the wave action of Corozal Bay. This erosion resulted in the exposure of a profile approximately 65 m long on the east-west axis of the site that reveals the entire depositional history of this area. This profile consists of a deposit of laminated lenses of light to very dark grey midden (almost 1.0 m thick in places), covered by up to three meters of the dry laid rubble ballast that comprises the fill of the main plaza.

Excavations conducted within this deposit have revealed ceramics belonging only to the Chicanel Ceramic Sphere (Robertson, personal communication 1980) in primary depositional contexts and in burials (Cliff 1976), demonstrating that it is entirely Late Preclassic in date. Excavations further demonstrated that the sub-plaza deposits at Cerros were produced by the primary deposition of habitation debris associated with perishable domestic structures and overlapped occupationally with an early stage of monumental construction in the central precinct. In terms of structural density and intensity of occupation, this area justifiably may be referred to as a nucleated village. While sub-plaza deposits have been found at a number of other sites in the Central Maya Lowlands (cf. Coe 1965; Ricketson and Ricketson 1937; Smith 1972; Thompson 1939), none have shown the intensity of occupation found in the deposits at Cerros. In addition, none have shown the distinct juxtaposition of domestic occupation with monumental religious construction that existed at Cerros.

Excavations into this village deposit have been situated primarily along the northern edge of the plaza in order to take advantage of the profile (Fig. 3.1). These were located on the eastern margin of the stratified deposits; on the western edge of the deposits where they appeared to end against an early stone platform; and, finally, in the approximate center of the erosion profile.

In addition to these three large block excavations, operations have also included several smaller test pits, burial salvage operations along the erosion profile, detailed recordings of the entire profile following careful cleaning operations, and excavation of a 31 m long north-south trench through the center of the main plaza. All of these operations have helped to clarify the evidence from the block excavations. While the final results are far from complete, some preliminary interpretations may be presented regarding the nature and history of this village area.

OPERATION 1

Operations on the eastern margin of the village were begun in 1974 with two test pits which were excavated in order to salvage several burials observed to be eroding from the deposits because of wave action. One of these excavation units, Op 1a, was excavated to the base of the cultural levels and revealed a complicated series of lensed deposits, including several fragments of polished plaster floor. The stratigraphy was made even more confusing by the presence of five burials within this small test unit[2]. The second of the two tests in this area, Op 9a also revealed a burial dug into earlier *in situ* deposits consisting of a large patch of well preserved and polished plaster floor and sub-floor midden. Because all of the burial vessels and the ceramic material recovered from the midden deposit itself belonged to the Chicanel Ceramic Sphere, these excavations demonstrated that the sub-plaza deposits dated to the Late Preclassic Period. Moreover, they showed that several levels of plaster floors existed within the deposit since the floor in Op 9a was far too high to be associated in any way with the floor fragments in Op 1a.

The area of Op 1a was expanded in 1976 to a total size of 48 m², including what had been Op 9a. It was hoped that such an exposure would clarify a number of questions arising from the operations of the first season. These excavations in Op 1 were continued into the 1977 and 1978 seasons with some changes in methodology.

45

The basal deposit in the area of Op 1 was found to be a very dark grey, heavy clay. Aside from a layer of cultural debris at the top, this stratum was entirely sterile. This ancient soil is almost identical to descriptions of soils presently forming along the banks of the New River and the Rio Hondo and therefore is likely of alluvial origin (Wright, *et al.* 1959:61). Cultural material found directly on top of this clay included concentrations of small whelk shells (identified as *Melongena melongena*, Andrews IV 1969; Anthony Andrews, personal communication 1977), large sherds smashed in place, and floors of hard fired clay. In addition, the erosion profile also revealed the presence of shallow pits that were excavated into this clay and subsequently fired. These features were apparently hearths, although no evidence of charcoal remained within them.

Almost the entire sub-plaza midden deposit of Op 1, with the exception of the uppermost 5 to 10 cm, consisted of superimposed floors and primary trash lenses dating to the Late Preclassic on the basis of associated ceramics. The floors were associated with perishable, pole-and-thatch structures that were apparently houses. Thirteen construction episodes and two structures have been identified in the area of Op 1. The earliest structure in Op 1 faced to the east, but approximately halfway through its construction history the building evidently was re-oriented 180 degrees to face west. The second structure found in Op 1 was not complete enough to determine whether or not a similar re-orientation had occurred with that building as well. Surrounding these structures through time were a series of trash pits, burial pits, and midden areas, representing the refuse of day-to-day living. While the sample is small, it seems that burials were placed directly behind the structures, and that midden and trash pits were placed either to the rear or to the side of each building.

The midden debris from these structures consisted of large amounts of smashed pottery, ranging in size from whole vessels to larger pieces and finally to extremely small fragments. In some cases, entire lots were composed of nothing but culinary ware sherds. Faunal remains recovered include numerous examples of not only the whelk species *M. melongena* mentioned above, but also large quantities of fish bone representative of numerous species. The surprisingly few large mammal remains recovered include dog, fox and deer (Carr, this volume).

Large quantities of organic remains have been recovered utilizing flotation techniques; and, while much of the material has yet to be sorted, preliminary results show evidence for maize consumption. Cobs and maize kernels are present. In addition (Crane, this volume), examples of the hard seed from the small fruit known locally as *craboo* or *nance* (*Brysonima crassifolia* (*L.*) [Standley and Record 1936:206]) were found in almost every lot which was floated.

The length of time represented by the deposits in Op 1 is at present uncertain. However, by applying an average period of 30 years for each of the 13 episodes (Puleston 1973:151), a figure of 390 years is obtained. In view of the minor nature of some of the architectural modifications this figure must be seen as a maximum estimate. A broader estimate of 300-400 years for the length of the village occupation seems to agree with the ceramic information available. Material belonging to all three Late Preclassic ceramic complexes at the site has been found in Op 1 (Robertson, personal communication 1980). The actual occupation in the area of Op 1 spanned both the Ixtabai and C'oh Complexes while some evidence exists that the area was at least open, and possibly still occupied, during the Tulix period as well.

Three types of floors were noted within the sub-plaza deposit of Op 1. The first of these consisted of what is apparently light yellowish-brown to pale brown fired clay of variable thickness and consistency. Such hard, fire-baked clay areas were reported throughout the sequence of occupations at Altar de Sacrificios, where they were referred to by the Spanish term, *tierra quemada* (Smith 1972:3). This type of flooring was present throughout the entire architectural sequence in Op 1 and was apparently used for plaza or courtyard flooring as well as structure floors.

The second type of flooring in the deposit consisted of hard plaster surfaces (in some cases highly polished) similar to those that occur on sub-structure platforms elsewhere at Cerros. The remnants of the plaster floors in the Op 1 area were not extensive and were built on either horizontally-laid midden and marl layers, or on the same type of burned clay flooring mentioned above. Elsewhere along the erosion profile, such plaster floors extended for some distance and were associated with open plaza areas. Based on this evidence, plaster was generally used as a floor-surfacing material throughout the sub-plaza deposits at Cerros. A distinction could be discerned between plaster floors inside and outside of structures, with the outside floors being much thicker and harder.

The third type of floor in use in the Op 1 area was simply a surface of white marl (or *sascab*) of variable thickness and purity. Similar floors have been observed in association with domestic architecture in Yucatan (Wauchope 1938) and inside modern houses in northern Belize (personal observation). Like the other two, this type of floor construction appears to occur throughout the depositional history of Op 1.

It is possible that the distinction between plaster floors and *sascab* floors represents a functional one. Soft marl floors may have been associated with kitchens whereas hard, formal plaster floors may have been associated with houses. Unfortunately, analysis has not yet proceeded far enough to assign such functional distinctions to structures. Considering the presumably significant differences in labor investment for the three types of floors, it is also possible that differential socio-economic status or wealth may have been involved in the type of flooring surface chosen for a particular structure and plaza area. Again, as with the question of function, this must also await more complete analysis.

The lack of any associated formal platform construction is of particular interest with regard to the structures exposed in Op 1. The term "formal" is meant to refer to the construction of platforms by utilizing stone retaining walls and a fill of rock and/or earth. The earliest structure in this area was apparently constructed on a raised mound of burned clay about 30 cm above the surface of the ground and faced onto a ground level, hard plaster patio, or plaza, of unknown extent. The exact shape of this platform is not known, but it was probably approximately square or rectangular with no formal retaining walls. The margins of the platform simply sloped away to ground level on all sides.[3] Elsewhere, the erosion profile reveals that some of the early structures at Cerros were constructed directly on the original ground surface without benefit of any sort of platform whatsoever. Later structures appear to have been raised above the surrounding ground surface simply because they were located on earlier mounded housesites. When formalized platform construction does appear near the end of the occupation in the village area at Cerros, none were built in the area of Op 1.

This process of mounding through the accumulation of primary debris was demonstrated quite well by a segment of the erosion profile which revealed at least five superimposed plaster floors and a number of horizontal marl lenses (Fig. 3.2). The area of the superimposed floors was demarcated on either side by a very dark grey sloping deposit of primary midden, including large fragments of ceramic vessels and numerous bone, shell, and lithic remains. In contrast, the superimposed floors contained very little artifactual debris beyond minute fragments of ceramics and other material.

The final level of the sub-plaza deposits in Op 1 consisted of a 5 to 10 cm thick, very dark grey layer that showed no internal bedding whatsoever. This layer apparently represents a leveling process undertaken in preparation for the construction of the main plaza that covered the deposit. The uppermost levels of the midden deposit in this area seem to have been truncated and were presumably used as leveling fill for the low areas. It is also possible that, prior to its burial, the area served as a source of trash for use in construction fill. Neither the physical nature of the deposit itself nor the condition of the artifacts it contained indicated the presence of a weathering horizon at the top of the dark grey deposit. Indeed, a number of flat-bedded, unweathered sherds were found on its surface. Evidently the leveling of the ground surface in the area of Op 1 was followed almost immediately by the construction of the main plaza.

A large area of the plaza fill material was removed during the excavation of Op 1 and approximately 5 m of the retaining wall of the main plaza were exposed in the eastern extremity of the operation (Fig. 3.3). This retaining wall, as found, consisted of several courses of very roughly shaped limestone blocks laid in a mortar of yellow marl. These building stones varied in height from 10 to 25 cm, and averaged about 60 cm in length, and 30 cm in width. Only the front surface of these stones was worked while the back and sides remained rough. The exposed section of the retaining wall was not straight and its orientation varied from approximately 15 to 17 degrees east of true north. This agreed with the general orientation of the eastern edge of the plaza as originally reconstructed from surface contours. The remains of the retaining wall in this area stood approximately 60 cm high at the northern edge of the operation and increased to a height of 90 cm (or four courses) at the southern limits of the exposure. Since the Op 1 exposure indicates that the easternmost section of the main plaza was constructed at one time with no intervening floors, the retaining wall at the eastern edge of the plaza must have been at least 2 m and possibly 3 m high when the plaza was completed.

In general, the fill behind the retaining wall consisted of dry laid limestone ballast. The basal layer of the plaza fill was composed of medium to heavy limestone rubble, ranging in thickness from approximately 50 cm on the west to about 1 m on the east where the rubble sloped up behind the retaining wall. This large rubble was generally dry laid, with the exception of the fill immediately behind the retaining wall that was laid in a matrix of white to pale yellow marl. Above the large rubble basal layer, the remainder of the fill consisted of dry laid, small limestone ballast. Because of the closeness of Op 1 to the eroded coast and the prevalence of stone robbing from the northern margin of the plaza, the rubble fill in this area was not intact and no evidence of the plaza floor was found.

One dry laid construction wall was noted. Located approximately 7 m to the west of the retaining wall, it rose to a height of about 1.30 m above the surface of the midden. It seems evident that after the large rubble was laid on the surface of the midden, interior construction walls were built and the interstices filled in with small limestone ballast.

Contemporaneous with the construction of the retaining wall and the main plaza, or shortly thereafter, a cache was deposited about 30 cm east of the retaining wall. This cache consisted of a small necked olla placed in the upper part of the dark grey midden layer that underlay the main plaza construction. It had been carefully placed upright and the top of the rim was nearly flush with the surface of the midden. Although no artifacts were found inside this vessel, three worked chert discs in a triangular arrangement were located on the southeast side of the vessel. One of these discs rested on the neck of the vessel and may have functioned as a lid at the time of deposition. No evidence for an intrusive pit could be found. Thus it seems most reasonable that the vessel was carefully deposited at the time the leveling operations were undertaken in preparation for the construction of the main plaza.

This cache and the surface of the midden that lay beyond the limits of the main plaza were sealed by a thick, hard deposit of white marl. This marl apparently represents wash from the retaining wall of the main plaza following its abandonment but prior to its collapse. The occurrence of a large stone that had fallen from the retaining wall and crashed through the white marl wash layer to the midden sealed beneath supports this time framework. Moreover, the lack of any noticeable weathering horizon between the midden deposit and the marl wash would seem to indicate that very little time elapsed between the completion of the retaining wall of the main plaza and its abandonment.

While no stucco or marl plastering remained on the retaining wall, the thickness of the wash layer (up to 20 cm in some instances) indicates that it was probably

heavily plastered at one time. In addition, several fragments of plaster were found in the wash layer, confirming that at one time the retaining wall was coated with a plaster layer at least 4 cm thick. The surface of this marl wash showed evidence of heavy erosion in the form of small runnels leading away from the edge of the retaining wall, down the slight slope formed by the wash. Above the white marl wash was a deposit of weathered grey marl that graded to dark brown humus and presumably represents totally post-abandonment deposits.

OPERATION 33

The second large exposure, begun in 1977, was continued during the 1978 season. It was located in the approximate center of the erosion profile between the area of Op 1 on the east and Op 34 (see below) on the west where the primary deposits ended.

This operation, designated Op 33, was deliberately located over what appeared to be a series of stratified plaster floors that easily could be seen in the erosion profile along the coastline. During the 1977 season an area of approximately 28 m² was removed to the top of the first of these plaster floors, and a 1 x 1 m test pit was excavated to the base of the cultural deposits. The test pit, coupled with the detailed record of the profile on the northern margin of the deposit, allowed a preliminary evaluation of the earlier deposits, while the more extensive exposure of the uppermost floors revealed a series of constructions dating to the final occupation of the village area. During the 1978 season, several exploratory trenches were excavated to the west and south of the main operation, and further excavations were carried out within the limits of the original operation.

As in Op 1, the basal deposit in Op 33 consisted of a very dark grey, heavy clay of alluvial origin. Directly above this clay layer was a deposit of dark to light grey midden above which was found a poorly preserved plaster floor. Resting directly on a fragment of this floor was a cluster of three green stone beads and eleven coral beads. The arrangement of these beads indicates that they were deposited as a complete string, probably a small wristlet or armlet. Because it was resting directly on the surface of the floor, it is difficult to believe that this green and coral ornament could have been lost accidentally. Moreover, considering the scarcity of such jewelry elsewhere in the village area, it is much more likely that the ornament was deposited as an offering. Presumably this was done at the time that the floor level was raised.

The fill above this floor consisted of several layers of dark grey midden separated by a layer of mottled, pale brown *tierra quemada*. On the surface of these layers another floor was found consisting of thick, hard plaster. This same alternating pattern of fill and floor was followed for the next seven floors in this sequence. Usually, the basal fill beneath the plaster floor consisted of pale brown to dark brown fired clay that was sometimes mixed with layers or patches of unburned midden.

At the top of this sequence of nine plaster floors, evidence of a masonry structure was found. This evidence consisted of a small segment of wall, presumably part of a building platform. It was approximately 45 to 50 cm in length and 25 cm in height. This wall segment paralleled the erosional margin and was located on the edge of the cut. The remainder of the platform has undoubtedly eroded away. This wall was built on top of a layer of very dark greyish-brown midden. Subsequently, a plaster floor was laid down which abutted against the wall and was continuous with the layer of plaster overlaying the building stones. The preserved masonry consisted of unshaped, small stones that had been laid in a mortar of dark brown mud. Nothing more can be said about this wall except that it was generally oriented east to west.

Some time later a new floor was constructed, apparently abutting the earlier platform. It in turn consisted of a base of small rubble gravel in a matrix of grey marl, capped by 3 to 4 cm of plaster. This was the first time that a limestone gravel base was used in floor construction, and the remaining two floors in this sequence were constructed similarly. The developmental sequence from a burned clay base to a limestone gravel base was also found in the Late Preclassic Structure B-I at Altar de Sacrificios (Smith 1972). Edwin Littman, who analyzed the floors at Altar, believed that the use of burned clay as a floor base was related to the problem of proper drainage:

Clay...is...highly impervious to water and would tend to block the drying of the floors by natural seepage through the plaster. When burned, however, the clay forms a porous mass, easily broken into small pieces, through and around which water could pass rather freely. Burned earth is found under the earliest floors examined [of Structure B-I] whereas *almejas* or lime-encrusted shells [or broken stone] occupied a similar position in later floors (Littman 1972:270-271).

The use of clay and lime-encrusted river shells as building material at Altar seems to have been predicated upon a lack of good limestone and sandstone in the immediate site vicinity (Smith 1972). Cerros may have suffered from a lack of high quality building stone in the early period as well. Today there appears to be little or no good quality limestone in the immediate site environs (Scarborough, personal communication 1980). However, this may be due to massive stone-quarrying for the Tulix period architecture rather than to any original lack of native stone. Considering the strong marine orientation which apparently characterized the Ixtabai period, it is quite possible that sources of limestone in the interior of the peninsula were not exploited at that time.

The subsequent floor was apparently related to the construction of a building platform on the eastern side of the operation over the earlier platform. Prior to this activity, an apparent dedicatory cache was deposited in the center of the exposed plaza floor. This cache consisted of two vessels deposited in a pit that was dug into the earlier floor. The first vessel, referred to as a "beer mug," was deposited in the bottom of the pit and covered by a worked sherd lid. The second vessel was placed upside down over the first vessel and was ceremonially killed by having a small hole punched in the bottom. Both vessels appeared to date to the very early part of the Tulix period (Robertson, personal communication 1981). This activity seems to have been associated with the burning of something on the surface of the floor to the north of the cache, since a fire-blackened spot was found in that area. The new floor was laid down over the entire area exposed by Op 33. A new platform was then built on top of this floor.

This small building platform was located on the northeast margin of the excavation area. Unfortunately, a large portion of it had been eroded away prior to its discovery. What remained appeared to consist of a rectangular building platform with an adjoining round-cornered terrace on the west side (Fig. 3.4a). A 2 m segment of retaining wall was preserved on the south side of the building platform to a height of about 60 cm. The southern retaining wall for the terrace began about 25 cm north of the southwest corner of the building platform and projected approximately 1.5 m from the building platform. Portions of the terrace were preserved to a height of about 40 cm. On the west a 1.5 m segment of the terrace retaining wall was preserved and the terrace of about 1 m in length was found. Given the extensiveness of the plaster floor to the west, and the location of the cache, also to the west and almost in a straight line with the second projection, it seems likely that the platform was oriented to the west and that the projection is the remains of a front stairway or step.

The platform itself was largely constructed of medium-sized, loaf-shaped limestone blocks. The lowest course of the terrace was composed of larger, more squared blocks. The construction stones appeared to be either unshaped or very minimally shaped and were laid in a mortar of hard, white marl. The fill behind the platform retaining wall was composed of small limestone rubble in a matrix of marl.

This platform was subsequently modified by the addition of a new front retaining wall on the west side that resulted in increasing the preserved east-west dimension of the terrace to approximately 2 m. The new terrace had a square corner on the front and an increased surface area, but the orientation remained unchanged (Fig. 3.4b). As with the earlier platform, the addition was constructed of rectangular, unshaped limestone blocks in a marl mortar. Although neither this episode, nor the preceding one, showed any evidence of a plaster coating on the retaining walls, it is reasonable to assume that the completed platforms were heavily plastered.

The final floor in this area consisted of a limestone gravel base with a marl cap laid around the building platform to a height sufficient to cover all traces of the earlier, westward facing stairway. The resulting building platform was rectangular in shape with a rectangular terrace projecting approximately 2 m² from the western side. The orientation continued to be to the west.

The relatively elaborate platform associated with the upper plaster floors in this operation appears to be well within the range of variation for Late Preclassic building platforms elsewhere in the lowlands. It bears some resemblance to the Late Facet Pakluum Structure XXVII at Becan (Ball and Andrews V 1978), for example, and is similar in type of masonry construction to the less elaborate Cauac Phase Structure 26-61 at Tikal (Haviland 1963) and Structure F-2 at Chan Chen in northern Belize (Sidrys and Andresen 1978). The uppermost plaster floors associated with this structure at Cerros appear to be extensive plaza surfaces, that, judging from the erosion profile, may have been anywhere from 200 to 500 m in area. The estimated area

compares quite well with the plaster pavements at Becan that have been associated with Late Facet Pakluum plazuela groups (Adams 1977).

Prior to its burial beneath the main plaza, the final activity in this area was the excavation of a deep pit close to the medial axis of the platform in the northeastern area of the operation and the interment of Burial 23. Excavated from the top of the final floor down 1.35 m into the sterile, dark grey clay, the pit was deep and extremely narrow. Since the pit appears to have had an expanding base and originally may have been plastered, the possibility that it initially was constructed as a *chultun* could not be ruled out. Nonetheless, Burial 23 eventually was placed in the bottom of the pit. This burial consisted of the poorly preserved remains of a young adult of indeterminate sex who had been interred in a sitting position, facing approximately northwest. Associated vessels were a smashed Sierra Red: Xaibe Variety plate, a Conop Red-on-Red Trickle: Conop Variety collared bowl, and a complete Savannah Bank Usulutan: Variety Unspecified plate (Robertson, personal communication 1980). Other grave goods included a ceramic whistle in the form of a blowfish, the tip of an antler tine flaker, and a chert biface accompanied by a single flake struck from the bit end of the piece. At some point in time after this interment the area was abandoned and the platform on the eastern side of the operation was left to deteriorate. Still later, the entire area of Op 33 was buried beneath the dry laid rubble fill of the main plaza.

With the exception of a period of abandonment before burial, these remains indicate a continuous domestic occupation of the area throughout the period prior to the construction of the main plaza. Throughout the sequence, the plaster floors appear to be associated with primary trash, as opposed to construction fill. Large sherds were smashed in place on top of several of the floors within the 1 m² test pit, for example, and large areas of thin domestic trash were associated with several of the upper floors. In addition, several of the lower floors were associated with postholes that may have resulted from perishable structures.

However, the possibility must be considered that while the use of the area exposed in Op 33 may have been domestic, the function of the platform exposed on the east side of the operation may have been religious. Haviland (1981) reports that the majority of the structures that could be identified as shrines associated with domestic groups at Tikal were located on the east side of the plaza, as is the structure described above.

OPERATION 34

The third area of extensive block excavations, referred to as Op 34, was located at the extreme western edge of the village. The erosion profile in this area showed a relatively thin deposit of midden (only about 30 to 40 cm thick) overlain by approximately 60 cm of small rubble ballast. The profile indicated that the midden deposits ended against the side of a crude rubble structure on the west. This structure was originally believed to have been an early construction phase of the main plaza (Freidel 1976), implying that the dense occupation represented by the midden levels was contemporaneous with the early construction of monumental public architecture in the site center. Op 34 was begun in 1977 to test this hypothesis.

An area of approximately 24 m was cleared of rubble 4 m² south of the erosion edge and 6 m east-west along the axis of the eroded northern edge. Following the total removal of the rubble layer overlying this entire area, selected portions of the midden deposit were excavated.

As in the two previously mentioned operations, the cultural layers were underlain by a deposit of dark grey, alluvial clay. However, excavations in Op 34 proceeded to below water table. This was much deeper than those in the other two operations and showed that the dark grey clay gradually graded into the chalk or marl clay that underlies the surface soil of gravelly clay further inland (Wright, *et al.* 1959). This marl deposit was sterile, but, unlike the situation in the other two operations, the dark grey alluvial clay above it was not. This clay contained whole artifacts, including a large chert dagger and large fragments of pottery. Much of the ceramic material from this clay showed evidence of water-erosion, and, because there was no possibility of this material being recently deposited beach rubbish, it would seem that the material was deposited in the clay when it was still permanently or seasonally inundated. The surface of this dark grey clay sloped upward toward the south and the east, while in the northwest area of the operation the stone structure that had been noted in the erosion profile went into, and was surrounded by, this clay. This indicates that the structure had been built when the area was still partially inundated as well. This conclusion was reinforced by observations that the density of artifactual material in the grey clay was highest next to the platform. Moreover, the base of the structure to the south rose along with the surface of the clay that became increasingly more sterile.

This structure, a crude stone platform, was preserved for only a distance of about 1.25 m south from the erosion edge, giving it a total excavated length of 2 m when the 1977 excavations ended. It is estimated that erosion action and beach clearing activities during the two previous years accidentally had removed an additional 1 m of its length. Clearing and excavation below beach level during the 1978 season in Sub-operations 34b-h revealed that the platform angled northward at about 16° east of north and extended at least 4 more meters. The platform is reconstructed as cornering at about this point, giving it a minimum north-south dimension of 6.5 m (Fig. 3.5). What was apparently the base of the northern retaining wall of the platform was followed for a distance of 38 m before excavation ceased. On the southeast margin in Op 34a, the platform was constructed of very large, completely unshaped limestone boulders that were simply angled on the top of one another in a matrix of dark grey clay. No evidence whatsoever was found to indicate the former presence of a retaining wall or plaster layer on this portion of the platform. Nonetheless, the remaining *in situ* stones formed a relatively straight side, oriented approximately 20° east of north. The bulk of the eastern and the northern sides of the platform were faced with a retaining wall of medium to large limestone blocks, roughly faced on one side and oriented about 8° east of north.

At the southern end of the platform in Op 34a, floors of burned clay and marl, along with primary trash deposits, similar to those found elsewhere in the village deposits, abutted against it. However, approximately 1.5 m north of the beginning of these floors, the deposits gave way to a complicated inter-fingering of dark grey, silty clay and tan sand lenses that seemed to be water-lain. These later deposits reinforce the view that the platform was constructed while a portion of the area of the original Op 34 was still permanently or seasonally inundated. In fact, it apparently stretched from dryland deposits into a body of water—either a lagoon, river, or bay.

Although the artifacts associated with this feature have not been analyzed, it is believed that this structure represents a dock or wharf facility of some size and complexity. It seems to have been contemporaneous with the earliest village deposits in the Op 34 area and to have been used until at least the final construction phase of the main plaza.

This functional interpretation is further strengthened by the discovery of a crude stone feature that can best be interpreted as a waterfront jetty or breakwater based on a similar, but undated, feature found at the site of Nohmul (Pring and Hammond 1975). The jetty at Cerros was located 4 m to the east of the dock and was oriented in approximately the same direction. Time did not allow more than a partial uncovering and mapping of this feature, but this showed it to have been at least 1.5 m long, running north to south, and of an unknown width. It was constructed of small, unshaped limestone rubble in a matrix of dark grey clay, and, like the dock, was found in the alluvial clay deposit.

As was stated above, slightly later primary floors were located to the south and east of the dock. These deposits consisted of the same type of *tierra quemada* and soft marl flooring, alternating with layers of grey midden noted in Op 1. Several postholes were found throughout these deposits, but at the present stage of analysis it has been impossible to determine if they belonged to perishable structures. The upper 15 to 25 cm of these deposits consisted solely of dark grey midden that completely covered the area of Op 34a and may have been primary trash resulting from the occupation of a structure revealed in the erosion profile to the east (Fig. 3.6a).

On top of these deposits, the remains of several stone substructure platforms were uncovered. These platforms were apparently constructed and abandoned prior to the construction of the main plaza over the area. The exposed portions of these platforms consisted of segments of two retaining walls approximately 4.5 m apart. Both walls were oriented approximately north-south and were generally parallel to one another, with the first retaining wall on the eastern side and the second retaining wall on the western side of the construction.

The first retaining wall faced west and was constructed of medium to large limestone blocks that were crudely faced on the western side. These stones were laid in a marl mortar and apparently had been heavily plastered on the outside. The fill of this platform consisted of small limestone gravel in a matrix of greyish-brown to reddish-brown loam. This platform was preserved to a maximum height of 30 cm. Its poor condition indicates a period of abandonment prior to its burial.

About 3.5 meters of a second wall were uncovered facing the first one. It was quite different from the retaining wall described above as this wall was preserved to a maximum height of 65 cm and was constructed of a single course of large, flat, rectangular limestone blocks set upright on end. On top of this course, a second one of flat, rectangular stones was then laid horizontally. There was no good evidence for plastering and the wall was not sectioned. Thus, there are no data on the fill behind the wall. Nonetheless, it appeared to have been laid in a marl mortar. The use of bedrock slabs laid upright in mud mortar to form terrace retaining walls has been noted at the Formative Structure 450 Complex at Dzibilchaltun (Andrews IV 1965; Andrews V 1981).

Following the building of these two platforms, the entire area of Op. 34 may have been used as a trash dump until its burial under the rubble fill of the main plaza. The lack of any discernible weathering horizon on top of the basal midden deposits indicates that the time interval between the final deposition of midden material around the abandoned platforms and the burial of the entire area beneath the main plaza was a relatively short one.

OPERATION 38

For a complete picture of the nature of the village deposits at Cerros, preliminary findings from two other operations must be mentioned. The first of these is Op 38. This designation was given to all of the profile cleaning and recording operations that were carried out along the erosion profile in the 1977 and 1979 seasons.

The cleaning and recording of the erosion wall along the coast resulted in a detailed profile of the northern margin of the village deposits. This profile extends from the edge of the dock platform in Op 34 on the west, to the area where the deposits taper out to a thin layer of homogenous dark grey midden on the east (Fig. 3.2). This profile is about 66 m long from east to west and shows a total of at least 4 structure-locations. The term "structure-location" has been used because each of these four areas seems to represent a general location for repeated building activities. The same type of construction modification and mounding discussed in connection with the structures in Op 1 was observed in each separate structure-location.

The first of them was excavated in Op 1. The final phases of a second were excavated in Op 33, and a portion of a third was excavated in connection with the work in Op 34a. The last structure-location was found in the area between Op 1 and Op 33. The large space between Op 33 and Op 34 appears to have been occupied in the final phases by the large plaza associated with the building platform in Op 33. It is unclear whether or not this area contained a structure in the earlier periods of occupation. The second structure found in Op 1 did not show up in the profile at all, but began about 4 to 5 m south of the location or the erosion edge. The existence of portions of 4 structures along a 66 m profile yields a mean density of 36 structures per ha, a figure comparable only with some of the most densely settled sites in the Maya lowlands.

OPERATION 41

In 1979 the first leg of a planned L-shaped trench intended to link up the erosion profile with the Tulix phase monumental architecture of the center was undertaken. The initial step involved clearing a 4.5 m wide trench down to the surface of the village deposits for a distance of 31 m south of Op 34. It was hoped that more structure-locations could be isolated with standing masonry architecture similar to that found in Op 33 and Op 34.

Approximately 11 m south of the margin of Op 34 a large masonry platform, Structure 2A-Sub 4, was encountered within the trench. The overall size and elaborateness of the structure, as well as the obvious ceremonialism involved with its burial beneath the main plaza, point to its having been public architecture of a religious nature. Tests below this structure revealed midden material of unknown depth beneath it. Tests did not go into this midden, but from the surface it appeared to have been the same type of habitation debris encountered elsewhere in the village deposits and a portion of a burned clay floor was revealed.

The platform was constructed on top of this midden and was apparently associated with a ground level, plaster-floored plaza. Although only a small portion of the front of the structure was exposed, it appears to have been originally a simple two-level platform facing east toward the village (Fig. 3.6b). The structure is reconstructed as being approximately 16 m wide. The first terrace had a 90 cm high sloping apron, whereas the more elaborate second terrace was 1.4 m in height and consisted of a sloping wall with apron molding, plinth, and an outset panel on either side of the

stairway. The staircase was outset, approximately 4 m wide and gave access to the east onto the plaza. It had wide, shallow steps and no balustrades.

Subsequently, the plaza in front of the platform was raised about 15-20 cm and replastered. Later, the plaza was again raised by about 40 cm. These two episodes eliminated a total of about 55-60 cm from the height of the platform and gave it the appearance of a structure built on top of a raised platform. The final plaza floor apparently was associated with a stone retaining wall against which later midden deposits were banked until the wall was completely buried. Whether or not the second plaster floor was associated with a retaining wall is unknown. At some point, this structure was apparently abandoned long enough for a great amount of marl melt to accumulate against the walls and for the surface of the plaza to deteriorate.

Just prior to its burial by the fill of the main plaza, the area in front of the northwestern retaining wall was the scene of a ceremony, presumably associated with this burial. A deep hole was excavated through all three of the plaza floors in the corner formed by the north wall of the stairway and the retaining wall. A few rocks and several pieces of painted plaster, possibly all that remained on the walls after the period of deterioration, were dumped into this hole. It should be noted that the same types of holes were excavated in the corners formed by the stairway and retaining walls of Structure 5C-1st, where they apparently functioned as places for the burial of painted and molded stucco that had been stripped off the walls. In addition to this hole, a large amount of pottery was broken in the area, including numerous examples of reconstructable "beer mugs," necked jars and a great many sherd lids. During the ceremony the top of the first terrace was used as a makeshift altar. Something was burned on top and in front of this terrace, probably copal incense. In addition, numerous small fragments of jade and at least one fragment of magnetic hematite were scattered on top and in front of the altar. It is quite tempting to visualize a small group of Maya priests uncorking a number of storage jars containing a vintage *balche* and proceeding to get ceremonially intoxicated. The ritual smashing of their drinking mugs and *balche*-jars and the scattering of jade fragments would have followed (cf. Garber 1981; Robertson-Freidel 1980). Following this ceremony, dry laid rubble construction walls were carefully built up to and over the structure, and the platform was completely buried by the fill of the main plaza.

SIZE AND POPULATION OF THE VILLAGE

The exact areal extent of this village cannot be determined at this point. It may have changed its size over the 300-400 years of its occupation. However, circumstantial evidence suggests that, even at its greatest expanse, it was no more than 4 ha. A small amount of testing beyond the limits of the plaza revealed thin midden deposits but no trace of habitation debris or structures. This was found to be the case to the east, south, and southwest of the main plaza. Unfortunately, the deposits underlying the construction fill under the area of the raised acropoli to the west of the main plaza (Structures 4A and 6A) could not be reached. Therefore, nothing could be learned of the pre-Tulix occupation in these areas. Deposits diagnostic of the village were found beyond the limits of the main plaza only underneath plaza 5A (Freidel, this volume), indicating that the village could not have been much larger than the approximately 2.81 ha covered by the main plaza and the Tulix acropoli to the west.

Additionally, it was noted in Op 1 that the retaining wall for the main plaza was placed directly over the margin of the village deposits and followed the village edge for at least 5 m. This observation, together with the unusual orientation of the eastern edge of the main plaza when compared with that of Structure 4A and the center in general, strongly suggests that the main plaza was deliberately constructed to totally and completely cover the area of the earlier village. Without further testing a maximum estimate of 2.81 ha for the area of the village seems reasonable.

This figure of 2.81 for the village includes both the nucleated habitation area and the space containing public architecture. In order to arrive at a realistic population estimate, we need to estimate what amount of this 2.81 area was, indeed private space. Extrapolating from the Tulix settlement at Cerros is one way of obtaining such an estimate. During the Tulix period the public architecture in the central area covered 5.5 ha (Freidel, personal communication 1980). The approximate extent of the entire site as defined by the canal that encircles it is 37 ha (Scarborough 1980). From these figures we can derive a proportion of public to private space of 14.8%. While some people may disagree with the use of Tulix phase Cerros to model the earlier nucleated village of the Ixtabai and C'oh phases, there is some justification for so doing. Some data do exist to indicate that the later site layout does

indeed mirror the earlier village arrangement. Both have large west-facing plazas, and Structure 2A-Sub 4 and Structure 4A are oriented in exactly the same direction. In fact, one seems to be an earlier version of the other. Applying the above proportion of public to private space, we arrive at a total area of 2.39 ha for the private sector of the village. Multiplying this figure by an average density of 36 structures/ha, we get a total count of 86 structures with each occupying an average area of 278 m², (approximately a 16.6 by 16.6 m area).

The question that arises at this point is how many of the estimated total number of structures in the village represent households or houses containing a nuclear family. While the problem of differing structure function has yet to be carefully examined, some preliminary observations can be made. Of the five definite structures currently isolated in the village deposit, four seem to be too large and too elaborate in floor plan to have been kitchens or other types of outbuildings. The fifth structure, despite its very limited exposure, shares several characteristics of elaboration with the others, indicating that it should be classed along with them. In addition, none of the five located structures appear to be arranged spatially with any of the others in a recognizable Maya plazuela pattern. Thus, the evidence indicates that all five structures represent different households, and that each represents a house as opposed to some other type of building. The density figure of 36 structures/ha may be interpreted as referring to households, and population figures may be computed accordingly. Using the figure of 5.6 people for the average Maya nuclear family (Haviland 1969; Puleston 1973), we arrive at a preliminary population estimate of 482 people for the nucleated village at its maximum.

CONCLUSIONS

The excavations into the sub-plaza deposits at Cerros definitely indicate the existence of an intensely occupied, nucleated village in the Late Preclassic Period. The earliest occupation isolated so far in the area of the site center apparently consisted of a fully nucleated village of perishable domestic structures. These structures were constructed with floors of tamped and burned earth and marl and were associated with plazas or patios of hard plaster. No evidence could be found for more than one structure per household. The evidence available indicates that the occupation of this village was restricted to the central area of the later site and did not occur in the surrounding peripheral areas. No occupation debris dating to this early period could be found outside the site center. The only other evidence for Ixtabai occupation on the entire peninsula comes from the area surrounding a large *aquada* about 1.65 km southeast of the site center, and about halfway to the present village of Copper Bank on Laguna Seca (Scarborough, personal communication 1981). Good evidence linking the early village with the construction of monumental religious architecture in the center has not yet been found, although such architecture might be to the west below Structure 4A. The ceramics from these early levels have been identified as being exclusively Late Preclassic in date (Robertson, personal communication 1982).

This occupation apparently continued without any appreciable break during the Late Preclassic period, spanning the Ixtabai and C'oh ceramic complexes at the site (Robertson, personal communication 1982). It had been occupied during the early Tulix period as well. The existence of quite easily discernible houses and midden "moundings" in the erosion profile indicates that the location of the perishable structures did not change greatly (if at all) throughout the total period of occupation. The village area does seem to have grown in at least one direction. It is almost certain that the continuing occupation resulted in, or was accompanied by, a withdrawal of the water from the site and further northward. Regardless of whether this was the result of an inadvertent filling of the waterfront edge or a drop in the level of the water itself, the effect on the occupation area was the same. The village apparently expanded to absorb the new space. Some time during the occupation of the village, possibly during the Late Ixtabai or C'oh period, a large public plaza was constructed with a temple platform built on top of it.

Indications of structure re-orientation in Op 1 may correlate with this construction. If so, the construction of the large public platform probably dates to the C'oh period.

This period of continuing occupation and growth may have been associated with the emergence of a new class of elites in the area, possibly associated with the function of the administrative center itself as a trade nexus. If this was indeed the case, it cannot yet be positively demonstrated. By the end of the occupation in the village, masonry platforms certainly had replaced several of the earlier clay ones and were associated with large plazas of plaster. One of these areas apparently consisted of a large area of well constructed plaster flooring at ground level with no retaining wall. This floor was associated with a small building platform that probably supported a domestic building. The location of this building platform establishes continuity from the earlier occupations and would seem to lead to the conclusion that the remains are the result of a single group's increasing status through time. Elsewhere in the village some deposits of primary trash were apparently leveled and covered by platforms. Some of these were at least 50 cm high. Whether or not in the final stages of its existence the village was occupied by individuals of elite or of middle-class status (possibly a service population) cannot be determined from the architectural remains in the village alone. Exactly when the occupation of the village ceased is equivocal in view of the great amount of surface modification that occurred at the end of the occupation. Normally, it would simply be a matter of examining the ceramics for evidence of the most recent sherd material. However, the evidence indicates that the area occupied by the village remained open for some time prior to its final burial under the main plaza and raises the problem of distinguishing between material resulting from the final occupation and that resulting from dumping trash in the area after its abandonment. Without a definite date on the final habitation of the area, we cannot adequately correlate the architecture in the village with that in the peripheral area or adequately determine if there was a period of overlap in occupancy.

In any event, the data do indicate that some time during either the Late C'oh or the Early Tulix periods the village was abandoned and utilization of the area for domestic space ceased. After an unknown period of time during which the area was left vacant and probably used as a source of trash for construction fill and as a trash dump, the final construction phase of the main plaza was built over the area, contemporaneous with the rapid transformation of the village into the monumental core of the extensive Tulix phase community.

NOTES

1. Thanks must be given to those whose labor contributed to the success of the field excavations, including Melanie Porter, Julia Minor, Jude Lizama, Linda Goss, Maria Vega, Lynn Steele, Harriet McQuarrie, Jim Garber, Vivian Ducat, Herman Byrd, Mike Caruso, Rick Boston, Truett Roberts, and Karen

Jackson, The author wishes to express his special thanks to Beverly Mitchum and Sorayya Carr, who carried out independent excavation operations in the sub-plaza deposits. The local Belizeans who aided are too numerous to list, but special mention must be made of Venacio Novello, Foreman during the 1974 season, and Valeriano Tun, Foreman from 1976 onward.

Unless otherwise noted in the text, judgements concerning the significance of ceramics from the sub-plaza deposits are my own, but they formed during numerous long discussions with Robin Robertson, the project ceramicist. Any errors in interpretation are my own. For specific type identifications, I am indebted to her.

Finally, I wish to express my thanks to David Freidel, David Pendergast, Robin Robertson, and Vernon Scarborough for reading and commenting upon earlier versions of this paper.

2.   Due to its location on the margin of the erosion-cut, the areal extent of this operation varied from only 2–3 m² in any single level.

3.   The same type of informal burned clay platforms were used as a base for the domestic architecture at the Early Classic site of Ceren in El Salvador (Sheets 1979). Sheets reports that at Ceren, such platforms consisted of "wet-laid clay floors which were first allowed to dry and were then fired in place..." (1979:38).

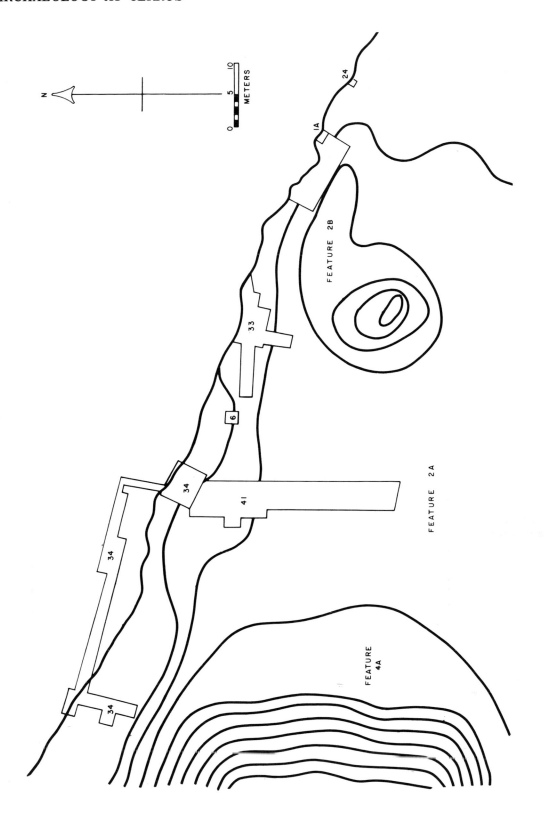

Figure 3.1. Locations of the major excavations in Feature 1A.

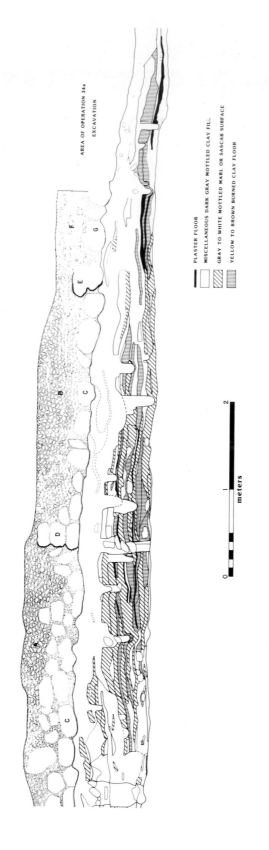

Figure 3.2. Profile of erosion wall segment east of Op 34a illustrating the superpositioning of domestic construction layers and household midden.

Key: A, Very small limestone gravel ballast, in a matrix of friable, grey silty clay and humus; B, Small dry-laid limestone rubble ballast, fill of Main Plaza, Feature 2A; C, Large limestone rubble ballast in a matrix of friable grey-brown silty clay, basal fill for Main Plaza, Feature 2A; D, Dry-laid rubble construction wall for the Main Plaza, Feature 2A; E, Rear of Structure 2A-Sub.5-1st retaining wall; F, Small limestone rubble ballast, fill of Structure 2A-Sub.5-1st; G, Large limestone rubble ballast, basal fill of Structure 2A-Sub.5-1st.

Figure 3.3. Excavated segment of Feature 2A retaining wall located in the eastern portion of Op 1.

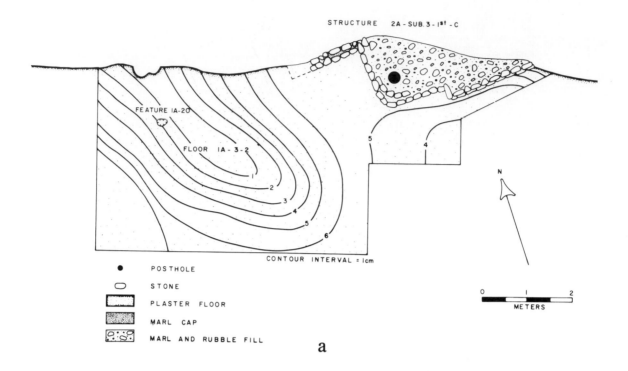

a

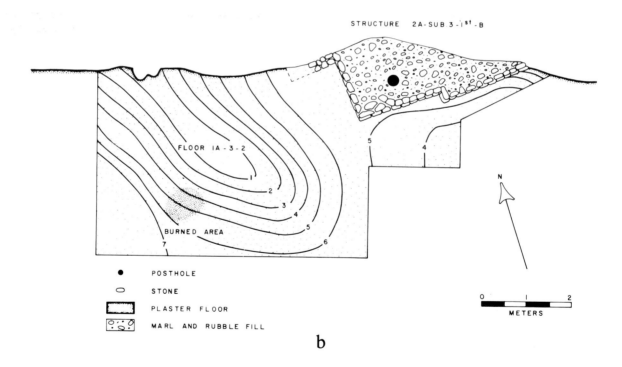

b

Figure 3.4. Structure 2A-Sub. 3-1st plans. a, 2A-Sub. 3-1st-C; b, 2A-Sub. 3-1st-B.

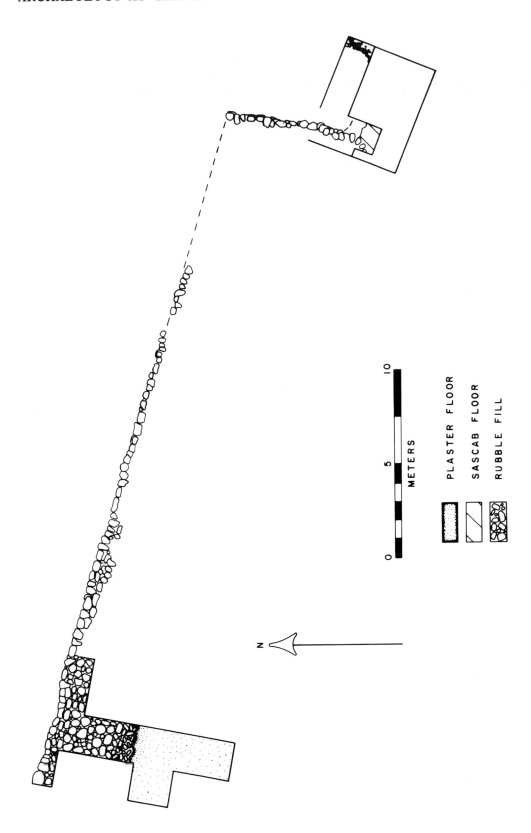

Figure 3.5. Plan of the excavated portion of Structure 2A-Sub. 2, showing reconstructed northeastern segment.

Figure 3.6a. Op 34—exposed surface of midden in Op 34a showing heavy concentration of artifactual debris.

Figure 3.6b. Op 41—excavated portion of the small, two-level platform, Structure 2A-Sub. 4, revealed by the Op 41 trench in the Main Plaza.

FEATURE 11 AND THE QUEST FOR THE ELUSIVE DOMESTIC STRUCTURE: A PRELIMINARY RECONSTRUCTION BASED ON CHIPPED STONE USE

Sue Lewenstein

Since 1974, excavations at Cerros have yielded a rich sample of material culture that includes thousands of chipped stone artifacts. Much of this collection consists of remains recovered from small structures and other features located outside the ceremonial-administrative precinct (Freidel 1978, 1979). This paper will discuss attempts to determine the uses associated with the Maya stone tools recovered from one carefully excavated group of low mounds located approximately 450 m southwest of the ceremonial district. I will use the inferred functions and tool frequencies, along with archaeological context, to reconstruct (whenever possible) the activities that took place during several sequential occupational episodes.

The spatial distribution and magnitude of productive loci and other specialized tasks at Cerros are clues to the local economy. Restricted association of certain activities to limited geographical areas within the site or to a narrow range of architectural features or status indicators has important implications for the reconstruction of the Preclassic Maya social order (Haviland 1963:506-518; Michels 1976, 1979; Santley 1977: 322-325) and also indicates the degree of political and administrative involvement in production and exchange (Hay 1978; Spence 1979; Lamberg-Karlovsky 1975).

This is not the first attempt to apply the lithic use wear approach on a broad scale to the interpretation of a Mesoamerican archaeological context (cf. Clark 1980; Hay 1978; Puleston 1969). The use damage preserved on stone implements is produced by the use of tools for a wide range of tasks, many of which leave no other trace. This is especially true at lowland sites like Cerros, where preservation of faunal remains, textiles, bone tools, pollen, seeds, postholes and hearths is often problematic. Functional lithic analysis is not a substitute for ceramic or other lines of evidence, but it can provide supplementary data for the identification and characterization of activities already under study, such as weaving (Parsons 1975; Stark and Heller 1980), pyrite mirror manufacture (Pires-Ferreira 1975), jade and other lapidary work (Andrews and Rovner 1973; Kidder et al. 1946:118-124; Terzuola 1975), stone carving (Becker 1973), and shell working (Suárez 1977).

In addition, there are many other tasks, equally important in understanding the archaeological record, which involve perishable materials. Stone tools often were used to process many of these substances. Therefore it is reasonable to expect that the analysis of lithic use wear will lead to the identification of some of these activities. Bone working, woodworking, butchering, hide processing, fiber, bark and resin exploitation, fishing, and the processing of edible plants appear to be promising avenues of research in use wear studies (Hayden 1979; Hester and Heizer 1971; Keeley 1980, Lewenstein 1981; Odell 1980; Semenov 1964).

Not every identified activity area represents specialized craft production. Nor is every small mound a vestigial domestic structure (Stenholm 1979; Haviland 1970:183). In order to address economic and socio-political issues on the site level, it is imperative to be able to (1) correctly distinguish residential from non-domiciliary structures in the settlement zone, and (2) identify the range of household activities (Flannery and Winter 1976; Stenholm 1979). Once the quantity and spatial patterning of domestic behavioral residues are understood, these can be factored out of the artifact distributions. It is then that anomalies corresponding to non-domestic tasks and loci of specialized manufacturing will be evident. Ultimately it may be possible to deal with the issue of the processual relationship between social stratification and occupational specialization at Cerros. Several questions are raised by this goal: 1) what degree of social differentiation characterized the earliest occupation of the site? 2) did specialized productive activities precede status differences? 3) what role did special knowledge, manufacturing and marketing skills play in the evolution of lowland Mesoamerican chiefdoms? 4) did overspecialization of the site level contribute to the downfall and abandonment of Cerros at the end of the Late Preclassic era?

A STARTING POINT

In order to answer these questions, I intend to draw on data generated by the analysis of the chipped stone collected from all excavations in the dispersed settlement and in the nucleated coastal midden at Cerros. The first mound group investigated, Feature 11 (Figs. 1.1 and 2.2b), is a small plazuela group described by Scarborough (1980 and this volume) as an elite residence on the basis of the fine quality of its late Preclassic stone masonry. The group is situated less than 40 m from the present coastline in thornscrub savanna. Three structures share a common platform. Structure 11B, the largest, is 3.5 m high and occupies the east plaza, facing west. It contains two rectangular rooms arranged in tandem (cf. Harrison 1970:97 and Fig. 11), and a western patio area.

Structures 11C and 11D are not well preserved, but appear to have been smaller. They are about 1.5 m high and were oriented east toward 11B. All three mounds were tested. In each case Late Preclassic construction and occupation were documented. The upper levels were mixed with the debris from Late Postclassic reuse of the plazuela.

Almost 700 lithic artifacts were recovered from Feature 11. All stone items were examined for use traces under a binocular microscope with a 40x capability. Additional eyepieces that increase magnification to 80x were available and occasionally used in sorting utilized from non-utilized pieces. In a few cases it was possible to study a tool with the scanning electron microscope. Because of the time and expense involved this procedure could not be used on the entire sample. Artifacts identified as utilized tools were drawn and described on 3×5 index cards. Each was re-examined microscopically in order to confirm the presence of use damage, which was recorded on IBM coding sheets for future manipulation. Among the attributes recorded were:

1) size and shape,
2) raw material,
3) heat treatment or other physical/chemical alteration,
4) edge angle,
5) location of use,
6) degree of intentional retouch,
7) clues as to hafting or prehension,
8) zones of polish or dulling,
9) edge abrasion or crushing,
10) the distribution and orientation of striations, or linear scratches,
11) microflake scar symmetry, size, shape, distribution, and termination type (Ahler 1979; Crabtree 1972; Hayden 1979; Odell 1980; Semenov 1964).

The functional interpretation of the wear patterns was based primarily on comparisons with experimentally produced use wear on modern replicas of the prehistoric implements. Replicas were made of chert from Rancho Creek, near Colha, Belize, and from grey translucent obsidian collected from the El Chayal outcrop near Guatemala City. The tool replicas, many of which are unretouched flakes, were used for a variety of tasks such as cutting, scraping, whittling, perforating and incising. The materials worked with these tools include a number of substances that are known to have been exploited by coastal peoples during the Late Preclassic. These include hard and soft woods, several Central American fibers and vines, sherds, animal hide, turkey and deer bone, shell and fish. During the 1981 season experimentation continued, focusing on chopping, adzing, hoeing, and planing tasks. The range of contact materials was also expanded to include bark, twine, rope, palm, limestone, vegetables and tubers, resin, hide processing, and the butchering of birds and animals. The analysis of these materials has not been completed.

In addition to edge damage comparisons between archaeological and experimental tools, several other lines of evidence proved useful in making functional inferences. Of particular importance were considerations of the following:

1) archaeological provenience. With what other tools was a specimen associated? Were there non-lithic items such as shell fragments or grinding stones correlated with the occurrence of certain wear patterns? (Flannery and Winter 1976; Hay 1978; Santley 1977)
2) the growing literature on ethnoarchaeology and use wear experimentation (Frison 1979; Gould 1980)
3) raw material suitability for a hypothesized task (Crabtree and Davis 1968)
4) tool morphology (Semenov 1970)
5) natural or imported resources available for possible use by the inhabitants of Cerros (Feldman 1971; Record and Mell 1924; Large 1975)

6) ethnohistoric and ethnographic accounts of traditional life in the region (Gann 1918; Thompson 1936; Tozzer 1907).

The Feature 11 assemblage can be subdivided into 86 Preclassic lots, representing two sequential building episodes, and a large number of mixed upper levels corresponding to Late Preclassic, Early Classic and Late Postclassic occupations (Robertson, personal communication 1982).

A GLIMPSE AT LATE PRECLASSIC ACTIVITIES

Unfortunately, no utilized lithic implements were recovered from unmixed early contexts in Structures 11C and 11D. Excavations on Structure 11B opened a horizontal exposure of more than 125 m². This represents almost the entire western half of the mound (Fig. 2.3a). The result was 54 edge damaged chipped stone tools of Late Preclassic date from within the structure, on the patio, and from the various loci adjacent to the building. Five of these are obsidian blades.

The earliest occupational activity was identified beneath the platform at ground level, associated with a friable lens of red-brown clay. Artifactual remains from this lens were limited to only two of the excavation units (Op 103h and i). This deposit included a jade fragment along with six chipped stone artifacts, two of which were grey obsidian blade fragments. Use wear was detected on only one of the six lithic artifacts—an obsidian blade. The edge damage observed on this implement indicates extended use in scraping and cutting a moderately soft substance. This wear pattern most closely approximates the damage recorded on experimental blades used to scale and clean fish. Lack of an adequate sample precludes any further reconstruction of stone tool-using activities during this initial occupation. Excavations in other nearby features also probed this level and recovered contemporaneous lithic materials. Further inferences will be possible when analysis of these materials is complete.

The major Late Preclassic occupation of Structure 11B is associated with the buildup of the platform and the subsequent construction and use of a building having two long rectangular rooms and a recessed wall niche in one corner. The niche was adorned with a panel of painted plaster molded on carved stone. Two pieces of jade, fragments of a bead and an ear flare, were recovered from the niche. Two hundred twenty-six lithic artifacts of chert or chalcedony were collected from unmixed Late Preclassic lots associated with this structure. Fifty-three of them show signs of having been used. The four obsidian artifacts recovered are prismatic blades. One of these has been retouched at the bulbar end into a thick perforator.

All utilized implements were examined microscopically and functional determinations were made before any spatial distributions and associations were considered. In some cases specific inferences as to mode of use and contact material, such as "flake used to whittle soft wood," were possible. Other times the assessments were more general, such as "cutting/slicing implement used on soft substance." Usually specific actions were indicated. Specific worked materials were identifiable less often.

Next the stone tools were plotted on a plan map of Structure 11B in addition to walls, features and non-lithic artifacts. Five spatially discrete clusters of utilized chipped stone were apparent on the map (Fig. 4.1). Three of these loci are located outside of the building. Cluster 1 is in the patio area to the right of the threshold. To the left of this threshold and extending around the corner to the north lies Cluster 2. Cluster 3 is behind the building to the north, Clusters 4 and 5 occupy the west half of the anterior room and the rear room, respectively. All but a few of the stone tools were spatially associated with one of the clusters. Although not all tools within a group are necessarily related functionally, nor will all components of a tool kit necessarily be found together, there are major differences in wear patterns among the five clusters of tools (Fig. 4.2). These traces can be useful in retrodicting some of the activities carried out by the people occupying Structure 11.

Cluster 1 appears to be a bone and woodworking area. The tool kit is made up of a large core tool bearing traces of use as a hammer, chopper and adze on a hard substance, four flake scrapers, one steep scraper, two perforators, one graver/perforator, and one double perforator. All of these tools appear to have been used on bone and wood. One flake was also used to cut or slice a soft substance like twine or some other fiber.

Hide processing and leather working may have been performed in Cluster 2 on the other side of the threshold. Two of the seven implements found, a thick chalcedony flake and a biface fragment, were used as scrapers on a soft substance similar to hide. Three chert flake knives and one obsidian blade fragment also were used for cutting and some light scraping. The function of the large biface recovered has not been identified.

Behind the structure a third cluster of utilized stone tools was found. These included an unused adze preform, one perforator, one graver/denticulated plane, three flake scrapers, two whittling knives and one large preformed flake with both a cutting and scraping locus. The use wear on all of these specimens indicates contact with wood. The location of these implements suggests an area where woodworking, especially roughing-out operations took place, including the stripping of bark and initial shaping of wood to be made into furniture, bowls, shafts, etc., possibly at some other locale. This peripheral area may have been chosen for these tasks to avoid littering the plaza on the other side of 11B. It also afforded an ideal spot to store lumber, wood scraps, and stone tools until they were needed.

Cluster 4, in the anterior room of 11B, produced very few lithic artifacts. The only utilized lithics were an obsidian blade fragment (used on soft material), a scraper (used on soft material), a resharpening flake and a single segment of a broken macroblade tool. No specific activity area is indicated here. In fact this area appears to have been kept relatively free of lithic tools and debris.

The innermost room is characterized by a high density of chipped stone, including core and flake tools as well as unutilized flakes. Twenty-one utilized tools were recovered in Cluster 5. These include three hammerstones, two chopping tools, a retouched flake notch, three perforators, a triangular shaped chert graver, two whittling knives, a steep-angled scraper, two planes, four cutting implements and two flake scrapers. The activities hypothesized for this area are the manufacture of chert flakes for cutting and scraping, the storage of core tools and the production of fine woodwork. The woodworking may have occurred in a ritual context, judging from the concentration of woodworking tools close to the niche.

It is interesting that all of the activities described above usually are thought to be within the domain of adult males. There is no evidence that mundane household chores such as food preparation or storage, clothing manufacturing or mat-making were performed in Structure 11B during the Late Preclassic. Hearths, grinding implements, faunal and other food remains, bell-shaped or other storage areas, bone needles, awls, and spindle whorls are absent. Although a semi-cleared area in the rear room of the structure was expected, this locus appears to have been the scene of a great deal of active, *ad hoc* tool production. These two activities

appear to rule out a sleeping area. Lithic debris would be especially undesirable in a bedroom.

On the basis of the lithic and architectural evidence, Structure 11B does not seem to have been a Late Preclassic residence. Rather, it appears to have functioned as a gathering place for men, where ritual and craft activities were performed, and economic plans and political machinations discussed. At present it cannot be determined whether Structure 11B was used exclusively by the male residents of Structures 11C and 11D, the probable domestic loci, or whether it was the meeting place for relatives and allies who lived elsewhere.

GUILT BY ASSOCIATION: UNRAVELING THE MYSTERIES OF THE MIXED UPPER LOTS

Samples of utilized chipped stone occur in the mixed lots recovered from both Structures 11C and 11B. The assemblage from Structure 11C appears to be a mixture of Late Postclassic and some Late Preclassic materials. During excavation it was not possible to follow any structure walls or floors. Of 118 stone artifacts recovered only four show signs of prehistoric use. An obsidian blade possibly was used for fish scaling/butchering. A denticulated scraper made on a macroblade, a scraper re-sharpening flake, and a broken tang (used as a thick scraper/plane on hard wood) were made of chert. Among the knapping debris there is some evidence of chert tool finishing, sharpening, and retooling. Ceramic balls, shell fragments and ceramic *mariposas* were associated with the lithic artifacts. Although domestic activities are not precluded by the presence of this artifact assortment, there is little here which conclusively indicates a residential function. In all, a 24 m² horizontal exposure was achieved. The fact that only 24 m² were exposed coupled with the deteriorated state of the mound may partially account for this paucity of evidence.

Among the mixed lots from Structure 11B more than 90 utilized stone tools were discovered, many of which are retouched chert and chalcedony flakes. In interpreting these materials two questions were specifically addressed. How many of these artifacts consist of Late Preclassic tools whose context has been disturbed and what functional correspondence between the Preclassic and Late Postclassic activities can be inferred by comparing the two assemblages?

One way to answer these questions is to look at the mixed lots that were excavated directly above the two room structure discussed above (Fig. 4.2). The ten utilized stone tools found above the south room or Cluster 4 were separated out and labeled Mixed Cluster 1. Nine of these tools are from Op 103w. Two gravers, a scraper, two obsidian whittling knives and a perforator represent woodworking implements. A saw and a scraper represent boneworking activities. Soft substances like fibers or vegetables are associated with the two remaining scraping implements, one of which is denticulated. Obviously this locus was not a cleared entry-way throughout the entire period when the structure was in use. There appears to be little correspondence between the hypothesized Late Preclassic function and the contents of the superimposed mixed lots. It seems the Postclassic occupants of Structure 11B did not arrange their activities to conform to the ruins of the Preclassic building.

Mixed Cluster 2 is made up of nine utilized chipped stone artifacts retrieved from deposits above the interior room of Structure 11B. The presence of a large core tool or hoe and a high percentage of fine woodworking implements in these upper deposits correspond well with the function hypothesized for the underlying Preclassic room based on the tools in Cluster 5. In fact this group of stone tools may be primarily Preclassic in date despite their mixed provenience. There is no evidence to suggest a Postclassic refurbishing of Structure 11B, for example, and it may be that this area was not in use after it was abandoned in the Late Preclassic.

Eight utilized tools, making up Mixed Cluster 3, were recovered in the mixed strata at the north edge of the platform. The wear traces on some of this group suggest woodworking activities, indicating the tools may be part of the underlying Late Preclassic assemblage in Cluster 3. The other tools, consisting mainly of scrapers, were apparently used in food preparation and represent either Late Preclassic or Postclassic trash accumulation. There are very few lithic artifacts among the material remains recovered from the mixed lots at the southwest corner of Structure 11B above Cluster 2. Of note are two chert knives, one of which is geometric in form. Both bear wear patterns attributable to leather cutting. These functions are not incompatible with Cluster 2 which has been interpreted as a possible hide processing and leather working locus.

Mixed lot materials associated with the patio area south of Structure 11B are plentiful. They have been subdivided into Mixed Clusters 4 and 5. Mixed Cluster 4 is approximately 8 m × 4 m. The collection includes 175 chipped stone artifacts, forty-six of which show use wear. Among these are twenty-three utilized obsidian blade fragments. Associated items include a limestone maul, a spindle whorl, two ceramic gaming pieces, six ceramic *mariposas*, and a limestone cylindrical polisher. Four distinct tasks are indicated by these artifacts. Sharp flakes of chalcedony from nearby Progreso and of pink-to-light-brown local cherts were produced in this area in addition to fish nets. Six ceramic *mariposas*, thought to be net weights (Willey *et al.* 1965:408), were associated with six flakes whose edge damage indicates they were used to cut sherds. Once the two notches were cut in a sherd, the edges were shaped by grinding. Wooden sticks may have been used as well in producing the nets given the presence of five small notched wood scraping flakes and three whittling knives (cf. Hurley 1979 for examples of aboriginal weaving using sticks). The only other tools necessary for net making are fiber cutting knives. Use traces attributable to fiber cutting have been observed on at least ten obsidian blades and several chert flakes recovered from this context. This net production episode is assigned to Late Postclassic times on the basis of the fully ground platforms seen on all proximal fragments of obsidian blades in this artifact cluster (Rovner 1976:49-50). A small leather working kit, consisting of a hide knife, four scrapers, and two perforators was also found in this area. Seventeen tools are believed to be food preparation utensils. These include chert knives and flake scrapers used on vegetables and in animal butchering.

Because all of the artifacts come from surface lots it seems all four activities took place during the final, Late Postclassic occupation of the group. However, the spatial association of the artifacts does not necessarily mean that these four tasks were carried out at the same location or contemporaneously. It is more likely that the group was deposited in one place as a result of periodic sweeping of the patio area during the Late Postclassic occupation.

Mixed Cluster 5 is south of Mixed Cluster 4. Although a mano fragment suggested a food preparation locus, a limestone maul, a shell fragment, a piece of land coral abrasive, two *mariposas* and two ceramic gaming pieces were also included in this collection. Moreover, the use wear observed on the chipped stone tools did not point to cooking or other kitchen tasks. Instead it supported a variety of scraping activities carried out on hard woods, bone and leather. Once again, this may be an area into which Postclassic residents swept the byproducts of activities that were conducted elsewhere in the patio. The mano fragment may be associated with the food processing implements attributed to Mixed Cluster 4, three m to the north.

SUMMARY AND CONCLUDING REMARKS

Analysis of the lithic artifacts from Group 11 indicates that during the Late Preclassic domestic functions were restricted to Structures 11C and 11D. The larger Structure 11B on the east side of the platform was a men's house reserved for ritual and related woodworking activities. The Late Postclassic reoccupation of this plazuela group can best be described as a scattered or sprawling household associated with perishable architecture.

Much of the behavioral reconstruction presented here is hypothetical at present. Further hypothesis testing can be achieved by reference to ceramic and faunal data, both of which are helpful in the identification of kitchens and other functionally distinct areas. However, determining and interpreting stone tool use can contribute to our understanding of the organization of past ways of life and sometimes provides insights that are not forthcoming from any other line of evidence.

Acknowledgments

The Arizona Chapter of the ARCS Foundation, the Social Science Research and the E. Blois de Bois Foundation helped make this research possible. I am deeply grateful for their support.

I would also like to thank the Department of Microbiology, Arizona State University, for allowing me to use their scanning electron microscope to observe and photograph the lithic use traces discussed in this paper.

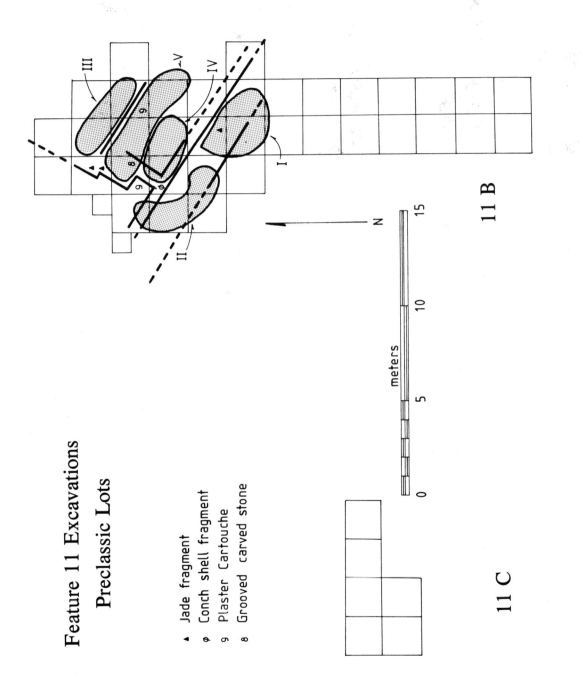

Feature 11 Excavations
Preclassic Lots

▲ Jade fragment
φ Conch shell fragment
9 Plaster Cartouche
8 Grooved carved stone

11 B

11 C

meters

Figure 4.1. Late Preclassic artifact clusters identified during the excavation of Structure Group 11.

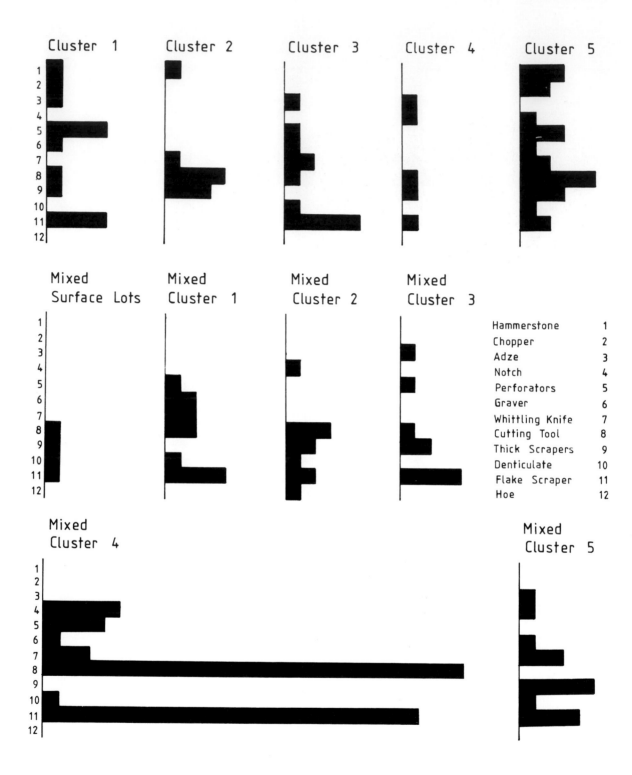

Figure 4.2. Histograms reflecting the frequency of occurrence of artifact types found in the clusters shown in Figures
4.1 and 4.3.

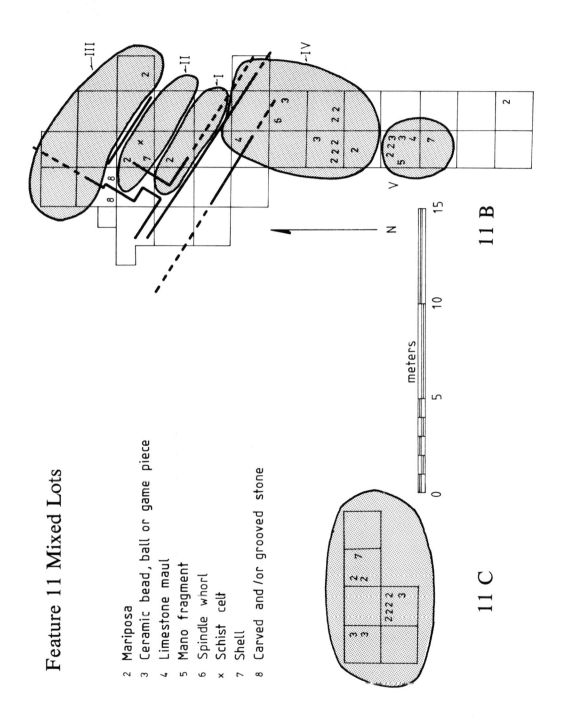

Figure 4.3. Artifact clusters identified in the mixed lots excavated in Structure Group 11.

DRAINAGE CANAL AND RAISED FIELD EXCAVATIONS

Vernon L. Scarborough

An excavation program was initiated to collect formal information about the canal system at Cerros. All naturally defined levels were routinely screened for artifacts and macrofossils. Flotation samples were run from each stratum in the field and preliminary microfossil interpretive statements have been made (Scarborough 1980). Pollen samples from 200 contexts are presently under study, as are chemical and physical soils tests. Although only limited interpretive statements have been gleaned from the soils analysis to date, an additional 300 contexts have been collected to aid in determining the origin and fertility of the sediments in question.

EXCAVATIONS IN THE MAIN CANAL

Five trenching operations across the main canal were placed perpendicular to the long axis of the main canal. Each trench was positioned to retrieve specific information about the immediate surroundings in which the excavation was carried out, while addressing the overall function of the canal system (Fig. 2.1). The two southern trenches are described in some detail elsewhere (Freidel and Scarborough 1982) and will not be discussed in this presentation unless specific comparisons seem appropriate. Except for the two southern-most trenching operations, the excavations were widely separated spatially in order to discern the amount of variability in the system and to answer such questions as (1) what was the precise gradient of the canal? (2) what was the unequivocal date of the canal? and (3) what was the function of the canal?

The West Trench

Our western-most trench (Op 157) through the main canal was placed at the foot of the 5 m high Structure 21 (Fig. 5.1). This location was selected because of the promise of obtaining midden debris from the structure in the canal, the possibility of defining a water control device in proximity to this large sentinel-like structure

and the beginning of the main canal, and the prospect of stratigraphically linking the canal with the previously dated Tulix phase Structure 21.

This trench exposed 16 m² to a maximum depth of 1.60 m. The main canal at this location was defined by a deeply buried caprock canal bank which dipped to form a symmetrical U-shaped cross section. The canal was approximately 6 m wide and only 1 m deep, though the original height of the canal bank walls may have been higher. The bottom of the canal was exposed by means of three posthole probes. The trench was within 35 m of the present shoreline and, depending on the conditions over Corozal Bay (i.e., dry season *norte* disturbances), would fill and hold half to full capacity of the original canal volume.

The basal matrix was typified by the same sterile, friable, white marl or clean *sascab* noted from the other exposures. Above the original canal cut lay 1 m of friable, blocky grey clay silt. Most of the matrix examined was taken from the upper 50 cm because of the rising water table. The entire matrix was heavily intruded by pebbles and cobbles, though the western half of the exposure contained a greater concentration of debris than did the eastern. Fall stones are believed to have slumped from the adjacent Structure 21 and probably indicate a contemporaneous abandonment of both the mound and the trough. Near the bottom of the exposure the clays were more compacted. The sediments were severely recemented, making microstratigraphic control impossible. Overlying the lower grey clays was 40 cm of viscous dark grey clay. The western three-quarters of the canal trough was heavily intruded by pebbles to small limestone boulders.

The eastern bank was composed of friable light grey clay with small gravel size inclusions of white marl. These clays appear to be resting behind a crude alignment of small boulder size stone. It is difficult to define the original sterile decomposed caprock behind the stone concentration because of the mottled nature of the matrix. However, at approximately 1 m from the surface of the exposure, indurated caprock was encountered behind the stone alignment.

In the western portion of the exposure, indurated

caprock was found at approximately 80 cm from the surface. Again, a concentration of stone, two to three courses high, occurred at the edge of the canal bank. The matrix behind the concentration consisted of a viscous dark grey clay similar to the sediments in the canal. The matrix near the caprock was less intruded by large cobbles to small boulders than that higher in the stratigraphy. Generally, the darker clays in this region were more mottled by intrusions and mound fall than elsewhere in the exposure. The artifact inventory was greatest in the higher reaches of the western side of the exposure. The entire trench was covered by a 10 cm thick viscous black loamy clay intruded by pebble to small cobble size limestone gravels.

Our exposure indicates that the main canal was excavated to a more shallow depth at the western end than at other locations. Although a severe amount of siltation buried the main canal course, the amount of soil overlying the caprock at both ends of the cut suggests the former presence of raised fields. If the banks of the canal were raised and defined by flanking field plots, then the height of the main canal bank would have been considerably greater and more in keeping with the critical depth of the main canal found in other exposures. Moreover, the degree of siltation which has occurred at this locus is significantly greater than at other locations, suggesting the erosion of raised field sediments into the main canal. This line of argument is further supported by concentrations of stones found at the edge of the canal bank which may represent the lower courses of buttresses supporting the field platforms defined elsewhere in the settlement.

In any case, the canal seems to have been infilled from its adjacent banks. Some of the sediment appears to derive from the margins of the canal, but the substantial amount of rubble limestone suggests a colluvial origin for the rest of it, probably from the summit of Structure 21. Preliminary examination of the ceramic collection from the cut indicates a Late Preclassic/Early Classic date. In addition to pottery, a small amount of bone and charcoal were noted from the matrix.

It should be mentioned that the absence of bay beach sands in the basal sediments of the canal suggests a change in the present shoreline. The proximity of the present beach sands and the elevated position of the bay level, relative to the bottom of the canal, indicate that the main canal would have been invaded by the bay if the bay level were the same today as in the past. It is suggested that either the land mass at Cerros was

formerly at least 1 m higher along the coast or that the water level was comparably lower.

The East Trench

Another trenching operation (Op 154) was placed on the eastern margin of the core zone (Fig. 5.2). A small ground level structure (Structure 165) on the immediate margin of the canal bank had been revealed during the intensive mapping of the main canal. The trench location was chosen to define the nature of ground level occupation with specific reference to the main canal. Abundant trash was anticipated within the canal trough.

The trench exposed 25 m² to a maximum depth of 1.55 m. The canal cut appears to have been a symmetrical U-shape, although the bank sloped downward at a gentle angle before dropping abruptly into the canal (Fig. 5.3a). The canal exposure at this location was 3.20 m wide and 1.70 m deep relative to the arbitrary vertical datum used for the entire site. The bottom of the canal was defined by the sterile clean white marl or sascab exposed at the base of the caprock. The basal sediments were covered by the dry season water table and the bottom of the canal was discernible only through postholing.

The bulk of the sediment in the canal consisted of a blocky grey clay loam containing numerous gypsum crystals. The matrix was severely recemented due to the effects of percolating ground water charged with calcite or dolomite. Pomacea burrows further disrupted the stratigraphy. A significant inventory of midden debris was retrieved from the exposure, the greatest concentration of material coming from the western margin of the unit below the ground level structure. Late Preclassic pottery, chert, bone, charcoal and ash were either collected or identified. The eastern portion of the unit exposed additional concentrations of sherd debris at the edge of the canal. Toward the center the matrix graded imperceptibly into a lighter grey clay loam containing a lower concentration of gypsum crystals and a greater frequency of limestone gravels. It contained some cultural debris. The bedding plane of the sherds indicates a lateral slope wash deposition for this sediment.

The canal was capped by a 10 cm thick, viscous, black gumbo clay containing few limestone gravels. At the boundary between this humic horizon and the underlying grey clay loam was a diminutive U-shaped trough in the center of the canal trough. It appears to represent a stone lined canal segment constructed some 1.10 m above the base of the original canal cut and after the major siltation process at Cerros. It may be associated with the Early Classic reuse of the canal system.

Because of the narrow width of the canal at this location, a sizeable area of canal bank was exposed in our 12 m long trench. The eastern bank revealed a pavement of tabular limestone cobbles. Because the pavement did not rest on a paleosol or a lens of grey clay loam, it seems the soil was scraped off the caprock before the pavement was laid. The pavement, not revealed at other canal bank locations, is similar to other plaza surfaces exposed in the settlement. A thin veneer of light grey clay loam overlaid the pavement and, in turn, was capped by the black gumbo.

On the west bank a ground level structure was identified, but no architectural features were apparent. This type of poor preservation has been reported frequently in the settlement. Even though the structure had been placed directly upon the caprock, no clearly defined postholes were noted. The quantity and quality of trash at the foot of the structure within the canal suggest that the structure was a domicile. In addition, a possible step into the canal trough was suggested during our excavation of the bank. However, the advanced deterioration of the canal bank at this location does not allow a positive conclusion. A thin humus layer covered the exposure.

The original canal cut is associated with a constriction in the canal, perhaps made necessary as a crossover point from the core area into the periphery of the site. The possible step in the western canal bank may be the location of a former log bridge (cf. Wilkens 1969). The pavement on the east side may be the continuation of a stone path into the eastern *hulub bajo*. The location of a structure on the west bank might be expected given a degree of controlled access to the core area. Following the infilling of the canal system a minor "echo" canal (cf. Haury 1976:149-50) was crudely constructed to collect water in a manner not unlike that demonstrated at the southern margin of the core area (Freidel and Scarborough 1982: Fig. 6).

The Northeast Trench

At the northeastern end of the visible main canal segment, another trenching operation (Op 156) was placed across an area of high ground (Fig. 5.2). The

unit rests approximately 150 m south of the present shoreline. This location was selected to examine the terminus of the present canal trough and to reveal, in part, the function of the canal by excavating a potential raised causeway location.

This operation was the most complex in the canalization program. The trench exposed 30 m² to a maximum depth of 1.80 m. The canal in cross-section was a stepped asymmetrical U-shape with a broad platform or sill positioned at the eastern base of the canal (Fig. 5.36). The canal dimensions at this location were approximately 5 m wide and 2.10 m deep relative to the vertical site datum. The canal bottom was defined by the same sterile white marl or *sascab* reported from other exposures. It was located 40 cm below the dry season water table and was demonstrable by the positioning of 13 postholes within the canal banks. The postholing also revealed the nature of the basal platform or sill which projects from the eastern bank approximately 2.25 m before abruptly dropping 75 cm to the bottom of the canal channel. In plan, the sill runs diagonally across the floor of the canal from the southeast side of the exposure into the northwest profile. In addition, the east canal bank revealed two carved steps inset into the indurated canal bank caprock. Although severely weathered, they appeared clearly in our south profile exposure. The west bank of the canal was poorly defined but appears to have been stepped, dropping precipitously into the canal course. It seems to have had one step but no projecting sill.

The matrix within the canal consists of a dark grey clay flecked with white marl. The matrix was severely recemented and affected by worm casts. *Pomacea* intruded throughout the matrix. The soils were generally better sorted in this exposure than elsewhere, though a few limestone gravels were apparent near the bottom. The highest incidence of gravel was reported at the flanks of the canal bank. Although little cultural debris was recovered from the sill surface, a great deal of trash (pottery, flint, bone, charcoal and ash) was collected from the basal course of the canal trough. Little debris was found directly on the canal floor. Instead it lay 40 cm above the present canal bottom. Most of the sherds were horizontally bedded or bedded in the plane of the canal bank contour. At the banks of the canal the matrix was a more sandy texture but mottled by grey clay fill.

The stratigraphy generally illustrates the nature of the main canal. Although lateral lensing is not clearly visible, the apparent concentration of sherd debris at the margin of the canal bank suggests that the matrices are entering the canal from the banks and not longitudinally down the canal course. The sill identified in the cross-section seems to be a landing or platform used to obtain water during the dry season from the deeper canal channel to the west. The lower canal course might be viewed as a dipping pool reached by resting on the low-lying sill. The canal cut is quite narrow at this lower location, approximately 2 m wide from the edge of the sill to the western canal bank. This constriction may have been a device for controlling the amount of water in a larger pool located immediately south of our trench as revealed by the contour map (Fig. 5.2).

Two vessels were recovered from this portion of the canal. The first a whole Tuk Red-on-Red Trickle: Tuk Variety collared jar, was located 1.50 m below a presumed Early Classic walkway bridging the canal after it was filled in. This Tulix phase vessel was found upright and resting 20 cm above the sill at the east end of the canal bank. Other large sherds, dating to the Tulix phase, were collected from this area as well.

On the western margin of the canal another vessel was discovered broken and disarticulated. It was a slightly larger version (12 cm in diameter) of the one found in the east end. It was resting upside down. It may have been placed on the step-like contour noted in the west canal bank. Neither of these vessels contained offerings and, judging from the context as well as form, appear to have been portable water containers.

Both vessels appear to have rested on carved caprock treads and subsequently slipped into the raised field muck early in the collapse of the adjacent field system. Their typological assignment and those of other pottery fragments in the canal indicate they most likely had some ritual significance (Robertson, personal communication 1983). Whether this ritual significance is related to the termination rituals found elsewhere at the site (cf. Garber 1981; Robertson-Freidel 1980) or not is unclear at this time.

At approximately 1.70 m above the basal sediments in the canal trough, and overlying the bulk of the canal sediments, was a narrow limestone walkway about 1 m wide and 10 m long. A single course high, the stones were water smoothed, small tabular limestone boulders, laid horizontally across the high northern end of the main canal. A dense concentration of coarse limestone pebbles was isolated at the west end of the walkway on the caprock bank. Their distribution was restricted to a 2 × 2 m area on the north side of the walkway. These stones appear to be associated with the construction of the causeway and may represent an infilling repair operation associated with the slumping of the underlying bank.

Immediately south of the walkway on the west bank another concentration of stone was identified. This concentration of medium sized pebbles consisted of a single course grid form alignment corresponding to the orientation of the walkway. The stones appear to have been placed in the viscous black gumbo clay humus slightly above the caprock bank. The entire exposure was capped by the same black gumbo humus found throughout the depressed canal trough.

The canal sediments are believed to have been deposited over a generation or more during the Terminal Late Preclassic. The extreme amount of sediment in this exposure and the complete infilling of the canal segment north of this location may indicate the presence of additional eroded fields.

The walkway is argued to be Early Classic in date due in part to the apparent attraction of this locus during this period. Our settlement survey and excavation program have demonstrated the continued presence of a sizeable population subsequent to the halt in nearly all private and public construction at the end of the Late Preclassic Period (cf. Scarborough and Robertson n.d.). The Early Classic population would have used this location as a crossover point because of the greater infilling and the accessibility of features reoccupied in the periphery zone. The diminutive, functionally enigmatic stone grid alignment on the west bank of the canal is believed to be Late Postclassic in origin. Given the amount of lateral erosion from the sides of the main canal, it is unlikely that this formation would have been preserved unless it were quite late in the sequence. The Late Classic and Early Postclassic periods are not demonstrable at Cerros.

The Eastern Lateral Canal Trench

On the eastern side of the core area, we traced the course of an apparent drainage network. Our survey team followed a lateral canal into the interior of the core community (Fig. 5.2). Only the depressed linear troughs were recorded because the amount of vegetation limited visibility. The canal-like depressions appear to be oriented to the cardinal directions. No field platforms were identified, but a few ground level structures were reported.

Our eastern lateral canal trenching operation (Op 155) was placed northeast-southwest across the course of a lateral canal approximately 35 m west of the main canal into which runoff was directed. A trench in this location was predicted to yield information about the amount of quarrying that occurred generally in this area, the presence of raised fields and the relationship between ground level residential space and the core area drainage system. Unfortunately, our limited exposure did not reveal as much information as anticipated.

This trench exposed 14 m² and was excavated to a maximum depth of 60 cm. As was the case with the shallow lateral exposure in the southwestern portion of the core area, only a limited amount of caprock appears to have been removed to produce the trough. The base of the ill-defined feature was approximately 2.5 m wide by 30 cm deep. However, the upper banks of the trough were separated by as much as 8 m, producing a dish-shaped cross section 80 cm deep. The bottom of the trough relative to the vertical site datum rests 45 cm below datum. The base of the trough is defined by indurated caprock with a thin deposit of granular limestone sand eroding from the caprock. The depression fill is defined by a dark viscous grey clay intruded by bits of limestone gravel. The grey clay on the high ground contained more limestone gravel than the trough. No buttress stones like those found elsewhere in the settlement were located. The entire exposure was capped by black gumbo clay humus. Late Preclassic slipped wares predominated in the sparse identifiable ceramic collection.

The exposure appears to be the remains of a shallow canal established to drain this area of the site. Raised fields are not demonstrable from our exposure. Kitchen garden plots are likely to have been present in this area, but clear archaeological associations are lacking. Given the presence of ground level structures, it is suspected that these minor canals diverted water away from residential space and into the main canal. Most of the thin layer of topsoil in this area is thought to be soil development subsequent to the Late Preclassic abandonment of the site.

THE FIELDS AND ASSOCIATED FEATURES

More extensive survey and excavation was conducted in the west central portion of the core area (Fig. 5.4), the focus of our raised field research because of the visibility of features, both on the ground and in aerial photographs. The south segment of the main canal in this zone, excavated at two locations (Op 153 and Op 116), revealed a 2 m deep, 6 m wide U-shaped canal cut, which was later modified by an Early Classic check dam and stone lined catchment pond (cf. Freidel and Scarborough 1982). The bottom of the canal at this location is 1.60 m below site datum. The sediments associated with the Late Preclassic infilling of the canal strongly suggest a raised field origin, given their depth and lateral lensing. The soil matrices are similar to those reported in the other three exposures within the main canal and appear to have the same depositional history. In addition, we exposed a broad shallow lateral canal linking the main canal to the raised fields. This lateral canal was 10 m wide and 80 cm deep and similar in form, depth, and depositional history to our eastern lateral canal exposure (Op 155).

The Field Trenches

During the 1979 field season, a trenching operation (Op 152), exposing 10 m² and revealing a stone lined canal segment, was placed between two earthen platforms across a flanking minor feeder canal (Fig. 5.5). At the time, the stones were interpreted as buttresses supporting the raised field platforms. The canal was 1 m wide by 1 m deep with its base located 1.10 m below site datum. Underlying and behind the stones defining the canal segment was impermeable *sascab*, forming a diminutive levee in profile and kept in place by the outside buttress stones. The canal sediments appear to have eroded off the raised platform surfaces, and phosphate concentrations were found to be very high relative to other contexts in the settlement.

In the 1981 field season, we expanded this trench in an attempt to clarify the course of the feeder canal. In extending the unit east, we found that the well defined stone buttressing terminated at the juncture of three apparent platforms. The sediment inside the canal basin was the same as that found on the adjacent fields. the *sascab* did not appear to be mounded up on the east side of the canal basin as observed elsewhere in the canal cross-section even though the buttress stones were intact. The matrix was mottled by *Pomacea* burrows.

The matrix inside the canal consisted of a grey clay having undergone severe recrystallization. Outside the canal in the platform matrix, the sediments were similar to those found in the canal. Below these grey platform clays the matrix was defined by severely eroding caprock. It consisted of a granular yellowish-grey sandy clay which overlaid the indurated caprock. The decomposing caprock in this area is 30–40 cm thick and the ill-defined boundary between the platform soils and the underlying matrices suggests some *in situ* soil development. The quantity of soil relative to other exposures in the settlement (Op 155 and underlying house mound sterile fill), as well as the presence of lined canal segments and high phosphate readings, indicates that this area was intensively exploited for agricultural purposes. The entire exposure was capped by a thin lens of viscous black gumbo clay.

At the other end of this canal basin (12 m south to southwest), we placed another trenching operation (Op 159) to further define the dimensions of this feature. Our 5 m² exposure at the termination of the visible trough revealed a *cul-de-sac* depression. The canal basin was shown to terminate with boulder-size limestone caprock defining the southern margin of the feature. The canal profile revealed a 1 m wide canal section excavated to a maximum depth of 70 cm. The base of the canal was 55 cm below site datum. Solid caprock defined the east bank of the canal basin but it had been quarried out on the eastern side of the exposure. The caprock bank appeared to be a vertical dike supporting or containing the eastern platform matrices. The western platform buttress stones were similar to those reported in the first trench (Op 152) but were less well preserved. The matrices in the canal were the same mottled grey clays identified elsewhere in the canal system. However, the eastern field platform appeared to be composed of a series of 3 cm thick *sascab* lenses separated by 10–20 cm thick grey clay lenses to a depth of 1 m. No stone intruded into the field exposures.

These two exposures define the northern and western margins of one field platform as well as the adjacent canal basin. The canal appears to have been formed partly by the removal of the caprock and partly by the introduction of soil for the fields. The platforms are buttressed by small boulders and, in one case, by natural caprock quarried to form an apparent dike support. The area to the south and west of Op 159 appears to be a less impacted and elevated, unquarried caprock zone. It may have been modified to catch and direct runoff into the otherwise closed canal catchment basin.

To confirm the association of stone buttressing with linear depressions, we excavated a 2 × 2 m unit on the north side of an adjacent platform (Op 161). The southeast side of this large platform had been examined by our 1979 trenching operation (Op 152). Our new unit exposed a lazy, asymmetrical U-shaped cross-section of the canal basin approximately 1.2 m wide and 1 m deep with its base 70 cm below site datum. Large stones were found to line the canal walls and reinforce the banks of the features to the north and south. The basin fill was the same recemented grey clay defined elsewhere, with the decomposed caprock underlying the exposure. *Pomacea* burrows and root intrusion severely mottled the profile. A small amount of badly eroded unidentifiable pottery was collected. The entire unit was overlain by a 15 cm thick lens of viscous black gumbo clay topsoil.

The trench confirmed the presence of another canal basin flanking and defining the north side of this large field platform, as well as the south ends of two other probable platforms. The canal sediments apparently represent former raised field platform fill.

The Reservoir Trench

Within the survey area, numerous depressions or seasonal reservoirs have been recorded. On the northeastern side of the *sacbe* (Figs. 2.1 and 5.4) a large amorphous depression was identified and examined to determine its depth and form relative to the other features in this area. Some of the largest structures in the settlement lie to the immediate north of this feature (e.g., the Structure 10 Group) and their occupants were believed to have used the basin as a catchment zone. The eastern side of this reservoir was clearly defined, in part, by six small tabular limestone boulders resting at a 45° angle against the bank of the feature. These stones appear to be the remnants of a retaining feature. Op 160 exposed 4 m² at the edge of the reservoir and demonstrated that the entire reservoir was not lined. The matrix was the same grey clay intruded by small limestone pebbles as well as *Pomacea* burrows. The impermeable caprock was only 80 cm below the stone-lined retaining feature. The entire exposure was capped by the black gumbo clay topsoil.

The reservoir is in a position to have held a great deal of runoff water from the low-lying plaza that is Structure 9A and probably functioned as a catchment basin. The rather limited amount of fill at the margins of this depression appears to be associated with the northern plaza runoff rather than with eroded raised field platforms, indicating their absence in the vicinity.

Sacbe Trench

A *sacbe* or raised causeway (Feature 126) connects the ballcourt Structure 50 Group with the plaza area on which Structures 10, 13, 14 and 15 rest (Figs. 1.1 and 2.1) and is oriented N46°W. It traverses the most low-lying *zacatal* in the settlement, and is well defined across 210 m of clay gumbo or *yax'om* soils. In addition to facilitating travel, the *sacbe* may have functioned as a dike or partition separating the private water source of the reservoir and greater *zacatal* from the more public water sources of the raised fields and major canal. Op 115 was positioned within the northern third of the feature across a well-defined segment perpendicular to the long axis. The exposure was intended to provide information about the extent of quarrying carried out in this area and the form and possible function of the *sacbe*.

This trench exposed 8 m² to a maximum depth of 50 cm. The surface level was defined by a 10 cm-thick lens of black viscous clay or gumbo analogous to that found in adjacent *bajo* settings. The top of the causeway appears to have been covered by these sediments during the seasonal inundation of this depression. The black gumbo was thicker on the eastern-most end of the feature than it was on the western end, possibly reflecting a more recent siltation of the deeper *bajo* located on this side of the *sacbe*. The first excavation level was terminated upon encountering the continuous layer of limestone cobbles and small boulders defining the present surface of the *sacbe*. The width of the *sacbe* revealed in plan was 6.8 m, though the absence of well-defined curbstones suggests that the width was somewhat exaggerated as a result of lateral slumpage.

The lower excavation level represented the construction core of the feature. Only the eastern half (1×4 m unit) was sectioned. The rubble cap (30 cm thick) was found to overlie a light grey glei clay. The original surface of the feature appears to have suffered from severe erosion producing a leached and mottled profile. The dark gumbo clay characteristic of the upper *bajo*

sediments filtered through the profile which was also extensively penetrated by rootlets. However, there is some evidence for an extremely mottled paleosol capping the underlying sterile matrix. An underlying thin grey clay lens was found to grade immediately into the decomposing caprock.

The *sacbe* rises above the flanking *bajo* by a meter or more, but it extends less than half a meter above the silting *zacatal* setting. Our field data indicate that the basal sediments in our exposure have not been altered or built up. The causeway was deliberately isolated as a linear island following the postulated quarrying activities on either side of it. The limestone rubble cap stabilized the surface which was less cambered than it is today. We have assigned an early Tulix phase date to the *sacbe*, even though the sherd inventory was very meager. The Tulix phase dates for the Structure 50 Group and Structures 13 through 16 further support a Late Preclassic construction date.

POSTHOLING PROGRAM

More than fifty postholes were systematically placed over the earthen platforms and adjacent canal basins over a 1600 m² area. A north oriented grid system controlled the placement of postholes at 5 m intervals. The postholes produced a series of schematized profiles which confirmed the nature of our excavation data. A sub-surface contour map of the original indurated caprock surface underlying the platforms was drafted in an attempt to illustrate the nature of the raised field complex. A comparison of the surface and sub-surface maps has led us to believe that the largest platform is underlain by elevated caprock.

It is believed that the margins and perhaps the planar surface of the underlying caprock were altered for agricultural space as well as quarried for monument fill. The field platforms were formed in part by simply excavating the margins of the high caprock. Some reworking of the soil matrices is suggested as well. The flanking canal basins were lined water reservoirs. The buttress stones were also used to support the bulk of the adjacent and overlying platform sediments. A thick lens of *sascab* overlying the grey clays, found at the north end of the southeasternmost platform, may be a concentration of *sascab* used in the reworking of some of the field soils. The source of this white marl is at a depth below the indurated caprock. Because this *sascab* matrix was localized in its distribution, we cannot equate our field platforms with the elevated *sascab* platforms defined by Puleston (1977) on Albion Island. However, there is a suggestion that the flat and more depresssed area to the east of the postholing operation may represent deliberate raised earthen platform space that has collapsed over time. Unfortunately, our postholing program only examined the margin of this area and no trenching has been carried out.

The confluence of the main canal with the major lateral canal in this same southwestern portion of the core zone was also probed with posthole diggers. This area seemed to have a high potential for locating flood gates or related control devices. Limited testing indicated an abrupt drop into the main canal from the lateral canal, but precise elevational data were not available. The pronounced elevational difference between the two canals suggests a drainage function for the canal system rather than flow irrigation into the fields.

In the east, postholing was conducted to determine the degree of lobate form to the canal plan. We placed a series of postholes across the main canal south of Op 156 and north of Op 154 to assess the width of the canal cross-section. Although the bottom of the canal could not be determined, the banks dropped rather abruptly. Our results indicate that the original main canal had irregular lobate walls. This appears to be related to the ponding of water for easy access during the dry season.

SUMMARY

Test excavation and contour survey suggest that canals and ditches were intentionally excavated into bedrock to divert and catch rainwater in a significant portion of the dispersed settlement zone at Cerros. The banks of some ditches show evidence of having been further built up with rough cobble or slab bedrock retaining walls to hold topsoils in place. The design of these hydraulic works indicates that they were a large-scale public enterprise carried out by the community as a whole. First, the main canal forms a series of lobate ponds defining the perimeter of the dispersed settlement. Second, survey in the southern and eastern sectors of the settlement within this perimeter shows that the shallow canals and ditches surrounding higher ground were oriented to the cardinal directions. Pending paleobotanical studies, we can only conjecture that these features functioned as agricultural fields or garden plots but these narrow catchments clearly contrast with the probable reservoir features within the *sacbe* perimeter. The rapidity with which these ditches and canals infilled due to lateral slumpage of soils from flanking high ground at the time of the political collapse of the center at Cerros underscores the communal organization necessary for their construction and maintenance. While the ensuing Early Classic residual population carried out refurbishment of some sectors of the main canal, it was evidently unable to keep the system going as originally designed.

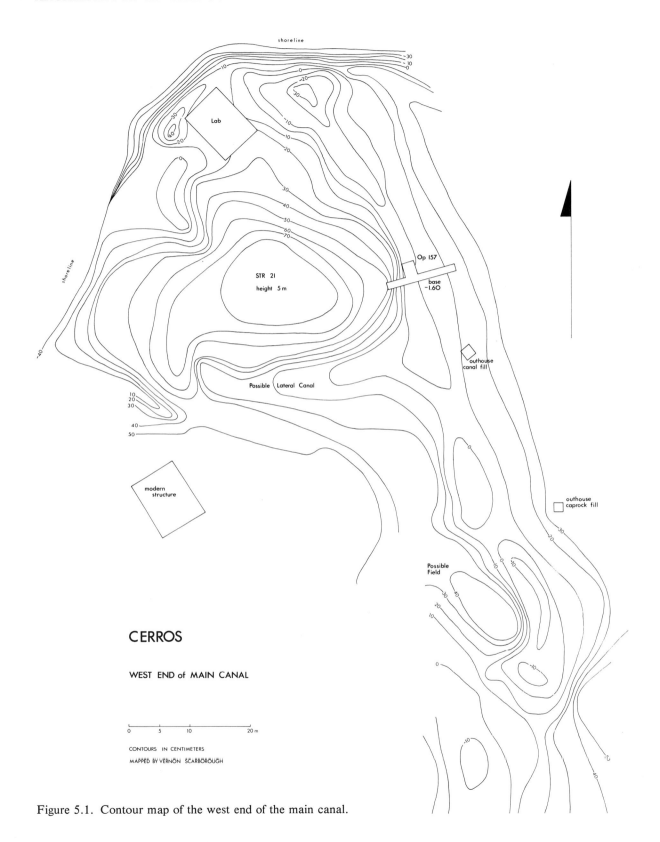

Figure 5.1. Contour map of the west end of the main canal.

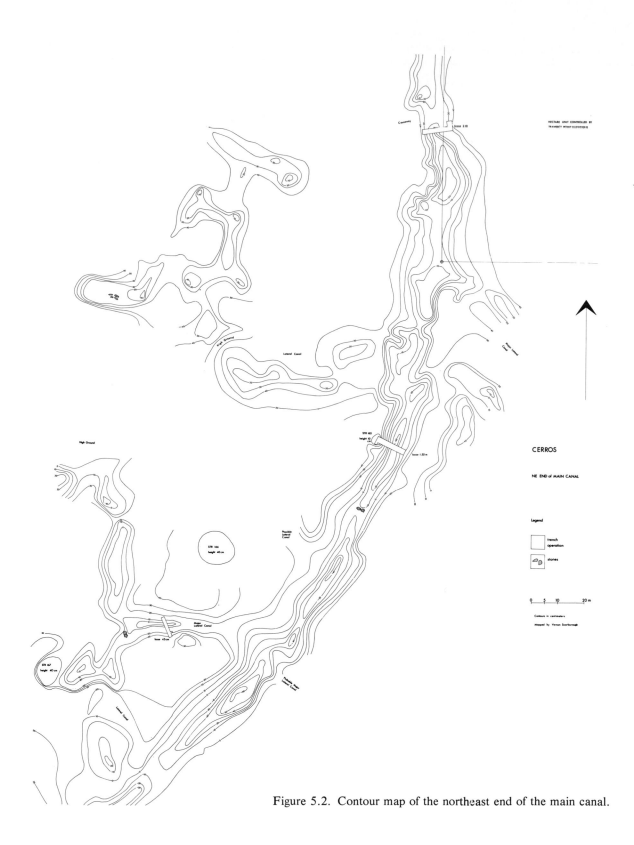

Figure 5.2. Contour map of the northeast end of the main canal.

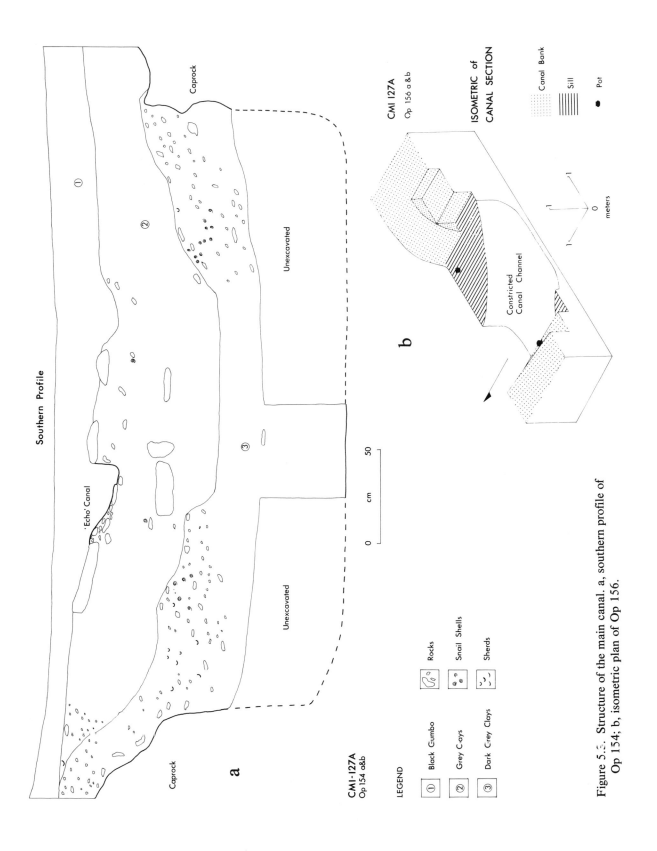

Figure 5.3. Structure of the main canal. a, southern profile of Op 154; b, isometric plan of Op 156.

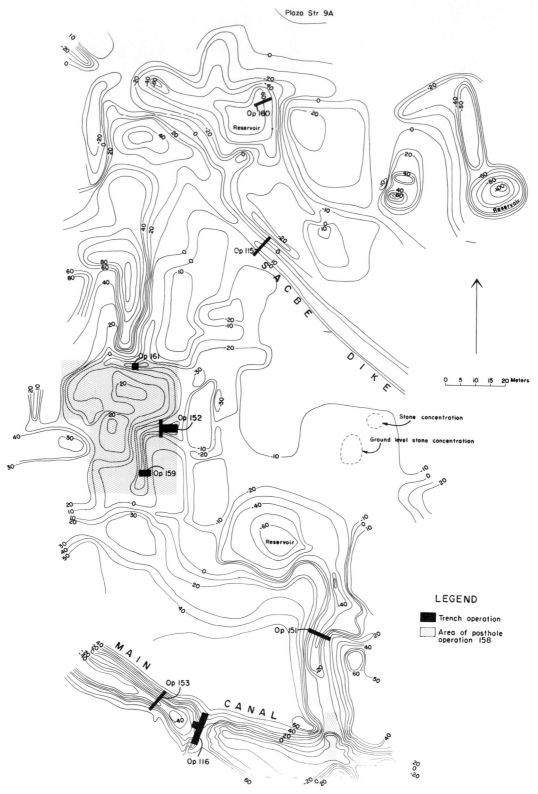

Figure 5.4. Contour map of the southwest portion of the main canal.

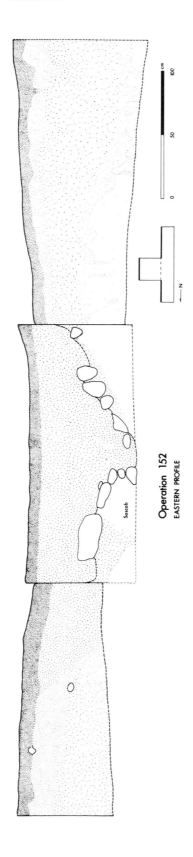

Figure 5.5. Profile of the mainor feeder canal excavated as Op 152.

THE CERAMICS

Robin A. Robertson

In the Maya Lowlands, Late Preclassic ceramic complexes have been traditionally divided into two facets: a long, regionally homogeneous early one and a short, more site specific, later one (Fig. 6.1 and cf. Adams and Culbert 1977: Fig. 1.3). The identification of the later facet has been based on the addition of a few new types to the earlier facet as well as the appearance of new modes (cf. Willey, Culbert and Adams 1967). Barton Ramie and Tikal, however, are exceptions to this general practice. At Barton Ramie, Gifford (1976) recognized two complexes, each with early and late facets. At Tikal three complexes are represented within this time period (Culbert 1977; Gifford 1976). Given these two exceptions and the fact that Cerros was apparently only intensively occupied from 350 B.C.–A.D. 150, one of the principle objectives of the ceramic research at the site has been to define and refine the ceramic chronology for the period in northern Belize and possibly, by comparison, in other areas of the Maya lowlands as well.

The potential for accomplishing this objective became apparent in the 1976 field season. The first two seasons of work at the site (1974 and 1975) produced large quantities of sherd material from the nucleated residential village underlying the main plaza and considerably smaller quantities of sherds from test pits placed into the monumental architecture of the center and immediately adjacent housemounds. Although the contexts seemed to differ typologically, the small number of sherds from the test pits and the extensive disturbance of the deposits in the nucleated residential village (Op 1) did not permit any clear-cut division of the Late Preclassic material by means other than seriation. In 1976, however, a flat test into a tree fall near Structure 22 (Op 107) produced a single component assemblage of 5,153 sherds that appeared to be significantly different from those found in the lower levels of the nucleated residential village. During the 1977 season, as excavations in the dispersed settlement intensified and large-scale exposures were put into the monumental architecture of the center, yet a third distinctive assemblage was noted on Structure 5C (Op 35). A reexamination of the original 1974 and

1975 sherds and those from later, less disturbed contexts (specifically Op 34) in the coastal erosion profile which sections the nucleated residential village confirmed the existence of these three assemblages and provided a means of stratigraphically relating them to each other (Robertson-Freidel 1980).

The lower levels of the nucleated residential village are associated with the earliest ceramic complex at the site, known as Ixtabai (300-200 B.C.). During the C'oh Complex (200-50 B.C.), residence gradually shifted to the mounds being constructed in the dispersed settlement zone. The transition from nucleated to dispersed settlement was completed during the Tulix Complex (50 B.C.-A.D. 150) and was accompanied by the construction of the monumental architecture in the center. All of these complexes lie well within what has been considered the Chicanel Ceramic Sphere (Willey, Culbert and Adams 1967).

At the end of the 1977 season, the sample consisted of 12,000 sherds. Over 95% of these sherds are Late Preclassic in date and over 75% of them come from primary habitation debris, ritual events associated with the interment of the monumental architecture, and caches and burials. Only 25% of the Late Preclassic material is from mixed contexts such as construction fill, or secondary occupation debris such as that found on the corners of structures. Its size and the high percentage of contexts consisting of primary, single moment in time, depositional events are what make this sample unique. Pring (1977), for example, had a sample of 120,000 sherds for the entire chronological sequence in northern Belize. With respect to the latter characteristics of this collection, Gifford (1976: 21) clearly describes the situation prior to the discovery and excavation of Cerros.

Middle American archaeology abounds with mounds containing structural stratigraphy while there is a dearth of midden deposits. Sequences of true midden stratigraphy are rare occurrences in the Maya territories. When the occasion arises that favors the discovery of undisturbed Maya midden deposition in quantity, it will be a find of inestimable value . . .

THE IXTABAI COMPLEX

The Ixtabai ceramic Complex is characterized by the normal thick, waxy slips of the Paso Caballo Waxy Wares (Smith 1955) found in other Late Preclassic complexes in the Lowlands (Fig. 6.2). The Sierra Group with its member types of Sierra Red: Sierra Variety and Society Hall Varieties (Gifford 1976), Laguna Verde Incised: Groove Incised Variety (Sabloff 1975) and Union Appliqued: Variety Unspecified (Pring 1977: 267-268) is the dominant slipped ware. Although the Flor Group is present but rare in the subsequent complex, the Cockscomb Group defined by Pring (1977: 284-288) for northern Belize is present in small amounts both in Cockscomb Buff: Cockscomb Variety (Fig. 6.3a-e) and in a rare Unnamed Buff Impressed and Incised. The Polvero Group is extremely rare (see Robertson-Freidel 1980: 373-378). It is represented by nine sherds of Bribri Black Incised and Unslipped: Bribri Variety (Fig. 6.4a), a type sharing varietal level similarities (Ball, personal communication 1978) with a Pakluum Special: Composite Black and Unslipped Incised vessel from Becan (Ball 1977: 114-116). The collection also contained five sherds of an Unspecified Incised Red Type reported by Ball (1978: 118) from the coast of northern Yucatan (Fig. 6.3a-e).

In addition to these slipped types, a new type, Hole Dull: Hole Variety has been added to the Late Preclassic inventory. The sherds belonging to this type have a thin, dull or low luster red (10R 5/6, 4, 8 and 5/8 and 2.5YR 5/6) slip characterized by reddish yellow (7.5YR 6/6), pink (7.5YR 7/4) and very pale brown (10YR 7/3) fire clouds. The exteriors are generally poorly finished prior to slipping with smoothing striations, scraping marks and traces of coils being present on the thick-walled (0.6-1.4 cm) jars. Thinner-walled vessels, specifically flaring sided bowls and beer mugs (Fig. 6.4b), however, tend to be somewhat better smoothed prior to the application of the slip.

It is within the category of unslipped pottery that the Ixtabai complex diverges most significantly from other lowland complexes. This divergence, however, may be more apparent than real. It is implicitly assumed in most ceramic reports that the unslipped pottery is not chronologically significant primarily because its production is determined not by aesthetic considerations but rather by domestic, functional ones. Because these functions presumably do not change through time, the pottery does not change. Censerware is an obvious exception to this rule and typically is typologically segregated (cf. Adams 1971: 53, who sees Morfin Unslipped: Morfin Variety and Corriental Appliqued: Corriental Variety as distinct from Achiotes Unslipped and Sapote Striated: Sapote Variety).

At Cerros this assumption seems to be invalid. Not only is the unslipped pottery as sensitive as the slipped pottery to temporal considerations, but, once the types have been established, even a non-ceramicist can easily differentiate them. Within the slipped wares, by contrast, the difficulties in differentiating Late Preclassic Sierra Red from Middle Preclassic Joventud Red, for example, have repeatedly been cited (cf. Sabloff 1975: 30 and Ball 1977: 17). An exception to this general neglect of unslipped pottery was Gifford's (1976) practice of establishing provisional types and varieties at Barton Ramie. The Cerros collections have confirmed the validity of these provisional designations in a number of instances.

There are six unslipped types within the Ixtabai Complex at Cerros. Sapote Striated: Chichem Variety closely resembles Sapote Striated: Sapote Variety, found elsewhere in the lowlands, in terms of wall thickness and neck height. However, the presence of vertical striation rather than criss-cross raking on the bodies and necks of the vessels provided the grounds for establishing a new variety (see Pring 1977: 235-236 for a discussion of the significance of the orientation of the striation). It is found at Barton Ramie (Gifford 1976: 106) in Sapote Striated: Variety Unspecified (Thin-walled, Cat. No. 21274). Chiculte Slipped Rim Striated: Chiculte Variety, identified as Sapote Striated Variety Unspecified Black-rimmed (Cat. No. 21271) and Red-rimmed (Cat. No. 21275) at Barton Ramie (Ibid. 107-108), are also in the Sapote Group. This type consists of thin-walled, round-bottomed jars which are brushed or lightly striated from the juncture of the neck with the body to the base of the vessel. The interior of the rim and neck is decorated with a Sierra Group slip (Robertson 1983: Fig. 4.4b, c).

Paila Unslipped, originally defined at Uaxactun (Smith and Gifford 1976) and subsequently identified only at Barton Ramie, where the variety was left unspecified (Gifford 1976: 108-110), is also present at Cerros as a minor unslipped type. With regard to the Corozal Project's work in northern Belize, Pring (1977: 231-232) thought it was impossible "to name the local [unslipped] material within the existing framework without adding to the confusion that exists currently in the description of unslipped types in the Maya lowlands." Consequently, he established a new type, Richardson Peak Unslipped: Richardson Peak Variety. Some of this type parallels the Cerros type Paila Unslipped: Variety Unspecified in terms of surface texture and form (Ibid: Fig. 52a, b and e).

Three new types have also been added to the inventory of unslipped types. Poknoboy Striped: Poknoboy Variety is a pink (5YR 7/4 and 7.5YR 7/4) to gray (10YR 7/1) matte slipped pottery decorated with post-fire scratches in the form of stripes (Robertson 1983: Fig. 4.3d, e). The vessels are invariably round-bottomed jars with outflaring necks and direct, rounded rims. The only difference between this type and Hillbank Red: Variety Unspecified (White-striped) in the Barton Creek Complex at Barton Ramie (Gifford 1976: 103-104) is that the Cerros type has a coarser paste. Some resemblance to Cenote White Striated: Cenote Variety at Aguacatal also appears to exist (Matheny 1970: 48) but, in the absence of illustrations and actual examination of the sherds, this conclusion must remain tentative.

To date, parallels for the other two types have not been found. Bobche Smudged: Bobche Variety (Fig. 6.4e,f) occurs in the form of black paste, thin-walled (0.3-0.5 cm), restricted-orifice bowls which have a light-colored, variegated exterior surface. Although this type has not been reported at other lowland sites, it is possible that the sherds have been discarded elsewhere because they are rarely more than 1.5 cm in size. Crabboe Washed: Crabboe Variety (Fig. 6.4c, d) is a common Ixtabai-Early C'oh type at Cerros. It consists of large, flaring walled plates, the exterior of which are so poorly smoothed that they resemble concrete. The interior surfaces bear a thin wash. It is possible that the suggested function of soaking corn or other substances in lime and water prior to its being ground up or consumed (Robertson-Freidel 1980: 61-62) was done in vessels of wood at sites where the clay resources were not as common as they are at Cerros.

The modes associated with the Ixtabai Complex support its identification with the early Chicanel complexes elsewhere in the lowlands. The most obvious characteristic is the lack of secondary surface manipulation. Adams (1971: 93) has pointed out that little decoration of this kind is present prior to Late Facet Plancha at Altar de Sacrificios. The same is true of other early complexes or facets at Seibal (Sabloff 1975: 78-83), Barton Ramie (Gifford 1976), Becan (Ball 1977: 129), and in northern Belize (Pring 1977).

In terms of forms, wide, everted rims or labial flanges, tecomates and simple outflaring walled vessels without medial angles or flanges are diagnostic of the Early Chicanel at Cerros, as well as at other sites in the lowlands.

THE C'OH COMPLEX

The C'oh Complex is a transitional complex in terms of surface treatment, but it is distinctive in terms of the modes which are found within it. Many of its component types (Fig. 6.2), including the dominant ones, could not have been isolated without the well-defined primary depositional stratigraphy at Cerros and the existence of very different types in the complexes bracketing it. The dominant redware in this complex, Canxun Red: Canxun Variety, for example, possesses a red (2.5YR 5/6-8) slip that is intermediate between Sierra Red: Variety Unspecified (Ixtabai Complex) and Cabro Red: Cabro Variety (Tulix Complex) in hardness and thickness. Its luster, however, is that of Sierra Red: Sierra Variety. Comparatively it seems most clearly related to the early Barton Creek type Hillbank Red: Rockdondo Variety at Barton Ramie. This type has a hard, medium thick, red-orange slip that does not flake easily. According to the description (Gifford 1976: 104) the degree of luster and waxiness are similar to the Cerros type as well. Unfortunately, parallels to the Cerros type should be coming from the late Barton Creek or early Mount Hope Complexes. The lack of comparability in forms substantiates this supposition (Fig. 6.5a-h). With the exception of small, medial angle bowls with slightly insloping walls above the angles and low flaring necked jars with direct rims and rounded lips, the Cerros forms are different from those associated with Hillbank Red: Rockdondo Variety and more closely resemble the Mount Hope Complex forms.

Given the similarity in the slips between Sierra Red and Canxun Red, it is possible that elsewhere the two types have been lumped. Supporting this lumping hypothesis are the Corozal Project ceramics. According to Pring (1977: 61), Sierra Red: Sierra Variety develops into the Late Cocos Complex Sierra Red: Big Pond Variety which, in turn, becomes the unnamed Tzakol red monochrome type. One of the characteristics of Sierra Red: Big Pond Variety is the increase in the percentage of medial angle vessels over those present in Sierra Red: Sierra Variety. If Sierra Red: Big Pond Variety is comparable to Cabro Red: Cabro Variety in its developmental position, then the later sherds and vessels in Sierra Red: Sierra Variety which are comparable in form to Canxun Red: Canxun Variety (Pring 1977: Figs. 58 and 59a-o) may be comparable to it in slip characteristics as well. Only examination of these collections will resolve the question. The absence of a type or types that are transitional between the Early Chicanel and Tzakol 1 makes it difficult to determine whether or not such lumping has occurred elsewhere. Because of its greater overall similarity to the earlier Sierra Group rather than to the later Cabro Group, Canxun Red has been placed in Paso Caballo Waxy Ware rather than in Chunux Hard Ware.

Included within the Canxun Group are five types which reflect different decorative techniques. Lanillo Groove Incised: Lanillo Variety is decorated with groove incised lines which encircle the interior of the rim or rim eversion and/or the exterior of the vessel at the basal break. Conop Red-on-Red Trickle: Conop Variety (Fig. 6.6d-f) is clearly related to the northern Yucatecan trickle pottery (Ball and Robles, personal communication 1978). Within the southern lowlands, Smith (1955: 27) lists liquid marking as one of the blemishes present on both Flores and Paso Caballo Waxy Ware at Uaxactun. It is possible that this liquid marking may in fact have been trickle decoration. Additionally, some sherds of this type have been lumped with Savannah Bank Usulutan: Savannah Bank Variety in the Barton Ramie type collections at the Peabody Museum. Yaxnik Through-the-Slip-Incised: Yaxnik Variety (Fig. 6.5i, j) possesses multiple line, through-the-slip incised, curvilinear designs representing finned or feathered serpentine creatures on the interiors of low, vertical-walled dishes. The exteriors of the rims bear purple paint. The presence of purple paint on the rims and the fact that the designs are representational rather than abstract distinguishes this type from Correlo Incised Dichrome: Correlo Variety at Uaxactun (Smith 1955: 117), Altar de Sacrificios (Adams 1971: 43), Tikal (Coe 1965: Fig. 2g) and Barton Ramie (Gifford 1976: 91). The last two types in this group are double slipped. Cassada Red-over-Black: Cassada Variety has a red slip that was applied over a black slip to produce muddy red and greenish gray mottled or streaky areas. It may be paralleled by three sherds from the Corozal Project placed in Matamore Dichrome: Shipyard Variety by Pring (1977:

301). Zorra Black-on-Red: Zorra Variety, on the other hand, reflects the practice of placing a thin black slip over a Canxun red slip around the rim and lower body or basal areas of the vessel to create fake fire clouds. This black slip can be removed with a razor blade. This attempt to imitate fire clouds differentiates this type from Repasto Black-on-Red: Repasto Variety or Variety Unspecified found at most sites in the lowlands during this time period.

Although the use of two slips arguably necessitates placing these last two types in a separate group (cf. Pring 1977), it seems that in this case the objective was not to create a two-color vessel as in Matamore Dichrome: Shipyard Variety (Ibid. 300-301) but rather to decorate specific areas of a monochrome vessel. Consequently, it represents a decorative mode within the Canxun Group. Similarly, Matamore Dichrome: Matamore Variety represents the intentional creation of fake fire clouds rather than a two-color vessel (Ibid. 298). The fact that it is succeeded, however, by a true dichrome in Shipyard Variety seems to provide a rationale for placing it in the Matamore Group. Thus, Pring's assignment has not been changed.

In the C'oh Complex, the Matamore Group is represented by Matamore Dichrome: Matamore Variety (Pring 1977: 297-299) and Tinta Usulutan: Tinta Variety. The latter is a pseudo-usulutan type in which the interiors of the vessels are buff while the exteriors are red. Multiple line, wavy or curvilinear designs produced by removing a thin red slip with a multiple toothed instrument are found on the buff interiors of these vessels. Consequently the type represents a decorated version of Matamore Dichrome: Matamore Variety and should be included in the same ceramic group. This type differs from Savannah Bank Usulutan: Savannah Variety in that the red and buff slips are waxy and can be scratched with a fingernail.

Cockscomb Buff: Cockscomb Variety continues from the Ixtabai into the C'oh Complex with an increase in frequency. In contrast, Iguana Creek White: Iguana Creek Variety (Gifford 1976: 96), a type belonging to the Flor Group, seems to make its first appearance in the early part of this complex (Robertson-Freidel 1980: 148-149).

Hole Dull: Hole Variety, typical of the Ixtabai Complex, continues through the early portions of the C'oh Complex. It is seemingly replaced by Hole Dull: Hukup Variety approximately midway through the complex. These varieties differ from one another in that the Hukup Variety slips do not have any luster at all and have a deeper red color. Additionally, the necks on the small, thick-walled jars so characteristic of this type are all flaring rather than vertical or slightly flaring as they are in Hole Variety (Fig. 6.6a, b). Hokab Impressed: Hokab Variety with its impressed medial angle vessels completes the Hole Group in this complex.

With respect to unslipped pottery, the Ixtabai Complex Paila Unslipped: Variety Unspecified, Bobche Smudged: Bobche Variety, Chiculte Slipped Rim Striated: Chiculte Variety (though in lower frequencies) and Sapote Striated: Chichem Variety (increasing in frequency) continue into the C'oh Complex. Crabboe Washed: Crabboe Variety is found in the Early C'oh Complex, but is replaced about midway through it by Chamah Washed: Chamah Variety (Fig. 6.6c). The latter type differs from the earlier one only in that it possesses a finer paste, thinner walls and a direct, rounded rim rather than an exterior thickened rim. Poknoboy Stripped: Poknoboy Variety is replaced by Teabox Unsliped: Teabox Variety which lacks the matte slip and the scratchings characteristic of the earlier type (Fig. 6.4g-j).The latter has a fine-grained, slightly gritty texture to the paste surface in contrast to the silky texture of the Poknoboy Striped vessels.

Sapote Striated: Chacah Variety consists of unslipped, moderate to thick walled jars (0.6-0.9 cm) that are striated on the neck and body. On the neck, and for approximately 4.0 cm down from the juncture of the neck with the body of the vessel, the striations are vertical. On the rest of the vessel the striations overlap with an orientation that varies from vertical to approximately 45°. It is similar to Pring's (1977: 233-235) Unspecified Variety of Sapote Striated on a varietal level.

From a modal perspective, the C'oh Complex is characterized by the appearance of medial angle and medially ridged vessels, nubbin feet, groove-hook rims, S-Z angle bowls, usulutan decoration, trickle decoration and punctation (2 sherds). Groove incision also increases as a decorative mode. Upon first reading, it may seem as though the ceramics at the site underwent a profound transformation during this complex. It should be noted, however, that there is a great deal of continuity in the types from the Ixtabai to the C'oh Complex and that these modes are gradually incorporated into the complex throughout its 150-year duration. Attempts to assign any significant proportion of these modes to a late or early facet of the C'oh repeatedly met with failure when the stratigraphic situation was taken into account.

THE TULIX COMPLEX

The Tulix Complex at Cerros represents the pinnacle of ceramic production at the site. Not only is there a substantial increase in the number of types (Fig. 6.2), but the pottery in general is technologically superior to that found in the Ixtabai and C'oh Complexes. The dominant Cabro Group (Figs. 6.6g, h; 6.7a-o), for example, contains seven established types and three unnamed provisional types which represent decorative variations of Cabro Red: Cabro Variety. The group belongs to Chunux Hardware and is characterized by glossy, non-waxy slips which are so hard that they usually cannot be scratched with a fingernail. They were fired at a higher temperature than the Sierra or Canxun Groups of the Paso Caballo Waxy Wares. This is indicated by the fact that some of the sherds have a vitrified appearance and most snap when broken or clink when tapped on a formica tabletop. Nonetheless, the slip surface is subject to root marks and erosion. Once damaged it erodes quickly, revealing a powdery, lighter colored surface which can be confused with the earlier redwares at the site. Liscanal Groove Incised: Liscanal Variety, Pahote Punctated: Pahote Variety (Fig. 6.7p, q), and Tuk Red-on-Red Trickle: Tuk Variety (Fig. 6.8), respectively, represent the groove-incised, pre-slip punctated, and trickle decorated types within the group. An Unnamed Red-on-Red Usulutan with Black Rim Bands is related to Tuk Red-on-Red Trickle: Tuk Variety. The narrow parallel lines resembling Usulutan decoration that decorate the sherds represent painting rather than the trickling of an organic substance onto the pots. This variation has not been named pending an increase in sample size.

Taciste Washed: Taciste Variety consists of flaring-walled dishes with convex bases (Robertson 1983: Fig. 4.10b) that have a Cabro Red related wash on the interior which has been blackened with soot around the basal break. The exterior surfaces are poorly smoothed and unslipped. The type probably represents a censerware (Robertson nd.). Munequita Appliqued: Munequita Variety with the related Unnamed Slipped and Unslipped Appliqued and Unnamed Composite Appliqued and Punctated may have served a different, but related, ritual function. These humanoid effigy vessels have appliqued features (Robertson 1983: Fig. 4.9c, d) resembling the Kichpanha figurine from northern Belize (Pring 1976: Fig. 68) except that the eyes of the

Kichpanha figurine are slashes and the ears are modeled rather than appliqued. It should be noted that on the basis of slip characteristics, the Kichpanha figurine probably belongs to the Cabro Group rather than to the Sierra Group, as Pring (1977: 268) asserted.

The final type in the Cabro Group is Sierra Red: Xaibe Variety. Although initially perceived as a later, northern Belizean version of Sierra Red: Society Hall Variety by Pring (1977: 245-250), the slip on this streaky pottery is clearly related to Chunux Hard Ware rather than to Paso Caballo Waxy Ware in hardness, luster and color. Consequently, although the name given by Pring has been retained, the group and ware designations have been changed.

In the Tulix Complex, the Cockscomb Group is replaced by the Nictaa Group. Nictaa Buff: Nictaa Variety has a hard, thin, buff to light brown slip with a greenish tinge when uneroded. With the exception of its buff color, the slip has all the attributes of the Cabro Group slips.

An orange pottery is added to the ceramic inventory in this complex in the form of Kuxche Orange: Kuxche Variety and its punctated version, Remax Punctated: Remax Variety. The slip is moderately thin, hard and uniformly orange, but lacks the pink paste surface of the Aguacate Group (Gifford 1976: 129). It differs from Happy Home Orange: Happy Home Variety in that the Kuxche Orange slip is harder and more orange. Iberia Orange: Iberia Variety at Seibal (Sabloff 1975: 90) has a waxy surface finish and a cream underslip. Closer to Cerros geographically, Chicago Orange: Chucun Variety from northern Belize has a non-lustrous, non-waxy, thin orange slip with a slightly pinkish or fleshy hue to it (Pring 1976a: 290-291). At present the type seems to be a local development related to, but distinct from, the Cabro Group.

Included in the Kuxche Group are two unnamed types. Unnamed Black Paint on Orange has dull, black painted rim bands. Unnamed Black Paint on Orange Incised with Purple Rim consists of one rim sherd from a low-walled medially ridged vessel. Two preserved groups of at least four narrow lines have been incised through the paint to the orange slip on the interior. The exterior of the vessel above the medial ridge has been painted with a purple paint.

Dichromes continue to be represented in this complex in the Matamore Group by Matamore Dichrome: Shipyard Variety (Pring 1977: 299-301) as well as by the new Chactoc Group. Chactoc Dichrome: Chactoc Variety consists of vessels slipped in red and buff.

These slips are identical to the slips found in Cabro Red and Nictaa Buff, respectively, rather than to the waxy red and buff slips which continue in this complex in Matamore Dichrome: Shipyard Variety. The assignment of Savannah Bank Usulutan: Variety Unspecified to this group rather than to the Sarteneja Group (Gifford 1976: Fig. 11) is based on the same arguments given above for the placement of the C'oh Complex Tinta Usulutan in the Matamore Group. Although the Barton Ramie slips are identical to the Cerros slips (and are not waxy as described by Gifford in Willey et al. 1965: 342), the way in which the designs were produced differs. At Barton Ramie they were positively painted, whereas at Cerros they were created by removing the upper red slip with a multi-toothed instrument to reveal the buff underslip on the interior of the vessel. Consequently, the variety has been left unspecified. The exterior is invariably red. Eight sherds at Cerros with positively painted usulutan designs have been left as Unnamed Positively Painted within the Chactoc Group.

Pixoy Usulutan: Pixoy Variety within the Chactoc group also has multiple line, curvilinear or wavy designs on the interior of the vessel, but the designs were not created by removing an upper slip. Instead of contrasting in color, the lines are lighter in color and more shiny than the undecorated areas. Arguably they were produced by pattern burnishing or by careful positive painting with the same substance used to produce trickle decoration. This type is present at Barton Ramie but was included in Savannah Bank Usulutan: Savannah Bank Variety (Gifford 1976: 116-117).

The only member of the Paso Caballo Waxy Wares present in the Tulix Complex at Cerros is Zapatista Trickle-on-Cream Brown: Zoon Variety. This type shows a strong resemblance to Zapatista Trickle-on-Cream Brown: Zapatista Variety at Becan (Ball 1977: 52). The varietal level differences, however, include a greater range of variation in slip color as well as the restriction of the type to high-necked, globular jars with three strap handles (Robertson 1983: Fig. 4.8c) in the Cerros collection.

The Tulix Complex version of Hole Dull (Hukup Variety) has been discussed above. Additionally, Sangre Red: Sangre Variety has been added to this group. This type consists of thin-walled, flaring sided bowls which are unslipped on the exterior below the rim and bear a dark red, dull, moderately thick, non-waxy slip on the interior. The type is most closely related to

Chamah Washed: Chamah Variety at Cerros and is probably ancestral to the Hermitage Complex Minanha Red: Rio Frio Variety at Barton Ramie (Gifford 1976: 159).

A single imported Verbena Ivory: Usulutan small, S-Z angle bowl (Wetherington and Demarest, personal communication 1980) has been recovered in this complex. The fine, cream-colored paste is atypical for the lowlands in this period, and the vessel fragment could not be picked out of Kaminaljuyu type collections when it was mixed in with them.

No new unslipped types are introduced in this complex. Instead, the unslipped types are marked by an increase in frequency of Chamah Washed: Chamah Variety, Sapote Striated: Chacah and Chichem Varieties and Paila Unslipped: Variety Unspecified. Chiculte Slipped Rim Striated: Chiculte Variety continues, but in lower frequencies, whereas Teabox Unslipped: Teabox Variety, and Bobche Smudged: Bobche Variety drop out of the inventory for functional reasons (Robertson 1983).

From a modal perspective, the trends begun in the C'oh Complex continue, particularly those related to more elaborate decorative modes. Although groove hook rims, nubbin feet, usulutan and trickle decoration, purple rim bands and S-Z angle bowls occur in the C'oh Complex, they are much more common in the Tulix Complex. Additionally, the complex shares the occurrence of interior folded rims and collared vessels with Pring's (1977) late facet of the Cocos Complex for northern Belize. Modeled effigy vessels represent an additional innovation in the complex. It should be emphasized that many of the traditional ceramic markers for the Floral Park Complex are missing. These include Gavilan Black-on-Orange, Guacamallo Red-on-Orange, Aguacate Orange, mammiform tetrapods, mushroom stands, pedestal bases and stucco painting. Cerros appears to have been abandoned prior to the incorporation of these particular traits into the lowland ceramic inventory (but cf. Robertson 1981).

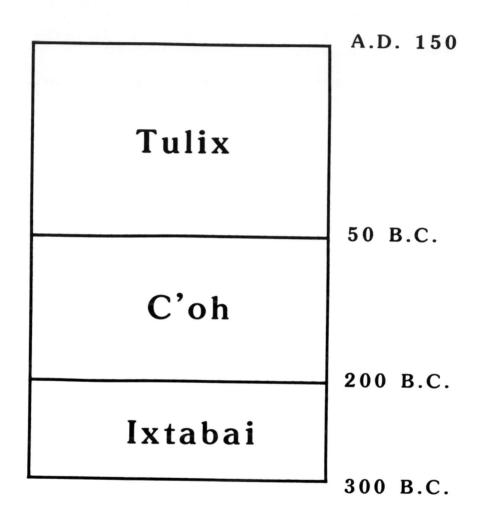

Figure 6.1. Ceramic complexes represented in the Late Preclassic assemblage.

Figure 6.2. Chronological placement of the ceramic types from Cerros.

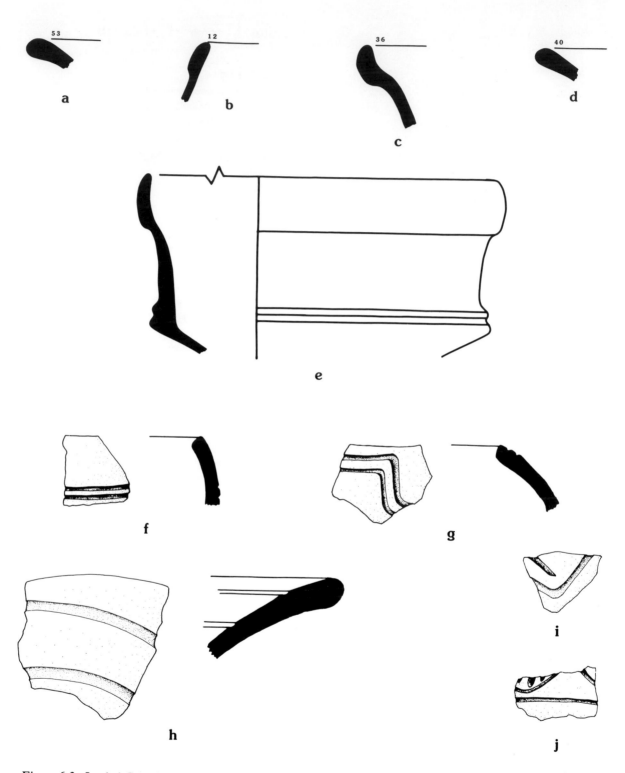

Figure 6.3. Ixtabai Complex types. a-e, Cockscomb Buff: Variety Unspecified; f-j, Unnamed Groove Incised.

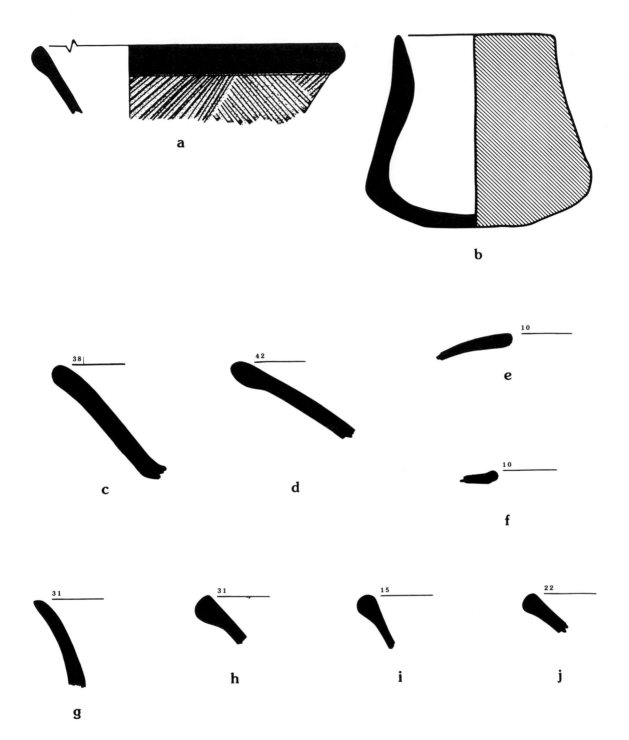

Figure 6.4. Forms and unslipped types characteristic of the assemblage. a, Bribri Black Incised and Unslipped: Bribri Variety; b, beer mug; c and d, Crabboe Washed: Crabboe Variety; e and f, Bobche Smudged: Bobche Variety; g-j, Teabox Unslipped: Teabox Variety.

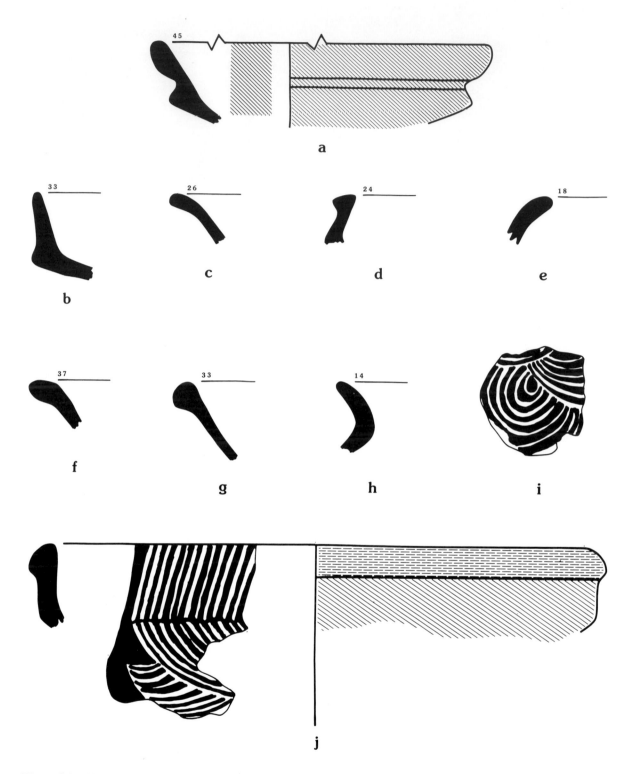

Figure 6.5. C'oh Complex types. a–h, Canxun Red: Canxun Variety; i and j, Yaxnik Through the Slip Incised: Yaxnik Variety.

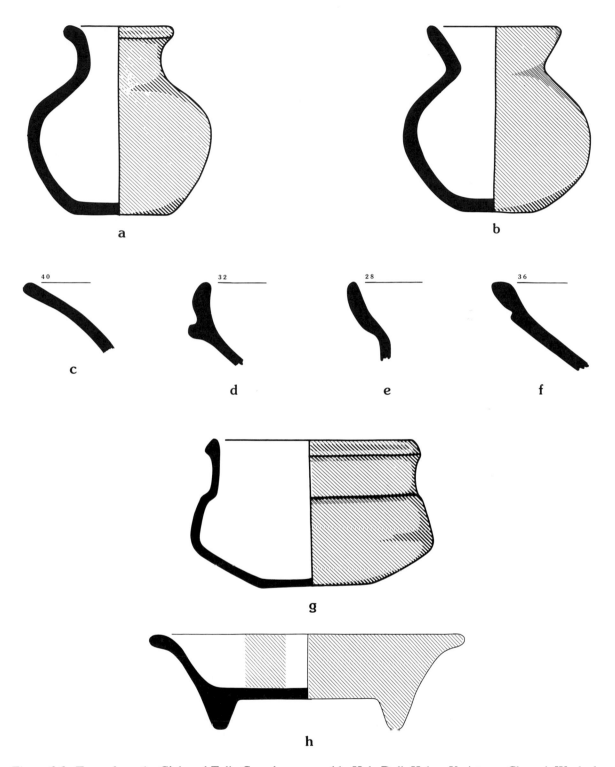

Figure 6.6. Types from the C'oh and Tulix Complexes. a and b, Hole Dull: Hukup Variety; c, Chamah Washed: Chamah Variety; d-f, Conop Red-on-Red Trickle: Conop Variety; g and h, Cabro Red: Cabro Variety.

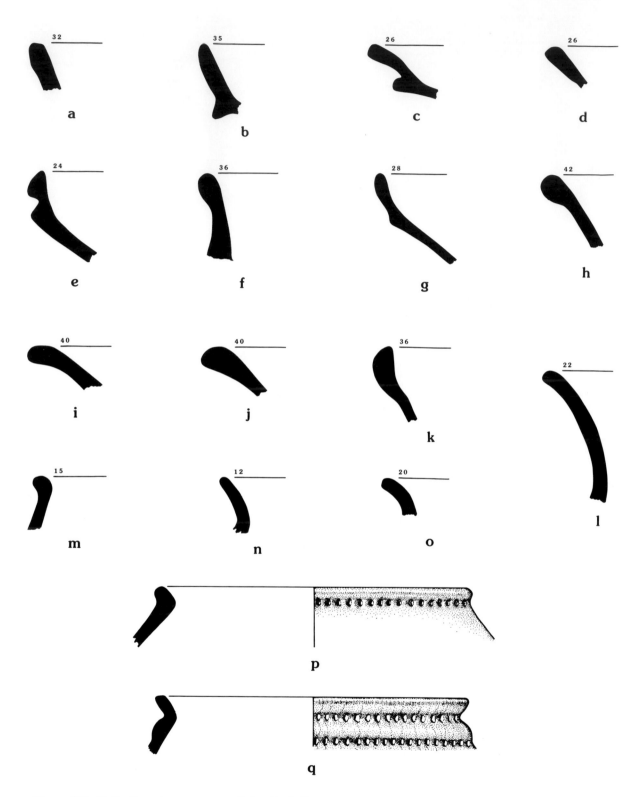

Figure 6.7. Tulix Complex types. a-o, Cabro Red: Cabro Variety; p and q, Pahote Punctated: Pahote Variety.

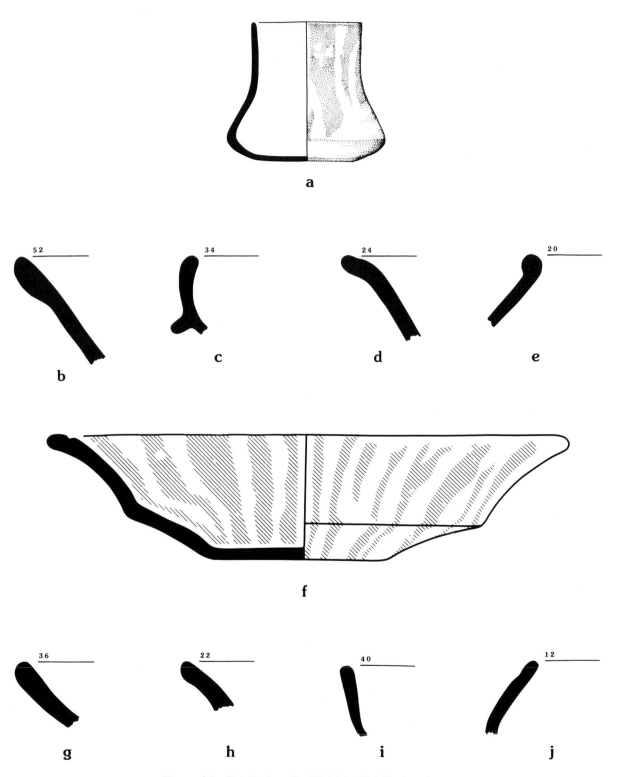

Figure 6.8. Tuk Red-on-Red Trickle: Tuk Variety forms.

CHIPPED STONE ARTIFACTS

Beverly A. Mitchum

This preliminary report on the chipped stone artifacts from Cerros deals with the material collected during the 1973 through 1976 field seasons, supplemented with information from the 1977 and 1978 seasons. It is primarily descriptive and generally follows the categories used in traditional typologies of Maya lithics (Willey *et al.* 1965; Willey 1972; Coe 1959; Ricketson and Ricketson 1937).

Although the tool categories are similar to those generally used in Maya lithic studies, they have been grouped to reflect the technological sequences used in tool manufacture. Recently, reduction sequence analysis has become one of the major areas of interest in Maya lithic studies (Rovner 1975; Sheets 1978) and future analysis of the Cerros material will define these in more detail.

At the present time, three general tool classes have been identified in the assemblage. The first consists of large bifacially worked tools, the second, of plano-convex tools produced from large blade (macroblade) blanks and the third, of small flake and blade tools. These tool categories reflect at least two distinct reduction sequences: one for the production of bifacial tools, and the other for macroblade tool production. The majority of the small flake and blade tools were manufactured on discarded flakes from these sequences.

The first section of the report contains descriptions of the major tool types from Cerros. Almost all of these artifacts are made of chert. The second section consists of a brief discussion of the obsidian artifacts. The final section contains the results of a preliminary analysis of the chert debitage from one excavation area at Cerros. This material is from Operation 1, a Late Preclassic nucleated residential village that was excavated during the 1974-1976 seasons (Cliff, this volume). This material was chosen for analysis because it comes from a primary occupation context.

Several terms are used in the report with specific definitions: blade—a parallel sided flake with its length equal to or greater than twice its width. (This also follows the discussion in Hester and Hammond 1976.)

Debitage—flakes and blades that could have been made into or used as tools. Debris—small chips, chunks or trimming flakes that could not have been used or reduced further.

The chert in the Cerros assemblage is honey brown, grey, greyish brown, banded grey and brown, black, white and tan. It ranges in texture from coarse to fine grain. Almost all of the formal tools were made from fine grain chert. Some of the hammerstone types and small irregular tools were made of coarse grain chert. To date, no attempt has been made to identify chert sources. No sources, however, are known to be located in the immediate vicinity of Cerros. Several high quality chert sources have been found in Northern Belize (Anderson 1976) and chert was probably brought to Cerros from one of them. The nearest source is located near Progresso, approximately 20 km from the site. In 1978, several members of the Cerros crew visited this source and observed numerous fragments of coarse grain chert on the surface (Scarborough, personal communication). Fine grain chert was not seen at Progresso, indicating that this material was probably brought to Cerros from sources farther south. The large chert source and knapping site of Colha, Belize, has produced chert and tool types very similar to those from Cerros (Hester, personal communication and personal observation) with one exception. Black chert has not been reported from Colha (Hester, personal communication; Wilk, personal communication). The sources of this black chert are unknown but may be south of Colha near Belize City. A number of black chert artifacts have been recovered from Moho Cay just off the coast from Belize City (Wilk, personal communication).

BIFACIAL TOOLS

This group includes large biface celts, knives, points and choppers. The quality of bifacial finishing ranges from crude shaping to fine workmanship.

Large Oval/Biface Celts

These are large celt-like chipped stone implements. Eight complete and 15 incomplete pieces have been recovered. They are lenticular in cross-section with the dorsal face being slightly more convex than the ventral. In outline, the bit ends range from convex to straight. The edges converge to a rounded point at the butt end. Four of the complete pieces have a patch of cortex on the butt. The edges vary from straight to slightly sinuous in profile and have been slightly ground in several cases. Most show evidence of use or battering along the edges in the form of small hinged retouch along the edge margins. This retouch is heaviest on the bit ends.

One of the smallest of the complete bifaces was found in association with Burial 23. The others are surface finds from along the coast or from excavation in the Late Preclassic nucleated residential village.

Length: 14.5-21.5 cm. Width: 6.75-8.25 cm. Thickness: 1.8-2.6 cm. (Figs. 7.1f, 7.2d).

Straight Stem Bifacial Point or Knife

A single complete specimen of this type was recovered. The body of the piece is twice as long as the stem. The edges of the body taper from the juncture with the stem to a blunt point at the distal end. The shoulders at the stem-body juncture are not pronounced. Instead they are slightly rounded so the stem is slightly narrower in width than the body. In outline, the stem is straight with a slightly rounded base. There is a pronounced medial ridge on the dorsal surface which produces a triangular ovate cross-section. The body edges are slightly sinuous in profile. Small hinged retouch is present on both edge margins, but is much heavier on the right edge. The piece was recovered from the surface of Structure 6B.

Length: 16.7 cm. Width: 3.3 cm. Maximum thickness: 2.4 cm.

Long Blade Tapered Stem Biface

Nine of these were recovered from a Postclassic cache on Structure 4A. They are lenticular in cross-section. In outline, the boulders range from sharply tanged to rounded. Both the stem and body edges converge from this juncture to points. The distal points generally are sharper than the basal ones. Bases range from pointed

to slightly rounded. The maximum thickness is near the juncture of the stem and body and the pieces are thinned toward both ends. The bodies are at least twice as long as the stems. The edges are straight in profile and have been lightly ground along the margins. They have been thinned by the removal of small parallel flakes extending from the edges across both faces.

Length: 14.2-25.2 cm. Width: 2.9-4.5 cm. Thickness: 0.6-1.5 cm. (Fig. 7.3b).

Unstemmed Bifacial Points or Knives

Five complete specimens have been recovered. The two larger ones are ovoid in cross-section and ovate-triangular in outline. In profile, the edges are straight at the distal end. They become sinuous toward the base as a result of the removal of alternate deep flakes from the edge margins. The bases are rounded. The smaller of these two has heavy secondary retouch along the edge margins at the midsection.

The three small unstemmed bifaces are lenticular in cross-section and elongated oval in outline. In profile, the edges are irregular. Two of these are moderately well shaped and have small hinged retouch along the margins of both edges. The third has this retouch along the proximal edges.

Length: 7.5-12.2 cm. Width: 2.5-4.4 cm. Thickness: 1.1-2.4 cm.

Bifacial Chisels

Four elongated fragments were recovered that were initially shaped through bifacial technique. The surfaces were then heavily ground, presumably through use. Two of these pieces are distal end and body fragments with the edges and surfaces converging to a distal point. Both have elongated scars extending from the distal tip down one surface. The longer piece has a double convex profile with one surface more steeply convex. In cross-section, this piece is flattened at the distal end.

The other two fragments were burned after they were manufactured and used. They are lenticular in cross-section. One is a midsection fragment. The other is a proximal fragment. Both are less heavily ground than the distal fragments. The grinding has smoothed, but not completely obscured, the bifacial flake scars.

Dimensions not taken on fragments (Fig. 7.2e).

Adzes

Eleven complete specimens were recovered. Even though some show only unifacial chipping, they are included with the large bifacial tools because the majority are at least partially bifacial and the unifacial types are made on large flakes instead of large blades. All are plano-convex in cross-section including those that are partially bifacially worked. They are divided into three groups on the basis of the flake scar pattern on the distal or bit end. Here, adzes are defined as tools with unifacially worked bits. The bits range from straight to convex in outline.

Tranchet blow bits: (Orange peel adze) On five of the complete pieces, the dorsal bit surface was formed by the removal of a single large flake with a *tranchet* blow. Three are triangular in outline. The others are triangular-ovate. The butts are rounded. Two of the triangular adzes are made on large side-struck flakes. The third has been bifacially worked so that the shape of its preform cannot be determined. Small flake scars, probably the result of use, are present on the bits. The bits form the widest part of these pieces. This *tranchet* technique has been described in more detail by Shafer (1976, 1980) in his analyses of material from Colha and Pulltrouser swamp.
Length: 12.1-16.7 cm. Width: 6.7-7.2 cm. Thickness: 1.7-2.1 cm. (Fig. 7.2a).

Oblique multiple blow bits: These small adzes are teardrop in outline. Both have a patch of cortex at the butt end. The bits were formed by the removal of multiple flakes extending from the distal end onto the dorsal surface. The bits are convex and are at oblique angles to the edges. There appears to be the remnant of a *tranchet*-blow scar on the right side of the bit of one of them. If so, the edge was then secondarily modified by the removal of multiple flakes. The smaller piece is bifacially worked at the butt end.
Length: 6.2-8.1 cm. Width: 3.3-4.5 cm. Thickness: 1.9-2.2 cm. (Fig. 7.2b).

Irregular bit adzes: The four pieces in this category show greater variability in shape than the adze types. All are bifacially worked with planed ventral surfaces. The dorsal surfaces vary in cross-section from steeply convex to shallow convex to trapezoidal. The steeply convex piece has a pointed butt. In outline, the edges of the shallow convex piece converge slightly, but the butts are straight. The adze with a trapezoidal cross-section has an oblique butt. The bit angles are steeper on these than on the other adze types. In one case, the angle approaches 90°. The bit edges are irregular and are formed by the removal of multiple flakes struck from the bit end and extending onto the dorsal surface.
Length: 6.7-9.8 cm. Width: 4.8-5.1 cm. Thickness: 1.8-2.0 cm. (Fig. 7.1e, h).

Bifacial Point or Knife Fragments

Nineteen pieces were classified as bifacial point or knife fragments. Most of these show the same quality of workmanship as that found on the complete bifaces or points (excluding the types from the Postclassic cache). However, they fall outside the size range of these types.

Four fragments appear to be stems from tapered stem shouldered bifaces with ovate cross-sections. Seven are pointed distal end fragments. These show more controlled flaking technique in their manufacture than do the general utility choppers. Six are ovate mid-section fragments.

Two large distal fragments may be fragments of long blade tapered stem bifaces. They were shaped by the removal of regular parallel flakes extending from the edge margins across both faces. The edges are straight in profile and have small hinged retouch along the margins.

Dimensions not taken on fragments.

Miscellaneous Bifacial Tools

Twelve tools or tool fragments were recovered that were produced through bifacial technique. These pieces appear to have been secondarily modified from fragments of other bifacial tool types. There is little standardization in the shape of these fragments or in the appearance of the working edges. Tool forms include denticulates, concave bit gouges, and scrapers (Fig. 7.4c).

MACROBLADE TOOLS

These are large plano-convex unifacially worked tools made on macroblade or blade fragments.

Tanged Daggers

Seven complete and forty-eight fragments have been recovered. In outline, the body is an elongated triangle. The shoulders are rounded and the stems taper slightly. All were made on large blades from opposed direction cores with the platform end of the blade re-worked into the dagger stem. On all except the smallest, the stems were bifacially thinned. The ventral surfaces of the stems were thinned by flat flaking across the surface. On the dorsal surfaces, the scars extend steeply from the edge margins onto the surface. All but the largest have fine retouch along the body edges. The largest has retouch only near the distal end of the body. The distal tips have been shaped to form points.

Two small pieces show essentially the same shape and manufacture technique, but are smaller and asymmetrical in shape. On one, the body edges are denticulated. The other has double convex edges in outline.

Large complete daggers. Length: 13.3-25.0 cm. Width: 4.3-5.6 cm.
Thickness: 1.2-2.0 cm. (Fig. 7.3f, g, h).

Small daggers. Length: 7.8-10.9 cm. Width: 3.5-4.8 cm. Thickness: 1.3-1.7 cm.

Re-Worked Tanged Dagger

One piece is identical in manufacture technique and shape to the other complete daggers except that an oblique break occurred at the distal end. This edge was then modified by the removal of several flakes extending from the edge onto the dorsal face. This modification produced an oblique cutting or scraping edge on the distal end.

Length: 13.9 cm. Width: 4.5 cm.
Thickness: 1.5 cm. (Fig. 7.1a).

Borers

Six elongated fragments were recovered on which the unbroken end has been unifacially worked to form a point. Five of these appear to have been made on the initial blade removed to start the working surface of a prismatic blade core. The other appears to be made on a re-worked stem from a tanged dagger. This piece is plano-convex in cross-section. Two of the others are

triangular-convex. On these three, the edges converge to sharp points. The other three are trapezoidal in cross-section and have slightly rounded points. The edges converge gradually to the point. The dorsal surfaces were secondarily modified by the removal of irregular flakes extending from the edge margins onto the surface. Small hinged retouch is present on the dorsal edge margins. The pieces with rounded tips are thinned at the distal end.

Length: not taken on fragments. Width: 3.3-5.5 cm. Thickness: 1.5-1.1 cm. (Fig. 7.4m).

Chisel

This piece has steep retouch extending the length of both edges. The butt end shows the same manufacture technique as that found on the tanged dagger stems in that it has been bifacially thinned on the ventral surface. The edge outline is straight on the stem but becomes slightly denticulated on the body from the removal of deep flakes extending from the edge margins. The distal end is blunt and has been thinned by a flake struck from the ventral surface. Heavy hinged retouch is present along the edge margins.

Length: 17.9 cm. Width: 2.7 cm.
Thickness: 1.8 cm.

Miscellaneous Macroblade Tools

Fourteen other fragmentary or complete tools made on macroblade blanks were recovered. While there is considerable variability in the shape of these pieces, all show steep retouch along the edge margins of the dorsal face. All are plano-convex in cross-section.

The most interesting of these pieces is a complete macroblade which has heavy retouch along the edges and at the distal end. It has a faceted platform, and a large *éraillure* scar on the ventral face indicates that it was probably produced by a hard hammer technique (Fig. 7.1g).

Three pieces appear to be stems from some kind of large plano-convex tool. However, the only large macroblade tools with stems are the tanged daggers and these fragments exceed the dimensions and differ in shape from the dagger stems (Fig. 7.4a).

Other pieces are midsection fragments with denticulated edges. On one piece, the edges converge to form a point at the distal end. This was produced through inverse retouch on what appears to be a distal body fragment of a dagger. Three were modified on the distal end to produce concave endscrapers. The last is an oblique endscraper.

All of these tools appear to represent part of a large blade industry and are either fragments of tools which have not been recovered in complete form or are secondarily modified fragments of large tools or blades.

Dimensions not given on fragments (Figs. 7.3e, 7.4a, b).

Notched Blades

Two medium-sized blades have wide, shallow notches on the midsections of the right edges produced through inverse retouch. On one, the distal edges have been modified to form a blunt point at the distal end. The point asymmetrically slanted to the left. The platform for the removal of this blade is formed by the removal of a single flake. The second is a blade fragment.

Length: 8.4 cm. Width: 2.8 cm.
Thickness: 1.1 cm. (Fig. 7.4q).

Drills and Punches

This group includes tools made on a variety of small flake or blade blank types. Most are made from re-sharpening or biface thinning flakes. Others are made from the local coarse grained chert.

Eight punches or drills made on flakes were recovered. The drills have elongated projections at the distal end formed by steep retouch on alternate edges of the projection. There is little standardization in the overall shape of the pieces. Two are made on side struck flakes. One is on a biface trimming flake with the flake platform used as one edge of the drill, and the fourth has steep backed retouch continuing down the edges of the piece from the drill point. Punches are distinguished from drills in that the retouch on the elongated projection extends from the edge margins onto only one of the surfaces. These again show variability in overall shape of the piece and range from elongate to triangular to ovate in outline.

On both of these groups, the worked projections range from blunt to sharp. In cross-section, the pieces are plano-convex or trapezoidal (Fig. 7.4i, j, k, l).

Dimensions not available.

Flake Celt

This piece is triangular in outline. The butt end was bifacially thinned to form a rounded point. The left edge is broken. There is bifacial chipping along the margin of the right edge. The distal end is unworked and is straight in outline. The butt is ovate in cross-section whereas the distal edge is flat.

Length: 9.9 cm. Width: 4.2 cm.
Thickness: 1.6 cm. (Fig. 7.2c).

Denticulates

Six flake denticulates were recovered. These have a series of notches either on a single edge, multiple edges or around most of the perimeter of the piece. The notches were produced by single blows and show little standardization in size.

Scrapers

Several side and end scrapers made on flakes were recovered. In general, scrapers show more variability in the type of blank used for their manufacture than do other tool types because, in addition to this group, bi-facial and macroblade scrapers have been recovered.

Length: 5.6-6.1 cm. Width: 4.1-5.1 cm.
Thickness: 2.0 cm. (Figs. 7.1c, 7.4n, p).

Projectile Points

Eleven small points were recovered. Seven are side notched and were made on small blades. These are uni-facial points. The bodies are retouched along the margins and converge to distal points. On five of them the stems have been shaped to form a convex base. One of the others has a large irregular stem which is almost as long as the body. Two are obsidian and have concave bases. All of these were found in surface or Late Postclassic contexts.

A small, long blade tapered stem point was recovered from the Postclassic cache on Structure 4A. In outline, this piece is identical to the large long blade tapered stem bifaces recovered from the same cache. It is bifa-cially worked. The ventral surface is formed by the remnant of the scar left from the core removal of this blade. Its platform was removed to form the distal point.

Another point is a small plano-convex tanged form made on a blade. It has been thinned on the ventral surfaces of the stem and distal end. Retouch is present on the edge margins of the body and stem. The shoulders and base are slightly rounded. The edges of the stem are straight.

The final piece included in this group is a laurel leaf made on a small blade. It is plano-convex in cross-section. The widest point is slightly below the mid-section. From this point the edges converge to points at each end. The right edge has retouch on the dorsal surface, whereas the left edge shows inverse retouch. There is a slight S twist to the piece in cross-section.

Side Notched Points Length: 4.8-2.3 cm.
Width: 2.8-1.2 cm. Thickness: 0.4-0.2 cm.

Long Blade Tapered Stem Point Length: 7.1 cm.
Width: 1.9 cm. Thickness: 0.5 cm.

Plano-Convex Point Length: 4.2 cm.
Width: 1.0 cm.   Thickness: 0.4 cm.

Laurel Leaf Length: 4.4 cm.
Width: 1.1 cm. Thickness: 0.2 cm.
(Figs. 7.3c, 7.4f, h).

Miscellaneous Small Flake Tools

Several other small flake tools have been recovered. Most of these can be classified as simple retouched flakes. On these pieces the retouch was most likely produced by use. In addition, several notched flakes have been found. On these, the notches are produced by multiple flake removal (Fig. 7.1b). One flake fragment has small regular retouch along three of its edges, producing a semi-circular form (Fig. 7.1d). Finally, one small chert blade fragment has been lightly retouched along its edges to form a point at its distal end (Fig. 7.4g). This piece may be a projectile point fragment. However, because no complete projectile points like it have been found, it is included in the miscellaneous category.

HAMMERSTONES

Forty-six stone artifacts have been recovered that are heavily battered on one or more edges. These can be divided into three types on the basis of their shape and the degree that the piece was shaped before its use as a hammerstone.

Six are coarse grain chert cobbles. They are spheroid in shape and most of their surfaces are battered. Most of them still have some cortex left on at least one of the faces. The pieces were shaped by the random removal of flakes struck from multiple directions. The resulting form seems to be a by-product of use as opposed to intentional shaping prior to use.

The second group of hammerstones are made on fine grain chert. They range from ovate to trapezoidal in cross-section and from round to elongate in outline. Battering is present only on the edges. The ventral faces may be formed by a single large flake scar left from the detachment of the piece from a core. The dorsal faces are shaped by the removal of flakes struck from multiple or opposed directions. This group, which is the most variable in size of the hammerstone groups, contains 34 pieces (Fig. 7.4d, o).

The third group contains flat discoidal forms. Both faces show flake removal from multiple directions. Battering is found only along the edges. One of them was found in association with a ceramic vessel and may have been used as a potlid (Fig. 7.4e).

Length: 4.9-10.1 cm. Width: 4.8-9.5 cm.
Thickness: 1.6-6.4 cm.

OBSIDIAN

About 4% of the chipped stone assemblage is obsidian. This tabulation is based on the total number of chert and obsidian pieces (tools, debris and debitage) from all excavations. Although the lithic analysis has not yet progressed far enough for a relative comparison of obsidian from Late Preclassic versus Postclassic contexts to be made, it seems to be present in about the same proportions in both periods. Most of the obsidian from the Late Preclassic nucleated residential village consists of small blade fragments. The three complete blades are from Postclassic contexts. Two obsidian cores with fully ground platforms were surface finds and probably date to the Postclassic (Fig. 7.3k). The only subsequently modified pieces made of obsidian are two small projectile points (Fig. 7.4h).

Most of the obsidian ranges from translucent black and gray to opaque black in color. Two fragments of green obsidian blades were recovered from temporally mixed plaza fill and are assumed to be from the Pachuca source in central Mexico. One of them has a fully ground platform and thus probably dates to the Postclassic. Of the black and gray obsidian blades and blade fragments twenty-four have identifiable platforms. Following

Rovner's (1975) description, five have rounded or pointed platforms, six are edge ground and thirteen are fully ground.

LITHIC ANALYSIS

A preliminary analysis of the lithic debitage and debris from Operation 1 in the Late Preclassic nucleated residential village indicates that very little primary tool manufacture occurred in this area of the site. The two most common types of debris are biface trimming flakes from late stage biface reduction and biface resharpening flakes. A few large (over 5.0 cm. in length) primary elements from the initial stages of biface manufacture have been recovered. Since these are retouched along one or more edges, they seem to have been selected for tool use and brought to the area for this purpose. Re-sharpening flakes include those struck from the bit edges of standard bifaces and orange peels (Wilk 1975). The orange peels are most likely produced from resharpening the *tranchet* blow adzes.

About 20% of the debris appears to have been burned. The burning occurred after the pieces were discarded. It is identified by the presence of heat spalls, discoloration, heat cracking and the glossy appearance of the stone.

While there is a large amount of debris and debitage in the midden deposit, the amount of chert working represented does not seem to be sufficient to account for the large number of hammerstones. It seems likely that these were used for many activities in addition to stone tool manufacture.

SUMMARY

The lithic assemblage from Cerros consists of a fairly restricted range of tool types. The Late Preclassic assemblage is characterized by the large, well made biface celts, *tranchet* adzes and plano-convex tanged daggers.

These types are standardized in shape. Their presence in the Late Preclassic midden in residential contexts suggests that these are utilitarian implements. This context for the plano-convex daggers contrasts with other reports of their presence in tombs or caches (Thompson 1939; Ricketson and Ricketson 1937; Lee 1969). The form of the daggers from Cerros is most similar to those from a Late Preclassic tomb at Chiapa de Corzo, Chiapas (Lee 1969) and they differ slightly in form from other examples in Belize (Willey *et al.* 1965; Gann and Gann 1939; Anderson 1976). This difference in form may be a temporal distinction between the Late Preclassic and later forms.

The rest of the Late Preclassic assemblage consists of irregular bifacial or plano-convex tools and flake tools. These artifacts show little standardization in shape and seem to have been used for general cutting, scraping and drilling activities. The occurrence of bifacial and large blade tools (plano-convex forms) seems typical of assemblages from most lowland Maya sites (Willey *et al.* 1965; Rovner 1975; Andreson 1976; Wilk 1975). The illustrations of the Swasey lithic material (Hammond *et al.* 1979) suggest that these techniques of tool production are part of a tradition beginning in the Early Preclassic.

The Late Postclassic assemblage contains fewer types but shows a greater degree of standardization within these types. This may be due to the small sample size of the assemblage and to biased recovery of this material from caches and non-occupational contexts. The assemblage is characterized by large bifacially worked points and small projectile points made on blades. The large chert macroblade tools do not occur in this assemblage.

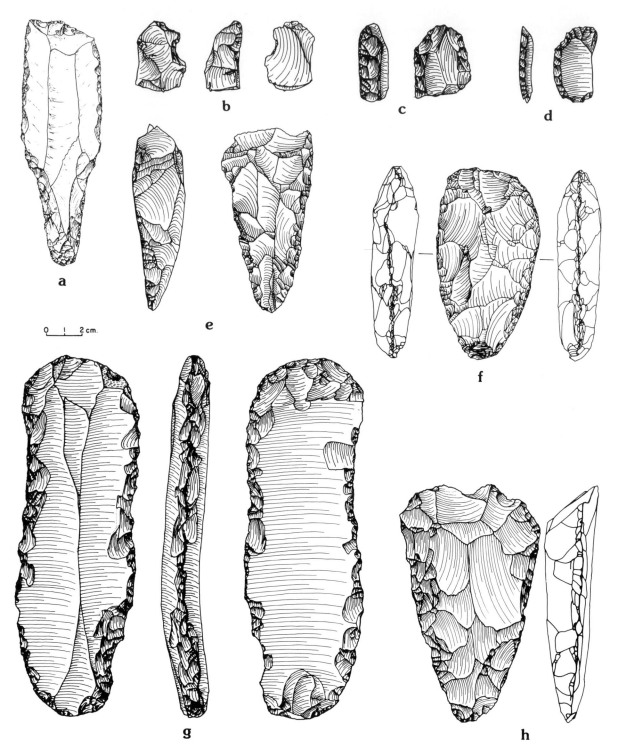

Figure 7.1. Chipped stone artifacts. a, reworked dagger; b, notched flake; c, side scraper; d, miscellaneous flake tool; e and h, irregular bit adzes; f, standard biface; g, macroblade.

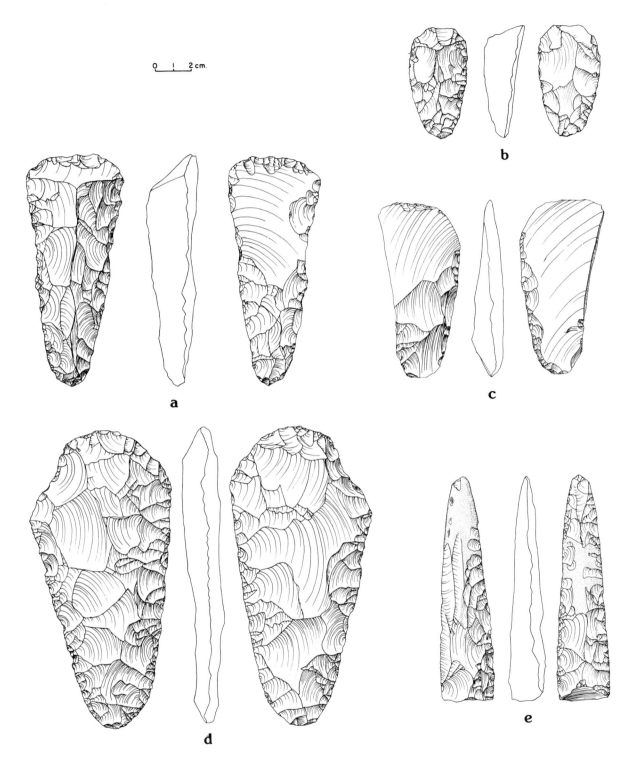

Figure 7.2. Chipped stone artifacts. a, orange peel adze; b, oblique multiple blow adze; c, flake celt; d, standard biface; e, bifacial chisel.

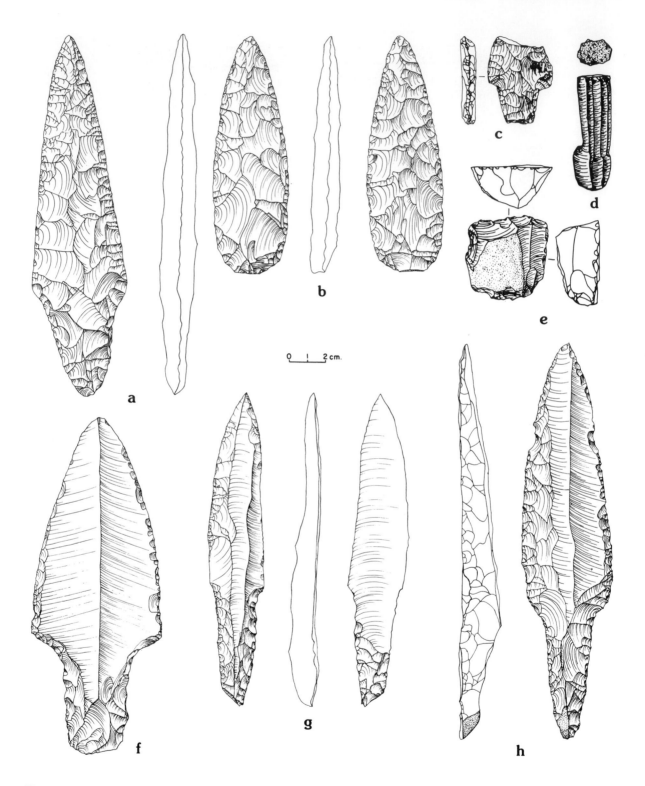

Figure 7.3. Chipped stone artifacts. a, long blade tapered stem biface; b, round base biface; c, projectile point; d, obsidian core; e, miscellaneous macroblade tool; f-h, tanged daggers.

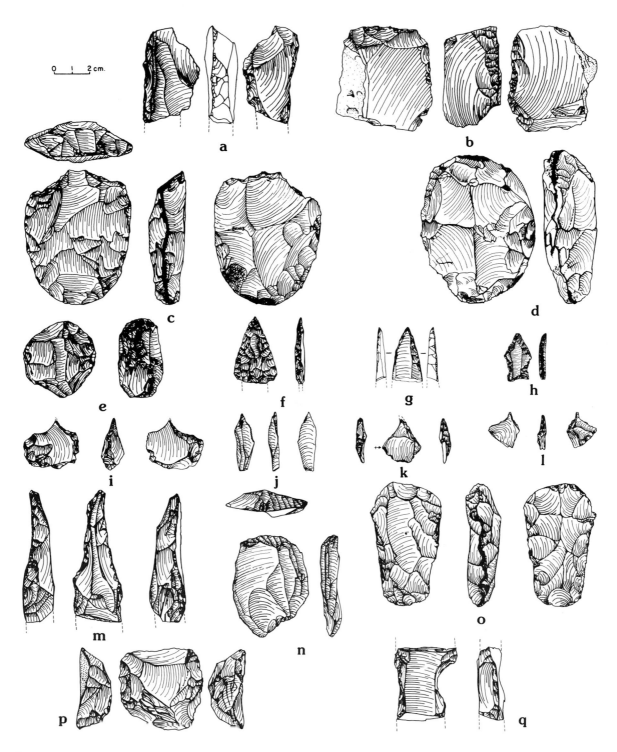

Figure 7.4. Chipped stone artifacts. a and b, miscellaneous macroblade tools; c, bifacial scraper; d and e, hammerstones; f, projectile point; g, miscellaneous small flake tool; h, obsidian point; i-l, flake punches; m, plano-convex borer; n, flake end scraper; o, hammerstone; p, flake scraper; q, notched blade.

THE ARTIFACTS

James F. Garber

During the course of excavations over 2,000 artifacts have been recovered from a variety of contexts. The artifact descriptions and contexts presented in this paper represent a brief summary of ongoing analysis.

The Maya site of Cerros, in northern Belize, functioned as a community from the Late Preclassic to the Postclassic Period. The orientation of this community shifts from political, religious and economic activity during the Late Preclassic, to domestic activity in the Classic, to domestic and religious activity in the Postclassic. A study of the artifacts has shown how these changes have affected the kinds of material culture that were acquired and consumed during each period and what this means in relation to the evolution of Maya civilization.

Maya artifacts traditionally have been organized by category of material (Coe 1959; Kidder *et al.* 1946; Kidder 1947; Phillips 1978; Proskouriakoff 1962; Ricketson and Ricketson 1937; Sheets 1978; Smith 1951; Willey 1972, 1978; Willey *et al.* 1965). These categories include chipped stone, ground stone, worked bone, worked shell, ceramics, re-worked sherds, plaster and metal. These categories of raw material roughly correspond to technological industries, in that each raw material grouping requires a different technology to work that material. Within each raw material, or industry, the artifacts have been sub-divided and grouped according to form. Although this categorization is necessary to facilitate description and inter-site comparisons, the description and placement of the artifacts from a site into these categories and groupings is all too often the end rather than the beginning of artifact analysis.

At Cerros the analysis was expanded to include a consideration of the behavioral patterns associated with the consumption and function of the artifact types. This was accomplished by analyzing the contexts from which the artifacts came. A typology was devised which is reflective of the behaviors associated with artifact disposal. Deposits were assigned a contextual designation on the basis of associated features and artifacts. These included:

1. cache
2. burial
3. habitation debris
4. pit fill
5. construction fill with rubble
6. construction fill without rubble
7. floor fill
8. on floor material
9. termination ritual deposits

Within other deposits the associations with features were absent or unclear and the nature of the deposit was not well known. This second group included:

1. surface
2. humus
3. fall
4. slump

The variable degree to which each of these two groups of deposits is understood is reflected in the contextual designations. In the second group, the contextual designation was based on the matrix or provenience.

In the first group the designations reflected their functions or associations. With the exception of termination rituals, these contexts have been used throughout the Maya lowlands and need no further explanation here. Termination ritual deposits, on the other hand, are defined as the activities associated with the termination or abandonment of a structure or area. They usually involve the intentional deposition and scattering about of decomposed limestone. This marl often contains smashed jade, stone spheroids (Fig. 8.1a), stone disks, sherd disks, crystalline hematite and smashed ceramic vessels, all of which are also associated with the termination activities.

In the case of the second group, the surface and humus categories need no explanation. Fall refers to tumble or construction fill which is no longer *in situ*. It can include material originally in the construction fill as well as material produced by the deterioration of the structure. It should be noted that on the surface or within the humus or fall may be material that actually belongs within domestic debris or some other context, but this was not readily apparent from the associated finds or features. Slump refers to deteriorated plaster, *sascab*, or marl which has slumped out of place. It can include material contained in the matrix when *in situ* as well as material which became incorporated into the deposit after the slumping began.

The utility of this typology can be documented by a consideration of the kind of information it produced. In the case of caches, for example, looking at the association of artifacts led to the identification of an additional artifact which was probably included in these ceremonial deposits. The Late Preclassic dedicatory cache on the medial axis of Structure 6B contained twenty-four artifacts of jade including five head pendants (Figs. 8.1, 8.2), ear flares (Fig. 8.1b), beads, mosaic pieces, ground fragments and a spangle. Also included were spondylus shells, small white shell disks, fragments of specular hematite, and sherd disk lids. These cached items were found in, on and among seven ceramic vessels. In terms of the jade, shell, hematite and pottery, the cache is similar to other Late Preclassic dedicatory caches at the site. With the exception of the extremely fragile specular hematite fragments, all of the artifacts from this and other dedicatory caches at Cerros are whole or reworked. Thus, the fragmentary condition of the specular hematite is, more than likely, a factor of preservation. Their co-occurrence with white shell disks may indicate that the tabular, reflective mineral fragments were the reflecting portions of mirrors that originally had shell backs. Over time the glue which held them in place decayed.

On a larger scale the analysis of contextual groups has led to the identification of a behavioral pattern that has received little attention or been unrecognized at other sites. This behavioral pattern is the termination ritual associated with the abandonment of architecture. First identified by the presence of burned and smashed ceramic vessels (Robertson-Freidel 1980), these rituals and their associated behavior includes the removal of plaster facading, the burning of ceremonial fires, the smashing of jade artifacts, the scattering about of marl or white earth, and the preparation and consumption of a ceremonial beverage (Garber 1981). Although one or more of these features may be absent from a given deposit, the scattering about of white marl, burning, and smashing of artifacts and pottery is consistent. Termination rituals have been identified on Structures 29B, 5C, 2A-sub 4-1st, 4B, 3B and in the Feature 1A residential zone. The pattern of artifacts present in a given deposit appears to depend on whether the context is associated with the abandonment of monumental or domestic architecture.

In the monumental architecture the smashed artifacts include jade beads, jade flares, sherd disks, bone beads, crystalline hematite, centrally perforated stone disks (Fig. 8.3b), burned stone disks (Fig. 8.3a, c) and spheroids (Fig. 8.1a), and miscellaneous pieces. Of all the Late Preclassic special finds at Cerros, 43.1% were recovered from these marl deposits. If the numerous burned disks and spheroids are not included in this calculation then the figure drops to 17.8%. Both figures loom especially large when one considers that the decomposed marl accounts for less than 5.0% of the fill excavated at Cerros, attesting to the relatively high expenditures of time, labor and material culture investment associated with the abandonment of monumental architecture. It should be noted that whole jades are associated only with structure completion and dedication, whereas intentially broken jades are associated with structure abandonment and termination.

Domestic architecture, however, merited even less expensive goods than the monumental architecture. No shell beads, for example, have been recovered from the termination deposits associated with the monumental architecture. Jade beads, in contrast, are quite common in the deposits associated with the abandonment of both domestic and monumental architecture. The jade beads frequently have been intentionally smashed, whereas the shell beads are rarely broken (Fig. 8.1d-k). Apparently the two kinds of beads were consumed quite differently. It is proposed that the less expensive shell was an inappropriate sacrifice for the abandonment of public architecture but was appropriate for the abandonment of private architecture.

Contextual analysis of the deposits at Cerros also has made it possible to propose specific functions for some types of artifacts and to clarify or confirm the function or functions of others. Numerous burned limestone disks and spheroids, for example, have been recovered from the termination deposits on Structure 2A-sub 4-1st (Figs. 8.1a, 8.3a, c). These are not found in domestic trash deposits. They appear to have functioned as vessel rests for the preparation of liquids or foods utilized in the ritual. Alternatively, they may have functioned as vessel rests and aerators in the firing of vessels to be smashed in the termination rituals. At present there is no evidence to support the firing of these vessels *in situ* (Robertson, personal communication 1982), making the former suggestion more likely.

Similarly, Mayanists have speculated for years on

the function of centrally perforated stone disks (Fig. 8.3b). Suggestions include: digging stick weights, maize shellers, counter-weights for doors, banner holders, club-heads, and spear shaft weights (Kidder, Jennings, and Shook 1946; Willey 1972). A similar stone was recovered from the remains of a Classic Period farmhouse associated with a cornfield preserved by volcanic ash at Ceren in El Salvador (Zier 1980). On the basis of this contextual information, Zier suggests that this specimen functioned as a digging stick weight. Several of the Cerros perforated stones have been recovered from deposits of domestic debris and probably also functioned as digging stick weights. However, seven of these centrally perforated disks have been recovered from a deposit on Structure 5C that is clearly not domestic in nature but rather is the result of termination ritual. These stones are associated with plaster facading which has been torn down and they may have functioned as armatures for moulded pieces. The central hole would facilitate attachment to the retaining wall of the structure with a wooden peg. In support of this hypothesis, the Temple of the Seven Dolls at Dzibilchaltun in Yucatan, Mexico, exhibits a frieze containing moulded plaster disks with holes or indentations (Andrew 1959; Coggins 1983:22). Similarly, at Palenque in Chiapas, Mexico, there are several stucco friezes, one of which utilizes these elements in the surrounding border (Digby 1964: Plate 1).

It may be that the centrally perforated stones used for architectural decoration originally functioned as digging stick weights, and that the Maya who provided the labor for the construction brought the weights as votives to be incorporated into the religious symbolism of the architectural decorations. Those recovered from domestic deposits and those associated with monumental architectural decoration are virtually indistinguishable from one another. The use of a domestic item as an element in iconographic designs represents a symbolic link between that which is profane and that which is sacred.

A similar pattern of behavior may be indicated by the inclusion of mano and metate fragments in the dry laid rubble construction fill of the Late Preclassic monumental architecture. Because this fill does not contain the other kinds of domestic debris, it does not seem that household trash was being used as construction fill. Like the centrally perforated stone disks, the broken manos and metates may have been selected as votive offerings by the laborers who constructed the mounds. They do, however, differ from the former

artifacts in that they have not been recovered from termination ritual deposits.

A consideration of the 248 ceramic disks recovered from the excavations confirms their earlier functional assessment as lids for narrow-mouthed vessels (Willey et al. 1965). These disks are re-worked sherds shaped by flaking and grinding. The larger disks (greater than 5.0 cm in diameter) apparently functioned as vessel lids because some were recovered *in situ* on top of the vessels in the summit cache on Structure 6B. Moreover, many of them have been recovered from the termination ritual deposits in the monumental architecture where they are associated with high necked jars of the appropriate diameter (Robertson, personal communication 1982). Sherd lids have also been recovered from the domestic debris in the Feature 1A residential zone where they probably are a component of the termination rituals associated with the abandonment of certain residential loci.

The smaller ceramic disks (equal to or less than 5.0 cm in diameter), in contrast, are much too small to have functioned as vessel lids, given the known vessel diameters. Moreover, they do not come from dedicatory caches or termination deposits but rather are found primarily in domestic debris. Willey's (1965, 1972) assessment of similar artifacts from Barton Ramie and Altar de Sacrificios as gaming disks seems to be an accurate one.

In some cases the suggested function of an artifact type can lend support to hypotheses about the subsistence base, which have been generated by other data bases. The 365 notched ceramic pieces or *mariposas* that have been recovered from Cerros illustrate this interaction well.

These artifacts are rarely associated with the monumental architecture. Most of them were from housemounds in the settlement zone or from the Feature 1A residential zone. Sixty-seven of these finds date to the Late Preclassic, 190 are from Postclassic deposits, 104 date to the Classic, and four are of unknown date. They probably functioned as net weights and line weights as has been argued by several investigators (Eaton 1976; Phillips 1978, 1979; Willey et al. 1965; Willey 1972, 1978).

Within this artifact group three distinct types of notched ceramics have been recognized (Fig. 8.4). The weight distribution of these three types is tri-modal. The most common type (231 examples) is end notched. These are made on sherds and are considerably lighter than the typical side notched pieces (fifty-six examples) which are also made on sherds. Specimens of the third type (thirty-two examples) are specially manufactured pieces of moulded clay that have been notched when the clay was wet. These are considerably lighter than either the side or end notched forms and are standardized in weight. Most of these pieces are of Postclassic date. Arguably the differences in weight between the three types reflect a difference in function. The most common, end notched or mid-range weight, was probably used on nets, whereas the heavier and lighter types may have been used on different kinds of nets or lines.

Mariposas are usually found in domestic debris or deposits such as humus or fall. Those found within the humus and fall are probably also domestic refuse but lack clear association with domestic features. No *mariposas* were recovered from caches or deposits resulting from termination. Their presence can be taken as evidence of a reliance, in part at least, on fish resources, assuming that the traditional assessment of their function as net weights is correct.

Over 50% of the *mariposas* recovered date to the Postclassic period. Although it could be argued that this is a reflection of sampling, only 25% of the manos and metates are Postclassic in date. Fishing with *mariposa* weighted nets need not be the only means of catching fish, but the increasing frequency of this artifact can be taken as evidence for an increase in this form of fishing. It also may represent an increased reliance on fish as a food source. As the silting in of the Cerros canal system in the Early Classic made the raised field system of agriculture inoperable (Scarborough 1980), the remaining inhabitants would have had to have found alternate sources of protein. Net fishing would have provided such a source.

Through an analysis of context, it can be seen that the patterns of artifact acquisition, consumption and disposal changed through time. These patterns were affected by the changing nature of the Cerros community and reflect the dynamics of long-distance trade at this site.

CERROS AS A TRADE CENTER

The raw materials of the Cerros artifacts can be divided into three groups: 1) those that are available in the area surrounding the site, that is northern Belize and the adjacent portions of Mexico; 2) those that are available regionally, that is within the Lowlands; and 3) those that are available by long distance trade.

Artifacts of materials available locally in northern Belize and adjacent areas of Mexico make up the majority of artifacts recovered. Some of the shell may have been imported, but the bulk of it, if not all, was probably available in northern Belize.

Artifacts of materials available regionally include ground stone tools of quartzite and pegmatite. The nearest source for these materials is the Maya Mountains in west central Belize, approximately 150 km from Cerros (Sidrys and Andresen 1976; Thompson 1964).

The artifacts of raw materials available only by way of long distance trade include: manos and metates of andesite and rhyolite, various ornaments of jade, mirrors of crystalline hematite, items of copper, gold and tumbaga and artifacts of obsidian. The nearest source for these materials is southern Guatemala, 400 km from Cerros (Sidrys and Andresen 1976). Additionally, until the analysis is complete, any of the *Spondylus* shell pieces may be of the *pacificus* species, meaning that they were imported by long distance trade.

Although pumice may have been imported, it does occur in blocks on the Barrier Reef and is known to float in from highland sources.

With the possible exception of some of the obsidian artifacts, none of the utilitarian or domestic artifacts of a Late Preclassic date are of a material that would necessitate acquisition through long-distance trade. The Late Preclassic artifacts of exotic materials are ornamental or nonutilitarian in nature. A great many of these are associated with the dedication and ritual abandonment of public architecture. If Cerros functioned as a trans-shipment point for nonperishable utilitarian items, it is expected that some of the items would have remained for local consumption. With the exception of a small quantity of obsidian artifacts possibly used for utilitarian purposes, no such artifacts have been recovered.

Rathje (1971, 1972) has proposed that basalt, obsidian and salt had to be imported by long distance trade to the Lowland Maya area because these items were essential to the subsistence economy in the lowland jungle. According to this model, centralized authority evolved in response to the need to organize and maintain long distance trade routes in order to insure the constant flow of these goods. Several investigators have questioned the validity of the assumption that obsidian and basalt are truly essential to lowland subsistence patterns (Freidel 1978; Rice 1976; Sanders

1973; Tourtellot and Sabloff 1972). Hammond (1979) and Rice (1976), moreover, note that nonutilitarian exotic goods are present as early as the Middle Preclassic.

Even though Late Preclassic long distance trade is almost totally restricted to elitist material culture of an ornamental or nonutilitarian nature, the importance of long distance trade in examining the development of complex society should not be downgraded.

Sanders (1973) and Rice (1976) feel that the importation of nonutilitarian exotics was probably organized from the source and provided little stimulus for the evolution of complex society. Although acquisition from the source may not be an important organizational stimulus, these objects, once acquired, could be the subject of socio-cultural manipulation in the lowlands. As Tourtellot and Sabloff (1972) note, however, long distance trade usually involved direct transfer rather than market exchange of prestige artifacts. These artifacts served as expressions of socio-political links both within and between the elites of different communities. Nonetheless, such trade in nonutilitarian goods is, in their opinion, only of secondary importance in bringing about changes in the level of socio-cultural organization from ranked to state society. In contrast, Freidel (1978) argues that trade in nonutilitarian goods is important in the development of Lowland Maya complex society because such goods figure prominently in the symbol systems of power. As population increased during the Late Preclassic period, it would have been necessary for social status to become recognizable. One means of accomplishing this end is through the manipulation of material culture and the creation of symbol systems.

In addition to the above mentioned socio-political functions of exotic materials, they must have served important economic functions as well. Given that the Late Preclassic period is characterized by increased interaction and information flow, indicated by the establishment of many administrative centers, exotics could have provided a medium for establishing standardized value systems which crosscut local economies while also being a medium for the expression of status and prestige (Freidel 1977, 1978, 1979). Such standardized value systems and symbols would have provided and established the basis of interaction between the elites of major centers. At the time of the Spanish Conquest, jade beads functioned as money (Tozzer 1941). Certain forms of jade and obsidian, and possibly other exotics, no doubt served similar functions in Precolumbian times (Garber 1981).

Exotic goods, manipulated in this manner, permitted the expansive interaction sphere which defines the Maya Lowlands. Sanders and Price (1968) and Tourtellot and Sabloff (1972) note that the diverse environments of the highlands necessitate trade and market systems in which a broad range of goods is regularly exchanged. It is this necessity for trade, produced by the diverse environment, that contributes to the evolution of complex society in highland environments (Sanders and Price 1968). It was the lowland trade in exotics that established the standardized value systems which aided in the establishment of a lowland cultural sphere rather than the group of individualized states found in the highlands.

During the Protoclassic, Cerros ceased to function as a locus of elitist activity but continued as a location for mundane, domestic activity. No monumental construction and no domestic construction of any consequence date to the Classic period at Cerros. Moreover, no jade or crystalline hematite artifacts have been recovered from any of the Classic period deposits at Cerros, indicating a lack of elite activity at the site during that period. Such goods are found at other Classic period sites in Belize (Hammond 1973, 1975, 1979; Pendergast 1976, 1979, 1981; Thompson 1931, 1939, 1964; Willey *et al.* 1965). It is during the Classic period, only after Cerros has ceased to function as a political or economic center, that utilitarian objects of raw materials obtained through long distance trade are imported to Cerros. The sources of manos and metates, for example, illustrate the changing nature of the trade networks. As Table 8.1 shows, in the late Preclassic 71.2% of the manos and metates were obtained via regional contacts from the Maya Mountains. None were imported via the long-distance

TABLE 8.1

MANOS AND METATES BY SOURCE
FOR EACH PERIOD

Source	Late Preclassic	Classic	Postclassic
Local	28.8	45.9	26.7
Maya Mts.	71.2	48.6	63.3
Long Distance	0.0	5.4	1.0
	n=52	n=37	n=30

routes despite the presence of jade, obsidian and crystalline hematite at the site from the same source area. In the Classic, however, 5.4% of the manos and metates are obtained through long-distance contacts, possibly indicating that long distance contacts were broadened in scope and were no longer restricted to nonutilitarian elitist material culture. Alternatively, it may be that Cerros' function as a redistribution node and trans-shipment point for products in northern Belize that were destined for inland exchange by way of the New River may have been eliminated during the Classic. This suggestion is supported by the increasing importance of local sources for these implements during this period. These alternatives can only be assessed as more Late Preclassic and Classic data from the interior and Yucatecan coastal sites become available.

The Postclassic Period at Cerros witnesses the re-emergence of elitist activity as evidenced by a large Postclassic cache containing many highly prized exotics including jade, gold, and tumbaga. This elitism did not include the construction of monumental architecture and is restricted to seemingly ceremonial activities, as indicated by the high proportion of incensarios. Many artifacts relating to Postclassic domestic activities have been recovered on many of the smaller mounds, but they appear to represent ephemeral deposits.

CONCLUSION

Cerros functioned as a community from Late Preclassic times through the Postclassic. However, the nature of this community changed drastically through time. These changes are reflected in the artifact assemblages and contexts in which they are found.

The Late Preclassic deposits at Cerros exhibit a wide range of artifact types and contexts. These contexts include: monumental architecture construction fill, dedicatory caches, domestic debris, and, at the close of the Preclassic Period, deposits resulting from termination rituals. The behaviors reflected by these contexts are in sharp contrast to those recognized for the Classic Period at Cerros which imply predominantly domestic activities. At the end of the Late Preclassic, Cerros ceases to function as a center for political, religious and elitist activity, but continues as a locus for more mundane activities.

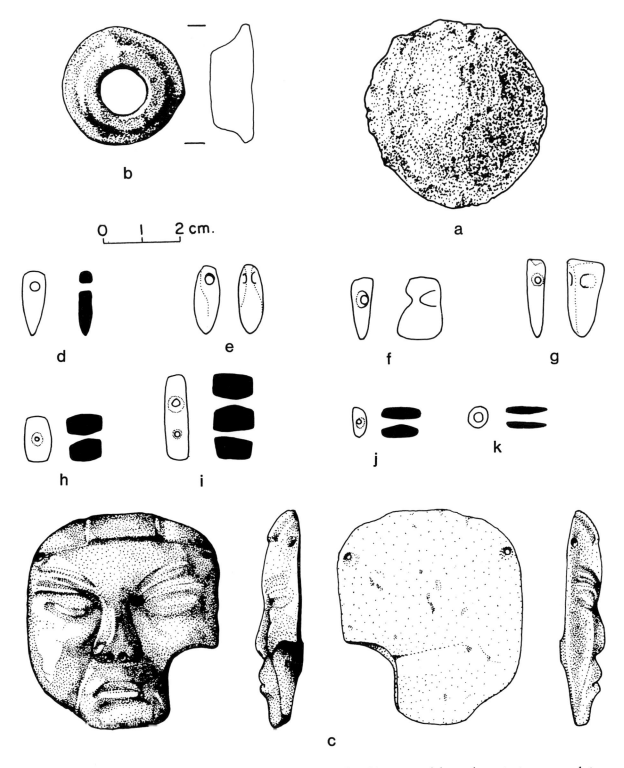

Figure 8.1. Artifacts from termination rituals in the monumental architecture and domestic contexts. a, ground stone spheroid; b, jade ear flare; c, Olmecoid jade head; d-k, shell beads.

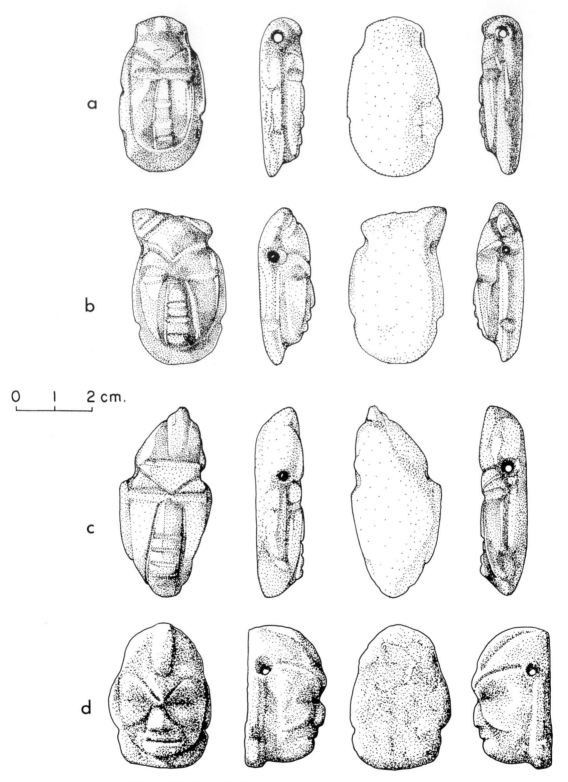

Figure 8.2. Jade bib head pendants from cache on Structure 5C.

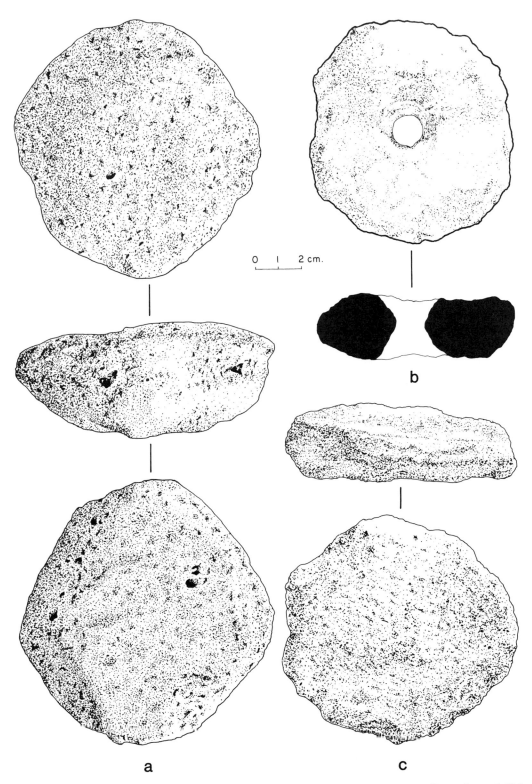

Figure 8.3. Ground stone artifacts. a and c, burned limestone disks; b, centrally perforated disk.

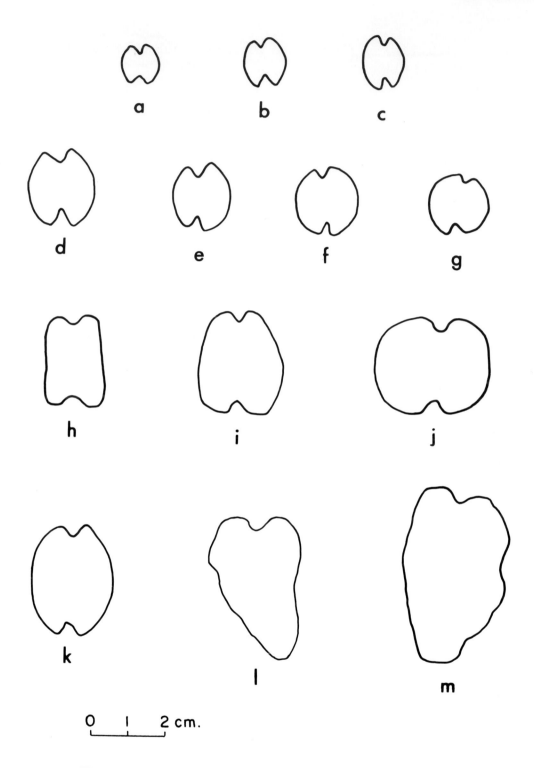

Figure 8.4. Mariposas. a-g, molded mariposas; h-m, notched sherds.

PRELIMINARY RESULTS OF ANALYSIS OF FAUNA

Helen Sorayya Carr

The excavations at the Late Preclassic Maya site of Cerros have yielded a relatively good sample of faunal remains, both vertebrate and invertebrate. The molluscan material is being analyzed by Anthony Andrews. The present author is conducting the analysis of the vertebrate and crustacean remains. This research is being carried out at the Florida State Museum of the University of Florida with the permission and guidance of Dr. Elizabeth S. Wing.

Faunal material recovered to date has come almost exclusively from excavations in the nucleated village area of the site on and near the shore of Corozal Bay. At present only the material from Ops 1a and 1b in the village area has been studied. This material consists of 1,119 fragments, two-thirds of which are from Op 1a. This material was recovered by screening with quarter-inch mesh. Flotation and finer-screened samples have been taken but have not yet been analyzed.

The present study is a preliminary one, the results of which serve to provide an initial characterization of the Cerros faunal assemblage and some ideas concerning the relative importance of various species and the environmental zones exploited. Further study will provide a more balanced view of faunal exploitation at Cerros and will no doubt involve modifications of the conclusions presented here.

GOALS AND METHODS OF ANALYSIS

The eventual goals of the analysis of fauna from Cerros are as follows:
1) to determine what fauna were used at Cerros
2) to determine what habitats were exploited as sources of fauna
3) to investigate the methods and scheduling of hunting and fishing activities
4) to estimate the relative importance of exploited species (to the degree that this may be determined, given the limitations of present analytical methods)
5) to discern any changes through time in faunal use and investigate possible reasons for such changes.

6) to examine any differences in faunal use between distinct social contexts within the site.

Ethnographic information on local faunal exploitation will be incorporated into the study. In addition, I began a comparative collection of modern fauna from the Cerros area during the 1979 field season and continued to add to it in 1981. However, because this collection comprises only a few specimens, the identification of archaeological faunal material has been based primarily on comparison with modern specimens from a variety of circum-Caribbean and Gulf of Mexico locations housed at the University of Florida.

Identification of crustacean remains was based on claw morphology and, in the case of the stone crab, the thick, stonelike nature of the claw. Certain blue crab identifications were checked with Terry Leithauser of the Invertebrate Paleontology Department at the Florida State Museum. He agreed that the identification was probably correct, but pointed out that claw morphology does vary between individuals (and even between claws on one individual) and thus generally is not used as a diagnostic characteristic in keys.

Chondrichthyes vertebrae were identified by inspection combined with the use of a key currently being developed by H. Stephen Hale of the Department of Zooarchaeology at the Florida State Museum. This key uses a height:length index and slope of the vertebral centrum for identification.

Much of the teleost material consists of unidentifiable spines and flakes of bone. There are also many unidentified vertebrae, most of which belong to a generalized percomorph type which probably cannot be more closely identified. The catfish bones were identified largely on the basis of surface texture.

Dr. Walter Auffenberg of the Department of Herpetology at the Museum aided in the distinction of certain *Chrysemys* and *Rhinoclemys* (pond turtle) shell fragments.

The agouti/Mexican porcupine identification was made on the basis of the size and form of a single worn incisor and thus could not be more specific. *Odocoileus* and *Mazama* were distinguished on the basis of bone size and antler morphology.

The quantification of archaeological faunal data has been the subject of a number of papers (e.g., Casteel 1977, 1978; Thomas 1969; Grayson 1979). There are three basic methods which are most commonly used: the fragments method, the minimum number of individuals (MNI), and the weight method. All of these have limitations and basic assumptions which make the validity of statistical manipulation of the data questionable. The final study will use all these methods, given that a comparison of the results of different methods provides at least some indication of the reliability of inferences based on them.

This preliminary study emphasizes the use of fragment counts and biomass estimates based on bone weight. The MNI has been recorded for each species in each lot. This is of limited utility at the present time, however, because the figures will change at a later stage in the study when certain lots which appear to belong to the same deposit are combined. At present, all the lots are being kept separate in order to identify and potentially significant differences among them. Moreover, although most lots were separated in the field on the basis of actual changes in the matrix, certain ones were arbitrary divisions within apparently homogeneous deposits. If no significant distinctions are noted in the material, data from these lots will eventually be combined. Since the calculated MNI varies with the degree of subdivision of the material (Grayson 1979:204), a large number of small lots, such as those from the nucleated village area at Cerros, will produce a relatively large overall MNI for the sample. If the arbitrary lots remained separated without indications of significant differences between them, the resulting MNI could be unjustifiably high. When the final MNI figures have been determined, meat weights will be estimated using the figures originally proposed by White (1953). Because of the variables which are involved in the MNI counts (discussed by Grayson 1979:203-213), size variations between populations within a species, and the fact that the assumption of use of all parts which are edible by our standards may be erroneous in specific cases, meat weights derived on the basis of MNI must be viewed as suggestive but not definitive.

The vertebrate biomass estimates used in the present study are derived from bone weights through the use of scaling formulas (Prange *et al*. 1979). Like other methods designed for the quantification of faunal data, this one has its drawbacks. A major problem is that the estimated biomass is affected by the state of preservation of the bones. Leaching will decrease bone weight and lower the biomass estimate, while mineralization will have the opposite effect. In the case of the Cerros sample none of the bones are heavily mineralized, but in certain lots the soil matrix was a cement-like mixture which could not be entirely removed from the bones without danger of destroying the bones themselves. Thus, a few of the bones scaled to improperly large biomass figures. Nonetheless, within any one lot the amount of adhering "cement" or degree of erosion from roots and so on was fairly consistent.

A major advantage of the bone weight-biomass method is that it does not involve the assumption that a single bone found in a certain context indicates the use of the entire animal in that context. Although this assumption is not a problem with very small animals, in the case of a larger animal, such as a deer, it may well be erroneous, particularly in a complex society where food-sharing among relatives, trade, tribute to elites, and the offering of meat for religious purposes might have occurred. While the biomass estimate resulting from the scaling of a single bone is not an exact reflection of the amount of biomass represented by that bone, it does not include parts of the animal not directly represented in the archaeological sample. Another advantage of the method is that it is applicable to classes as well as to species. Therefore it can be applied to a much higher percentage of the sample than can the MNI method, given that many bones may be identifiable only to the class level.

The biomass derived from this method is not a meat-weight. It includes the skeleton, viscera, etc., as well as the muscle meat. Although it may be converted to a meat weight estimate by taking a certain percentage of it, this procedure adds another level of assumptions and could result in inaccurate figures if the ancient people did not eat the same parts that we generally consider edible. Because it is possible to get some idea of the relative contribution of different species which is directly based on the biomass (Wing, personal communication 1980), this will be the method employed in this paper.

Testing has shown that fairly accurate determinations of weight may be made based on certain skeletal dimensions, using scaling formulas which apply to broad taxa such as teleosts or terrestrial mammals (Wing, personal communication 1980). However, this method can only be applied to a very small proportion of the elements studied to date and thus has not been used in this report.

Given that crustacea are a regularly occurring, significant component of the faunal assemblage at Cerros, some estimate of biomass should be used which allows the incorporation of the crustacea into estimates of the relative contribution of various species and of aquatic fauna as a whole. This is the weakest aspect of the quantification used here. Although Prange (1977:180) suggested, based on studies of spiders and cockroaches, that the mass of an arthropod exoskeleton should be proportional to the body mass in a way that is similar to the relationship between skeletal and body mass of vertebrates, attempts at using scaling formulas to derive biomass from exoskeletal mass of crabs have not proved successful to date (Sylvia Scudder, personal communication 1980). Thus, no formula was available which permitted the determination of crustacean biomass in a way analogous to that used for vertebrates. The only records available at this time are a series of total weights recorded for blue crabs in Florida and one total weight for a stone crab, both on file in the Department of Zooarchaeology at the Florida State Museum. In this report, the MNI per lot multiplied by the average recorded biomass for the species has been used as a very rough estimate of biomass represented by the crustacean fragments. This involves the assumption that a single claw represents an entire animal consumed at one place. This assumption is fairly safe when applied to crabs, as opposed to larger animals such as deer. The application of an "average weight" to a species which does not stop growing through the mechanism of epiphyseal fusion is, of course, a highly questionable procedure. Another problem is that there is no way to estimate biomass for the unidentified crustacea. Thus, relative proportions of different species in terms of biomass in lots including crustacea should be seen as tentative. Further work on the Cerros fauna will include an attempt to arrive at a better determination of crustacean weights.

DISCUSSION

Environment

The peninsula on which Cerros is located, together with surrounding water bodies, offers a variety of faunal habitats which, assuming no drastic environmental change has occurred, could have been exploited by the occupants of the site.

Climax forest, which in this area of pronounced wet and dry seasons would be deciduous (British Directorate of Overseas Surveys Maps 1958), may or may not have been available near Cerros at the time of occupation. It is not known to what extent the land was cleared for farming or other activities. However, even if the climax forest was not locally available, it is likely that certain areas were in a relatively advanced stage of floral succession, as is now the case, so that some type of "high bush" could have been exploited by residents of the site.

Land cleared for habitation and agriculture was certainly available in the immediate area of the site. Guamil or successional vegetation would occur in fallow milpas or any other area which was cleared and then left undisturbed. This vegetation, generally thick and brushy, may also occur in or around savannas.

Savannas, seasonally flooded patches of grassland, occur today in the vicinity of the site. Savanna vegetation may be maintained by flooding, poor drainage, or natural or man-made fires.

A large aguada, which is also seasonally flooded and supports short grass on what seems to be a vertisol soil during the dry season, is also available within an hour's walk of the site center.

The largest water body in the immediate vicinity of Cerros is Corozal Bay, a subdivision of Chetumal Bay. Although changes in the coastline have occurred since the time of occupation, as evidenced by erosion which has cut into the midden deposit in the nucleated village, the presence of an apparent Preclassic dock in the village area indicates that the shore was close to the village at the time of occupation. Corozal Bay is relatively shallow and brackish. The shoreline includes sandy and silty areas and patches of mangrove thicket.

Approximately 3 km to the east of Cerros, within easy walking distance, is Laguna Seca, a shallow lagoon (normally containing water, despite its name) lined with mangroves and connected with lagoons to the south by John Piles Creek. A lagoon environment is also provided by Saltillo Lagoon, about 4 km southwest of the site.

A riverine environment is provided by the New River at the south end of Corozal Bay. River banks in this area characteristically support a shrubby thicket (Neill and Allen 1959:15). The British D.O.S. maps (1958) also show some herbaceous marsh and swamp vegetation along the river.

Also exploitable by boat are the reefs and cays of the Carribbean Sea. The presence of a dock suggests that the use of boats occurred on a substantial scale and that these may have included sizable ones capable of traveling between Cerros and the cays.

The environmental situation suggests that a fairly wide variety of fauna, particularly aquatic species, may have been exploited at Cerros. This expectation is borne out by the identification of the remains, among which thirty-five non-human taxa have been distinguished, twenty-seven (or 77%) of which are aquatic.

Species Identified

1) Crustaceans
   a) *Callinectes* sp.—blue crab
   b) *Menippe mercenaria*—stone crab
   c) Unidentified crustacean (all other fairly complete claws seem to belong to a single type)
2) Chondrichtyes
   a) Carcharhinidae, including *Negaprion* sp. (probably *brevirostris*) and perhaps *Carcharhinus* sp.— requiem sharks, including lemon shark
   b) *Sphyrna tiburo*—bonnethead shark
   c) Sphyrnidae (other than *S. tiburo*)—hammerhead sharks
   d) Rajiformes—rays
3) Teleosts
   a) *Megalops atlantica*—tarpon
   b) *Elops saurus*?—ladyfish (could also be small tarpon)
   c) *Albula vulpes*—bonefish
   d) *Ictalurus* sp. or Ariidae—catfish
   e) Serranidae, including *Epinephalus* sp.—groupers
   f) Carangidae, including *Caranx* sp.—jacks
   g) Lutjanidae, including *Lutjanus* sp.—snappers
   h) Gerreidae, including *Diapterus plumieri*—mojarras, including striped mojarra
   i) Pomadasyidae, probably *Haemulon* sp.—grunts
   j) *Sphyraena* sp.—barracuda, sennet
   k) *Scarus* sp.—parrotfish
   l) *Sparisoma* sp. (Scaridae)—parrotfish
   m) Labridae, probably *Lachnolaimus maximus*—wrasses, probably hogfish
   n) *Acanthurus* sp.—surgeonfish
   o) Balistidae (Monacanthidae)—triggerfish, filefish
4) Reptiles
   a) *Staurotypus triporcatus*?—musk turtle
   b) Kinosternidae (other than *S. triporcatus*)—mud turtles
   c) *Chrysemys scripta*—slider turtle
   d) *Rhinoclemys* sp., probably *areolata*—black-bellied turtle
   e) *Caretta caretta* or *Lepidochelys kempi*—loggerhead or ridley turtle
5) Birds
   a) Only unidentified fragments whose thinness suggests bird bone
6) Mammals
   a) *Oryzomys* sp. or *Nyctomys sumichrasti*?—rice rat or vesper rat
   b) *Sigmodon hispidus*—hispid cotton rat
   c) *Dasyprocta punctata* or *Coendou mexicanus*—agouti or Mexican porcupine
   d) *Urocyon cinereoargenteus*—grey fox
   e) *Canis familiaris*—dog
   f) *Odocoileus virginianus*—white-tailed deer
   g) *Mazama americana*—red brocket

A large number of fragments were too incomplete to identify with any accuracy. Many of these could be identified to class, while others could not. These include some very tiny fragments. All fragments identifiable to class could be used in scaling formulas to derive biomass estimates. Of the fragments which are completely unidentified, most are probably mammalian, but a positive identification can not be made at this time.

The majority of identified fauna are teleosts. Of these, the best-represented taxon is the family Carangidae (jacks), which comprises approximately one-third of the teleosts identified beyond class level on the basis of both fragments and biomass.

Mammals comprise 42% of the sample by biomass and 13% by fragments. The dog and white-tailed deer predominate.

Contexts

The material examined from Op 1a comes from eight levels and four separately excavated burials, divided into a total of 31 lots. The material from Op 1b comes from five levels, one burial, and three features and is divided into thirteen lots (see Table 9.1).

A comparison of the fauna from Ops 1a and 1b

shows that among the categories for which biomass could be calculated (all fragments identifiable at least to the class level), the same groups contribute the most biomass to both samples. Unidentified teleosts provide the greatest amount in both cases, followed by white-tailed deer, blue crab, and dog. Together these groups comprise 52% of the biomass of Op 1a and 52.3% of Op 1b. Unidentified teleosts also rank highest with regard to fragment counts.

There are, however, certain differences between the operations. On initial inspection Op 1b contains a greater proportion of large fragments than does Op 1a. This is due partly to the different relative proportions of various species. Large inflated jack bones, for example, are particularly prominent in Op 1b and large tarpon vertebrae appear in Op 1b. The one vertebra of the tarpon family (Elopidae) occurring in Op 1a in contrast is much smaller and could be ladyfish rather than tarpon. In Op 1b the very few recognizable turtle fragments are equally divided between large sea turtles and pond turtles, whereas in Op 1a the smaller pond turtles clearly predominate.

Mammals other than rats constitute a greater proportion of the fauna of Op 1b than of Op 1a in terms of both fragment counts and biomass. Op 1a, unlike Op 1b, includes a large number of rat-sized rodent bones. With a single exception, these are all from one burial. During excavation the concentration of rodent bones was noticed and special care was taken to recover them. The one small rodent bone from another context was a tibia from a stratum described as midden with possible burial admixture.

When midden lots, unmixed with other deposits, are compared, the major distinction which appears between the operations is the greater number of turtle bones in Op 1a. These are mostly found in a rich black midden layer. A greater percentage of the bones in Op 1a than in Op 1b were classed as totally unidentifiable. There may have been somewhat more fragmentation of the material in Op 1a due to the intrusion of several burials and a few apparent animal burrows. It is interesting that a disjunction between these two operations was also revealed by the ceramics. The excavator has suggested that these differences are due to the large number of burial pits in Op 1a and the presence of a large trash pit and structure floors in Op 1b (Cliff, personal communication 1980).

Except for the careful recovery of rodent bones from Burial 1 of Op 1a, the excavation and recovery techniques employed were the same for both sub-operations and could not be responsible for the differences in collected material.

Functional Contexts

A number of functionally distinct contexts occur in Op 1. In addition to the ordinary trash deposits there are structural contexts, such as floors and walls, and burials. Trash pits, as opposed to layers of trash on the surface, also represent a different type of deposition.

Considering the floors first, Lot 40 (Level 9) in Op 1a consisted of marl or plaster layers with thin midden layers sandwiched in between. As expected, this lot yielded relatively little in the way of faunal material. The two recovered bone fragments may well have come from the sandwiched midden material. A white marl layer later in the sequence (Level 3) also yielded only two fragments. Similarly, Lot 16 (Level 6), consisting of tan and grey soil fill overlain by patches of flooring, was fairly extensive but yielded only ten fragments of bone.

In Op 1b, Lot 4 consisted of marl wash, most likely from a stone wall (Feature 3). It yielded much less faunal material (only 4 fragments) than non-construction lots of comparable volume.

Although burials may be expected to be distinctive in their contents, several factors obscure the distinction at Cerros. One is the practice of interring the dead in pits within the midden, fill, or other such deposits in the village. If a pit is dug in a midden, at least some of the fill may be expected to be this same midden material. Thus, faunal remains and other debris in the burial actually may not be associated with it in the sense of being offerings, leftovers from a funeral feast, and so on. A second problem is a related one: the burial may not be immediately distinguishable as a separate deposit during excavation, resulting in mixed lots where some of the burial fill is included with the surrounding matrix. This occurred to some extent with all four burials in Op 1a. Further confusion may be caused by the repeated disturbance of the deposit by multiple burials and other pits, which may overlap, as was apparently the case with Burial 15 and Feature 9 (a trash pit) in Op 1b.

Burial 1, represented by Lots 7 and 8 in Op 1a, was distinctive mainly in the preponderance of small rodent bones. A large number of tiny fragments belonging to small bones could not be identified for certain except as "small animal," but they are most likely rodent bones as well. Rats and rat-sized animals constitute approximately 42% of the fragments in Lot 7 and 88% of the fragments in Lot 8. Among the categories for which MNI could be computed, the rodents constitute the majority of the individuals in these lots. Lot 7 included a hardened deposit of tan soil. Other areas of tan to yellowish soil were interpreted by the excavator, Maynard Cliff, as probable animal burrows on the basis of the nature of the soil and the size and form of the deposit. The presence of material of this color in Lot 7 could well be associated with the heavy concentration of rodent bones. Burial 1 also yielded a number of other fragments representing a cross-section of the fauna found in the village area as a whole. The same is true of the other burials in Ops 1a and b. On the basis of this variety of fauna and the descriptions of the deposits which formed the fill of these burials, I am convinced that these bones are for the most part accidental inclusions in the fill of the burial pits. In the case of Burial 15 in Op 1b, the burial is known to have overlapped with the fill of a pit, which could be the source of many of the bones.

Two identified teleosts have been found so far only in a burial context (Burial 3): Labridae (hogfish) and Balistidae (triggerfish). However, each is represented by only a single, unmodified element, and does not provide a basis for speculation on a significant association between these species and burials.

One fragment in Burial 3, however, is puzzling and possibly may be more closely associated with the burial itself. This is the left frontal of a small grey fox with a round hole in it which may have been drilled. There are no other indications of modification on this bone. Although there is no known ritual emphasis placed on the fox by the Maya, and this frontal does not make a particularly attractive pendant, drilling seems to be the only explanation for this quite evenly-shaped hole. It was initially thought to be a modern intrusion into the deposit which had been shot, but the fact that a delicate bone protrusion within the skull just below the hole was undamaged makes this unlikely.

Three non-burial pits occurred in Op 1b. Feature 5, described as a pit with dark midden fill excavated into marl, was small in volume and yielded only seven faunal bone fragments. There was nothing unusual in the composition of the fauna.

Feature 6, also excavated into the same marl, was similar in volume to Feature 5. It is described as a pit filled with mottled soil and burned stones. It yielded a much higher volume of faunal material than Feature 5, including thirty-three fragments, of which 79%

belonged to teleosts. It may have served as a hearth at one time and later as a trash pit.

Feature 9 is also a pit that is somewhat smaller in volume than the others but also was filled with trash. It yielded forty faunal fragments. The identified bones in all of these features are of species that could have been eaten; the interpretation of these features as general trash pits is most likely correct. I am unable to explain the lower number of fragments in Feature 5, a pit of comparable size to the others.

One other type of feature should be distinguished from the midden material. This is the possible animal burrows. These features could not always be separated from the surrounding matrix in the field. However, Op 1a, Lot 14 is designated as a lot from a probable burrow. It was a very small lot and yielded only one unidentified fragment. An animal burrow was incorporated into Lot 18 of Op 1a but was mixed with burial fill. Op 1a, Lot 22, another burrow, yielded ten fragments, mostly of fish, which must have been incorporated from the surrounding deposits. None of these burrows contained bones which could be identified as belonging to the animals that probably made them, nor did the bones in the burrows seem to be gnawed more than those found elsewhere.

The remaining lots are largely midden material. The dark midden making up many of the lots in Op 1a is very rich in fauna, as is the grey marly deposit in Op 1b.

Chronological Considerations

Inspection of the amounts of bone in general, and of particular taxa, has not at this point revealed any notable trends through time. It has been suggested (Cliff, personal communication 1980) that there may have been a lower reliance on terrestrial animals early in the sequence which increased in upper levels even though marine resources continued to be heavily exploited. At present the faunal data from Ops 1a and 1b do not seem to support this suggestion. However, it is possible that the distribution of molluscs, which has not been examined at present, does point to such a trend. There is a slight tendency for the relative proportion of aquatic fauna to increase as the total number of fragments per lot increases. This is presumably due to sampling error in the smaller lots, as well as taphonomic factors.

Not surprisingly, great reliance was placed on aquatic resources throughout the sequence. While the few deer and dog bones that occur represent a great deal more meat than the individual small fish bones and indicate that these terrestrial species may have been quite a significant component of the diet, the aquatic species biomass figures and the number of fragments and the individuals they represent suggest that the primary orientation of the village occupants, with regard to time spent in procuring and preparing meats, was toward marine/estuarine resources. In support, Pohl (1976:157) has pointed out that straight bone counts may give a better indication of the focus of subsistence activities than meat weights in certain cases. Presumably as more operations are studied, diachronic trends in faunal utilization may begin to emerge.

Utilization of Fauna

The small rodents, including rats, which are concentrated primarily in Burial 1 of Op 1a, are interpreted as a natural, rather than cultural, inclusion in the deposit. The bones show no signs of modification (such as burning) and in some cases are more complete and in better condition than the other bones.

A few bones show evidence of butchery or cooking. Many of the teleost and crab fragments simply have darkened surface areas. In most cases it is hard to tell whether or not this is simply a stain from the soil and roots which may affect these materials more than other faunal material for some reason. Certain teleost bones and crab claws in contrast show definite indications of burning. Apparent burning also occurs on three turtle-shell fragments, the bones of one dog, the large rodent incisor, one possible bird bone, and several unidentified bones, including some from medium (cat- or dog-sized) to large mammals.

Butchery and skinning marks are very rare. Possible small butchery marks occur on two dog, two deer, and a few unidentified fragments.

Despite the general lack of butchery marks and burning, most of the species represented here, aside from the rats, are likely to have been eaten. At the present time, blue crabs, pond turtles of a type locally called *ixcanis*, which may be *Chrysemys* (Pohl, personal communication 1980), deer and various other mammals, birds, and a variety of fish are caught and eaten by the local people. Only a few of the archaeologically represented animals are not normally eaten now. One of these is the dog. However, dogs were consumed by the Maya in Yucatan at the time of Spanish contact (Pohl 1976:152), and Wing (1981:24, 26) states that in Formative times dogs were intensively used on the Caribbean coast of the Maya area. An interesting pattern is emerging which may prove to be significant. Dogs are represented at Cerros by a dentary, five teeth, one axis, and ten limb bones (which comprise 58.8% of the fragments). Of these latter, all the long bones belong to the forequarters. The hindquarters are represented only by metatarsals. It is tempting to suggest that the main meat cuts of the hindquarters were being consumed by other people or perhaps were used as an offering. Dogs were a popular sacrifice in Yucatan at the time of Spanish contact. Although dog sacrifice at that time stressed the use of the heart and blood (Tozzer 1941:114-115), the ritual use of certain meat cuts is perhaps somewhat analogous to the use of left sides of animals in ritual contexts in Classic Peten sites (Pohl 1976:173). It should be noted, however, that at this point the dog sample from Cerros is too small to form the basis for firm conclusions.

According to the local people, the fox is not eaten, even though the grey fox is hunted in Yucatan today (Birney *et al.* 1974:16). The significance of the apparently drilled fox frontal from Burial 3 may well have been of a ceremonial or even souvenir nature, rather than being related to subsistence.

Of the other mammals identified, deer, brocket, and agouti are edible. If the large rodent incisor belonged to a Mexican porcupine rather than an agouti, the animal's purpose may have been ritual in nature. The modern Maya use the quills in an acupuncture related manner for relieving illness (Pohl 1976:181). A group of mammalogists recently found a porcupine for sale in the market in Merida, Yucatan, which had supposedly been brought all the way from Chetumal, near the Belizean border in Quintana Roo (Birney *et al.* 1974:16).

The two identified crabs are edible; in fact, these types are currently the commercially important crabs in the Gulf of Mexico (Bender 1971:1).

Chondrichthyes vertebrae are uncommon. They may represent occasional catches for food, although there is no proof of such use. The only ray identified is not a stingray and probably was not captured for ceremonial purposes.

Of the teleosts represented at the site, most are currently considered good food fish, even though larger individuals of a few species (barracuda, groupers, and jacks) can cause *ciguatera* poisoning (Randall 1968:3,

22, 54-55, 61, 108-109, 128, 201-202). The Elopidae are currently valued by North Americans as game fish rather than food fish (Ibid.:20). Mojarras (*Gerreidae*) are among the fish commonly caught and eaten by the family living at the Cerros site.

Catfish are eaten in parts of Belize, according to Janet Gibson of the Belizean Department of Forestry and Fisheries (personal communication 1979). They are plentiful in Corozal Bay in the shallow water near the site, but they are not eaten by the family living at the site because they are known to relish the garbage that is deposited in the bay. Recognizable catfish bones occur in the archaeological collection but are lower in frequency than would be expected given their apparently high numbers in the bay at present. It could be that they were not favored in the Preclassic, perhaps for the same reason. The scarcity of catfish in the collection could also reflect the procurement methods used, suggesting netting rather than the use of hooks or spears. Groupers, which are generally caught by hook or spear, occur in comparatively substantial numbers in the sample. It is possible that spears were used in reef areas (where groupers often occur and where clearer water would make this method more efficient) but not in the muddy bay.

Loggerhead turtles, although not considered the best eating among sea turtles, are edible, as are their eggs (Ingle and Smith 1949:39). Of the non-marine turtles, *Chrysemys* and *Staurotypus* are definitely eaten in Belize today (Neill and Allen 1959:28, 29). A type of turtle called *ixcanis*, which is probably *Chrysemys*, is caught and eaten today in the area of the site.

Another possible use for faunal material is the making of bone artifacts. Artifact fragments are not common in this sample, even though several mammal bones do show striations and polishing. Some worked bone fragments may have been waste fragments from toolmaking, such as blanks. Other fragments are clearly parts of tools themselves. One teleost pterygiophore with a somewhat higher polish than most fish bones may have been used as a small awl-like tool.

Environmental Zones Represented

Although certain of the animals in the Cerros collection, such as brocket, could have been obtained in climax forest, there is no convincing evidence for the exploitation of this habitat. Brockets can occur in less forested areas although they generally stay far from

human habitation (Pohl, personal communication 1980). In this connection, it is not surprising that of the cervid remains identified in the Cerros collection, only two fragments were assigned (one quite tentatively) to *Mazama*. A few were uncertain, while several were assigned to *Odocoileus*, the white-tailed deer, which prefers the brushy low forest characteristic of second growth (Pohl 1976:136).

Cleared land, including fields, could have been the source of certain animals found at Cerros. Crops would be likely to lure such animals as the white-tailed deer and various rodents. Deer are attracted to recently burned land and thus may have been lured to burned fields late in the dry season. It has even been suggested that the Maya may have burned areas partly as a form of game management, as is done in some tropical areas today (Pohl 1976: 210). The grey fox will also venture into clearings and may be quite bold in approaching houses when there is not a lot of human activity there (personal observation and cf. Murie 1935:21).

Successional vegetation or "low bush" in fallow fields and bajos would have been another source of white-tailed deer. This zone is the most favored habitat of the species (Pohl 1976:136) and would have yielded grey fox as well (Burt and Grossenheider 1976:76).

The savannas and aguada are likely sources of the non-marine turtles in the Cerros collection. Specimens of *Kinosternon, Rhinoclemys*, and *Chrysemys* have been found in savanna and temporary rain pool habitats, although *Chrysemys* prefers permanent fresh water (Neill and Allen 1959:29; Neill 1965:115; Henderson and Hoevers 1975:55). *Ixcanis* turtles are also found in both the high and low bush areas of the site. In addition, savannas and aguadas would have been sources of small fish and game such as deer in the rainy season. Pohl (1976:45), for example, mentions that *nance* fruit lures game to the Peten savannas in the wet season. The presence of *nance* seeds in flotation samples from Op 1 at Cerros (Cliff, this volume and Crane, this volume) suggests that such may have been the case here as well.

It is difficult to pinpoint the source of many of the aquatic fauna in this area because of its estuarine nature. The water has a fresh, brackish, and salt gradient. Many species tolerate a fairly wide range. The workmen at the site report that a number of species occur in everything from savanna, rivers and lagoons to Corozal Bay. Fish found at Cerros which are available in fresh or brackish water are the tarpon, ladyfish, jacks, mojarras, grunts, catfish, and lemon shark (personal observation; Randall 1968:11, 20-21, 128). Moreover, the barracuda and bonefish occur in shallow water over muddy bottoms, which suggests that they might be found in Corozal Bay (Randall 1968:22, 54).

Reef fish represented in the sample include many groupers, parrotfish, surgeonfish, and triggerfish. Hogfish may occur in reefs but are more common over open bottoms (Ibid.:202, 217, 255, 258). Although snappers are generally deeper-water forms (Gibson, personal communication 1980), the presence of these fish does not necessarily indicate direct exploitation of reefs and deep water. These fish often are pushed into the bay by hurricanes (Gibson, personal communication 1980) and the grey snapper occurs near the shore among mangroves. Occasionally they even enter fresh water (Randall 1968:122). However, although they do not constitute the majority of the fish sample, these fish are common enough to strongly suggest fishing in reef and deep-water zones.

Loggerhead turtles may be found near estuaries as well as in deeper water (Ingle and Smith 1949:21). Sea turtles may also be captured when they come ashore to lay eggs, but whether or not there are any breeding grounds within a reasonable distance of the site is not known at present.

Crabs would have been obtained near the shore. At present blue crabs are caught in Corozal Bay immediately adjacent to the site.

Significance of Animals Not Represented

Very few of the bones in the Cerros collection appear to belong to birds, although *chachalacas* (*Ortalis vetula*) and parrots are now caught in the area and other birds, including the now rare wild turkey, have been mentioned by the Cerros workmen. The lack of bird bones may be partly due to their delicate nature. A similar paucity of birds was noted by Pohl (1976:112) at the Peten sites.

Identifiable land mammal remains in this sample show very little variety. Peccary and armadillo, for instance, are not represented, although they are certainly edible and would probably have been locally available. These data support the impression that subsistence activities stressed procurement of a variety of aquatic resources, with terrestrial meat sources largely restricted to the relatively profitable white-tailed deer and conveniently available domestic dog.

Procurement Methods

Spears, blowguns, nets, and presumably traps were available to the Maya for hunting and fishing. Notched sherds (*mariposas*), which are thought to be net weights, are common at Cerros, testifying to the use of this fishing method.

At present nets are used to catch the mojarra and other small shallow-water fish in Corozal Bay. Elopidae, bonefish, barracuda, groupers, and jacks may be caught on a hook and line, while at least certain groupers are easily speared (Randall 1968:20-22, 54, 58, 115). Both spears and nets are used to capture sea turtles in the water (Ingle and Smith 1949:36-37).

Dogs were used to hunt deer and birds in Yucatan at the time of Spanish contact. In the Peten today they are used for deer and small game. Maya polychromes show hunters with spears stalking game without dogs (Pohl 1976:214, 218). These techniques may have been used in the Preclassic as well.

At present the data provide no direct evidence for seasonal hunting and fishing. Most fish are available year-round, although tarpon are most readily available from May to July and grunts (represented by only one fragment) are most available from September to November (Gibson, personal communication 1979). Fishing in savanna areas occurs during the summer rainy season, but since the fish from these sources also occur elsewhere, it is difficult to determine seasonality from this evidence.

Deer might have been particularly easy to hunt toward the end of the dry season if they were attracted to burned-over fields. The one antler in the sample is very eroded at the proximal end, making it difficult to determine whether or not it was shed naturally.

Within the small sample studied to date, a clear clustering of certain species which might have been obtained at a certain season has not been noted. The concentration of *Rhinoclemys* remains in Levels 7 and 8 within the black midden stratum in Op 1a, however, is suggestive. As more of the Cerros material is examined, some indications of seasonal scheduling may emerge.

CONCLUSIONS

This study has served mainly to provide initial ideas which can be tested and refined with further study. The questions of procurement methods, scheduling, and environmental zones represented will be examined further, as will the question of diachronic change in faunal use. The lack of certain edible land mammals in the collection has served to suggest that the economy was oriented toward the use of aquatic resources, while the only terrestrial meat sources which were frequently used were deer and domestic dogs. The deer provided a large amount of meat and bones useful for tools and may have been found near fields. The dog bones at present show a pattern which suggests differential use of the fore- and hindquarters. The question of whether these characteristics of the faunal sample are simply artifacts of sample size or are valid reflections of faunal utilization patterns at Cerros should become clear as more material is analyzed.

TABLE 9.1

CONTENTS OF LOTS

Lot	Level/Feature	Species	Fragments	%	MNI[1]	%	Bone Weight (kg)	Biomass (kg)[2]	%
Operation 1a:									
3	L2	*Callinectes* sp.	1	50.0	1	50.0	0.0007	0.0394	52.5
		Medium to large mammal	1	50.0	1	50.0	0.0014	0.0356	47.5
			2	100.0	2	100.0	0.0021	0.0750	100.0
3 & 4	L2	Unidentified	1	100.0	1	100.0	0.0003		(100.0)
5	L3	Unidentified	2	100.0		(100.0)	0.0001		(100.0)
6	L4	*Callinectes* sp.	2	11.1	1	20.0	0.0007	0.0394	19.8
		Unidentified crustacean	1	5.6			0.0002		
		Menippe sp.	2	11.1	1	20.0	0.0050	0.0735	36.9
		Albula vulpes?	1	5.6	1	20.0	0.0001	0.0046	2.3
		Unidentified teleost	3	16.7			0.0016	0.0432	21.7
		Kinosternidae?	1	5.6	1	20.0	0.0005	0.0171	8.6
		Canis familiaris	1	5.6	1	20.0	0.0008	0.0215	10.8
		Unidentified	7	38.9			0.0053		
			18	100.2	5	100.0	0.0142	0.1993	100.1
7	B1	*Callinectes* sp.	1	1.1	1	16.7	0.0003	0.0394	29.3
	L7, 8	Sphyrnidae	1	1.1	1	16.7	0.0003	0.0447	33.3
		Unidentified teleost	4	4.4			0.0005	0.0168	12.5
		Unidentified bird	1	1.1	1	16.7	0.0001	0.0025	1.9
		Sigmodon hispidus?	1	1.1	1	16.7	0.0002	0.0062	4.6
		Oryzomys sp./*Nyctomys sumichrasti?*	3	3.3	2	33.3	0.0001	0.0033	2.5
		Unidentified rodent	18	19.8			0.0008	0.0215	16.0
		Unidentified small animal, probably rodent	16	17.6			0.0001		
		Unidentified	46	50.5			0.0075		
			91	100.0	6	100.1	0.0099	0.1344	100.1

[1]MNI was calculated only for bones identified at least to the genus level; crustacean claws belonging to a distinct, though single unidentified or class-identified bones occurring alone or with no other bones of the same class.

[2]All crab biomass estimates are based on the MNI, not the bone weight method (see text for a discussion of this). Since all identified reptiles are turtles, the turtle formula was provisionally used to derive biomass estimates for unidentified reptiles as well.

Table 9.1 continued

Lot	Level/Feature	Species	Fragments	%	MNI[1]	%	Bone Weight (kg)	Biomass (kg)[2]	%
8	B1	Scaridae	1	0.8	1	33.3	0.0002	0.0080	6.4
		Oryzomys sp.	12	10.1	2	66.6	0.0001	0.0033	2.7
		Unidentified rodent	18	15.1			0.0003	0.0089	7.2
		Large mammal	2	1.7			0.0046	0.1039	83.7
		Unidentified small animal, probably rodent	75	63.0			0.0004		
		Unidentified	11	9.2			0.0038		
			119	99.9	3	99.9	0.0094	0.1241	100.0
9	L5	Callinectes sp.	2	11.1	1	25.0	0.0009	0.0394	35.2
		Unidentified crustacean	1	5.6			0.0011		
		Sphyraena sp.	1	5.6	1	25.0	0.0002	0.0080	7.2
		Unidentified teleost	3	16.7			0.0005	0.0168	15.0
		Kinosternidae?	1	5.6	1	25.0	0.0006	0.0194	17.4
		Unidentified turtle	1	5.6			0.0002	0.0091	8.1
		Canis familiaris	1	5.6	1	25.0	0.0007	0.0191	17.1
		Unidentified	8	44.4			0.0010		
			18	100.2	4	100.0	0.0052	0.1118	100.0
10	L6	Callinectes sp.	5	5.4	2	14.3	0.0041	0.0788	6.0
		Unidentified crustacean	3	3.2	1	7.1	0.0021		
		Negaprion sp.	1	1.1	1	7.1	0.0004	0.0572	4.4
		Negaprion sp./Carcharhinus sp.	1	1.1			0.0001	0.0174	1.3
		Epinephalus sp.?	1	1.1	1	7.1	0.0009	0.0271	2.1
		Serranidae	1	1.1	1	7.1	0.0017	0.0454	3.5
		Carangidae?	6	6.5	1	7.1	0.0012	0.0342	2.6
		Lutjanidae	2	2.2	1	7.1	0.0007	0.0221	1.7
		Diapterus plumieri	1	1.1	1	7.1	0.0002	0.0080	0.6
		Pomadasyidae ((Haemulon sp.?)	1	1.1	1	7.1	0.0002	0.0080	0.6
		Sphyraena sp.	1	1.1	1	7.1	0.0001	0.0046	0.3
		Scarus sp.	2	2.2	1	7.1	0.0053	0.1139	8.7
		Acanthurus sp.	2	2.2	1	7.1	0.0005	0.0168	1.3
		Unidentified teleost	49	52.7			0.0460	0.6559	49.9
		Unidentified turtle	2	2.2	1	7.1	0.0005	0.0171	1.3
		Unidentified reptile?	3	3.2			0.0006	0.0194	1.5

Table 9.1 continued

Lot	Level/Feature	Species	Fragments	%	MNI[1]	%	Bone Weight (kg)	Biomass (kg)[2]	%
(Lot 10 cont.)		*Odocoileus virginianus*	1	1.1	1	7.1	0.0077	0.1651	12.6
		Unidentified mammal	1	1.1			0.0009	0.0239	1.8
		Unidentified	10	10.8			0.0032		
			93	100.5	14	99.5	0.0764	1.3020	100.2
11	L6	*Callinectes* sp.	3	11.1	1	16.7	0.0012	0.0394	11.3
		Unidentified crustacean	1	3.7			0.0003		
		Acanthurus sp.	1	3.7	1	16.7	0.0003	0.0111	3.2
		Sphyraena sp.	1	3.7	1	16.7	0.0002	0.0080	2.3
		Unidentified teleost	9	33.3			0.0041	0.0925	26.6
		Unidentified turtle	1	3.7	1	16.7	0.0009	0.0256	7.4
		Unidentified reptile (sea turtle?)	1	3.7	1	16.7	0.0006	0.0194	5.6
		Canis familiaris	1	3.7	1	16.7	0.0042	0.0957	27.5
		Unidentified mammal	1	3.7			0.0023	0.0557	16.0
		Unidentified	8	29.6			0.0010		
			27	99.9	6	100.2	0.0151	0.3474	99.9
12	L6	*Callinectes* sp.	1	25.0	1	50.0	0.0006	0.0394	42.1
		Unidentified teleost	2	50.0			0.0004	0.0140	15.0
		Unidentified mammal	1	25.0	1	50.0	0.0016	0.0402	42.9
			4	100.0	2	100.0	0.0026	0.0936	100.0
13	L7	*Callinectes* sp.	1	1.4	1	9.1	0.0008	0.0394	5.6
		Unidentified crustacean	2	2.9	2	9.1	0.0033		
		Unidentified Chondrichthyes	1	1.4	1	9.1	0.0001	0.0174	2.5
		Megalops atlantica/Elops saurus	1	1.4	1	9.1	0.0001	0.0046	0.7
		Sphyraena sp.	1	1.4	1	9.1	0.0002	0.0080	1.1
		Carangidae	1	1.4	1	9.1	0.0027	0.0660	9.4
		Diapterus plumieri	2	2.9	1	9.1	0.0007	0.0221	3.1
		Sparisoma sp.	1	1.4	1	9.1	0.0004	0.0152	2.2
		Acanthurus sp.	3	4.3	1	9.1	0.0006	0.0195	2.8
		Unidentified teleost	34	48.6			0.0129	0.2342	33.3
		Unidentified amphibian/reptile	1	1.4			0.0001	0.0056	0.8
		Rhinoclemys sp.	4	5.7	1	9.1	0.0034	0.0641	9.1
		Rhinoclemys sp.?	1	1.4			0.0012	0.0312	4.4

Table 9.1 continued

Lot	Level/Feature	Species	Fragments	%	MNI[1]	%	Bone Weight (kg)	Biomass (kg)[2]	%
(Lot 13 cont.)		*Odocoileus virginianus*	1	1.4	1	9.1	0.0082	0.1748	24.9
		Unidentified	16	22.9			0.0014		
			70	99.9	11	100.1	0.0361	0.7021	99.9
14	L7	Unidentified	1	100.0	1	100.0	0.0003		(100.0)
15	L7	Unidentified crustacean	1	9.1			0.0005		
		Carangidae	1	9.1	1	33.3	0.0005	0.0168	14.5
		Unidentified teleost	7	63.6	1	33.3	0.0032	0.0757	65.2
		Chrysemys sp./*Rhinoclemys* sp.	1	9.1	1	33.3	0.0008	0.0236	20.3
		Unidentified	1	9.1			0.0014		
			11	100.0	3	99.9	0.0064	0.1161	100.0
16	L8	Unidentified crustacean	1	3.1	1	12.5	0.0005		
		Ictalurus sp./Ariidae	1	3.1	1	12.5	0.0003	0.0111	1.8
		Sparisoma sp.	1	3.1	1	12.5	0.0005	0.0168	2.8
		Unidentified teleost	12	37.5			0.0028	0.0680	11.2
		Sea turtle	1	3.1	1	12.5	0.0069	0.1044	17.2
		Rhinoclemys sp.	4	12.5	2	25.0	0.0032	0.0615	10.1
		Unidentified turtle	1	3.1			0.0006	0.0194	3.2
		Mazama americana?	1	3.1	1	12.5	0.0086	0.1824	30.0
		Unidentified rodent	2	6.2	1	12.5	0.0002	0.0062	1.0
		Large mammal	2	6.2			0.0056	0.1240	20.4
		Unidentified mammal	1	3.1			0.0005	0.0141	2.3
		Unidentified	5	15.6			0.0008		
			32	99.7	8	100.0	0.0305	0.6079	100.0
17	L8	Unidentified crustacean	2	9.1			0.0007		
		Sphyraena sp.	1	4.5	1	20.0	0.0003	0.0111	8.7
		Epinephalus sp.?	2	9.1	1	20.0	0.0012	0.0342	26.8
		Acanthurus sp.	2	9.1	1	20.0	0.0004	0.0140	11.0
		Unidentified teleost	14	63.7	1	20.0	0.0020	0.0517	40.5
		Unidentified bird	1	4.5	1	20.0	0.0008	0.0167	13.1
			22	100.0	5	100.0	0.0054	0.1277	100.1
18	L8	Carcharhinidae	1	6.7	1	33.3	0.0001	0.0174	20.2
		Sphyraena sp.	1	6.7	1	33.3	0.0002	0.0080	9.3

Table 9.1 continued

Lot	Level/Feature	Species	Fragments	%	MNI[1]	%	Bone Weight (kg)	Biomass (kg)[2]	%
(Lot 18 cont.)		*Acanthurus* sp.	1	6.7	1	33.3	0.0007	0.0221	25.6
		Unidentified teleost	10	66.6			0.0014	0.0388	45.0
		Unidentified	2	13.3			0.0003		
			15	100.0	3	99.9	0.0027	0.0863	100.1
19	L8	*Callinectes* sp.	2	6.7	1	50.0	0.0004	0.0394	19.5
		Rajiformes	1	3.3	1	50.0	0.0002	0.0315	15.6
		Unidentified teleost	20	66.7			0.0016	0.0432	21.4
		Medium to large mammal	2	6.7			0.0038	0.0875	43.4
		Unidentified	5	16.7			0.0013		
			30	100.1	2	100.0	0.0073	0.2016	99.9
20	L8	Unidentified Chondrichthyes	1	25.0	1	50.0	0.0001	0.0174	28.1
		Medium mammal	1	25.0	1	50.0	0.0018	0.0446	71.9
		Unidentified	2	50.0			0.0001		
			4	100.0	2	100.0	0.0020	0.0620	100.0
22	L8	*Caranx* sp.	2	20.0	1	50.0	0.0096	0.1843	80.4
		Unidentified teleost	7	70.0			0.0014	0.0388	16.9
		Unidentified mammal	1	10.0	1	50.0	0.0002	0.0062	2.7
			10	100.0	2	100.0	0.0112	0.2293	100.0
23	L8	Unidentified teleost	1	100.0	1	100.0	0.0001	0.0046	100.0
24	B2	*Callinectes* sp.	1	7.1	1	100.0	0.0001	0.0394	33.8
		Medium to large mammal	3	21.4			0.0033	0.0770	66.2
		Unidentified	10	71.4			0.0019		
			14	99.9	1	100.0	0.0053	0.1164	100.0
25	B3	Balistidae/Monacanthidae	1	12.5	1	50.0	0.0003	0.0111	9.6
		Unidentified teleost	1	12.5			0.0001	0.0046	4.0
		Urocyon cinereoargenteus	1	12.5	1	50.0	0.0012	0.0310	26.9
		Large mammal	2	25.0			0.0029	0.0686	59.5
		Unidentified	3	37.5			0.0002		
			8	100.0	2	100.0	0.0047	0.1153	100.0
28	L9	Unidentified teleost	1	100.0	1	100.0	0.0003	0.0111	100.0

Table 9.1 continued

Lot	Level/Feature	Species	Fragments	%	MNI[1]	%	Bone Weight (kg)	Biomass (kg)[2]	%
30	L9	Unidentified	1	100.0	1	100.0	0.0002		(100.0)
31	L9	Unidentified crustacean	1	20.0	1	33.3	0.0001		
		Labridae (*Lachnolaimus maximus?*)	1	20.0	1	33.3	0.0030	0.0719	62.4
		Serranidae	1	20.0	1	33.3	0.0014	0.0388	33.7
		Unidentified teleost	1	20.0			0.0001	0.0046	4.0
		Unidentified	1	20.0			0.0003		
			5	100.0	3	99.9	0.0049	0.1153	100.1
33	B5	Carangidae	2	5.0	1	33.3	0.0011	0.0319	12.2
		Acanthurus sp.	1	2.5	1	33.3	0.0003	0.0111	4.3
		Unidentified teleost	10	25.0			0.0007	0.0221	8.5
		Rhinoclemys sp.	1	2.5	1	33.3	0.0022	0.0475	18.2
		Unidentified reptile?	4	10.0			0.0003	0.0120	4.6
		Medium mammal	2	5.0			0.0055	0.1220	46.8
		Unidentified mammal	4	10.0			0.0005	0.0141	5.4
		Unidentified	16	40.0			0.0030		
			40	100.0	3	99.9	0.0136	0.2607	100.0
34	L9	Unidentified	1	100.0	1	100.0	0.0005		(100.0)
35	L9	*Callinectes* sp.	1	5.3	1	33.3	0.0010	0.0394	13.4
		Unidentified teleost	1	5.3	1	33.3	0.0004	0.0140	4.7
		Canis familiaris	2	10.5	1	33.3	0.0111	0.2295	77.8
		Medium mammal	1	5.3			0.0001	0.0033	1.1
		Small to medium mammal	1	5.3			0.0003	0.0089	3.0
		Unidentified	13	68.4			0.0060		
			19	100.1	3	99.9	0.0189	0.2951	100.0
37	L9	*Callinectes* sp.	1	12.5	1	50.0	0.0005	0.0394	46.2
		Unidentified teleost	5	62.5			0.0001	0.0046	5.4
		Chrysemys scripta	1	12.5	1	50.0	0.0018	0.0413	48.4
		Unidentified	1	12.5			0.0004		
			8	100.0	2	100.0	0.0028	0.0853	100.0
39	L9	*Ictalurus* sp./Ariidae	1	14.3	1	50.0	0.0001	0.0046	9.9
		Unidentified teleost	5	71.4			0.0003	0.0111	23.8

Table 9.1 continued

Lot	Level/Feature	Species	Fragments	%	MNI[1]	%	Bone Weight (kg)	Biomass (kg)[2]	%
(Lot 8 cont.)		Sphyraena sp.	1	3.0	1	25.0	0.0001	0.0046	2.3
		Acanthurus sp.	3	9.1	1	25.0	0.0005	0.0168	8.4
		Unidentified teleost	21	63.6			0.0036	0.0833	41.9
		Unidentified mammal	2	6.1			0.0019	0.0469	23.6
		Unidentified	3	9.1			0.0001		
			33	99.9	4	100.0	0.0068	0.1990	100.0
9	L5	Callinectes sp.	25	14.7	7	41.2	0.0179	0.2758	10.5
		Unidentified crustacean	6	3.5			0.0003		
		Carcharhinidae	1	0.6	1	5.9	0.0002	0.0315	1.2
		Megalops atlantica	1	0.6	1	5.9	0.0021	0.0538	2.1
		Albula vulpes	1	0.6	1	5.9	0.0010	0.0295	1.1
		Epinephalus sp.	2	1.2	1	5.9	0.0075	0.1509	5.8
		Serranidae	2	1.2			0.0048	0.1051	4.0
		Serranidae/Lutjanidae	1	0.6			0.0022	0.0559	2.1
		Caranx sp.	1	0.6	1	5.9	0.0017	0.0454	1.7
		Acanthurus sp.	4	2.4	1	5.9	0.0009	0.0271	1.0
		Unidentified teleost	92	54.1			0.0393	0.5774	22.1
		Sea turtle	2	1.2	1	5.9	0.0072	0.1075	4.1
		Dasyprocta punctata/Coendou mexicanus	1	0.6	1	5.9	0.0002	0.0062	0.2
		Canis familiaris	4	2.4	1	5.9	0.0267	0.5057	19.3
		Odocoileus virginianus	1	0.6	1	5.9	0.0020	0.0491	1.9
		Cervidae	1	0.6			0.0074	0.1593	6.1
		Medium mammal	4	2.4			0.0078	0.1671	6.4
		Large mammal	1	0.6			0.0133	0.2701	10.3
		Unidentified	20	11.8			0.0075		
			170	100.3	17	100.2	0.1500	2.6174	99.9
10	L5	Callinectes sp.	5	17.2	2	33.3	0.0036	0.0788	15.0
		Unidentified crustacean	3	10.3			0.0006		
		Megalops atlantica?	1	3.4	1	16.7	0.0069	0.1411	26.8
		Carangidae	2	6.9	1	16.7	0.0097	0.1859	35.3
		Unidentified teleost	15	51.7			0.0038	0.0870	16.5
		Unidentified reptile?	1	3.4	1	16.7	0.0005	0.0171	3.2
		Unidentified mammal	1	3.4	1	16.7	0.0006	0.0166	3.2

Table 9.1 continued

Lot	Level/Feature	Species	Fragments	%	MNI[1]	%	Bone Weight (kg)	Biomass (kg)[2]	%
(Lot 39 cont.)		Unidentified	1	3.4			0.0005		
		Canis familiaris	29	99.7	6	100.1	0.0262	0.5265	100.0
			1	14.3	1	50.0	0.0012	0.0310	66.4
			7	100.0	2	100.0	0.0016	0.0467	100.1
40	L9	Unidentified teleost	1	50.0	1	50.0	0.0004	0.0140	3.4
		Odocoileus virginianus	1	50.0	1	50.0	0.0202	0.3934	96.6
			2	100.0	2	100.0	0.0206	0.4074	100.0
Operation 1b:									
2	L2	Mazama americana	1	33.3	1	100.0	0.0008	0.0215	100.0
		Unidentified	2	66.7			0.0005		
			3	100.0	1	100.0	0.0013	0.0215	100.0
4	L3	Unidentified teleost	1	25.0	1	50.0	0.0005	0.0168	18.8
		Cervidae	1	25.0	1	50.0	0.0031	0.0728	81.3
		Unidentified	2	50.0			0.0012		
			4	100.0	2	100.0	0.0048	0.0896	100.1
6	L4	Callinectes sp.	1	14.3	1	50.0	0.0006	0.0394	70.4
		Homo sapiens?	1	14.3	1	50.0	0.0011	Not included in meat calculations	
		Large mammal	1	14.3			0.0006		
		Unidentified	4	57.1			0.0017	0.0166	29.6
			7	100.0	2	100.0	0.0040	0.0560	100.0
7	F5	Callinectes sp.	1	14.3	1	33.3	0.0005	0.0394	56.8
		Carangidae?	1	14.3	1	33.3	0.0004	0.0140	20.2
		Gerreidae?	1	14.3	1	33.3	0.0002	0.0080	11.5
		Unidentified teleost	1	14.3			0.0002	0.0080	11.5
		Unidentified	3	42.9			0.0011		
			7	100.1	3	99.9	0.0024	0.0694	100.0
8	F6	Callinectes sp.	1	3.0	1	25.0	0.0002	0.0394	19.8
		Unidentified crustacean	1	3.0			0.0002		
		Albula vulpes	1	3.0	1	25.0	0.0002	0.0080	4.0

Table 9.1 continued

Lot	Level/Feature	Species	Fragments	%	MNI[1]	%	Bone Weight (kg)	Biomass (kg)[2]	%
11	L5	Callinectes sp.	8	8.0	2	13.3	0.0065	0.0788	3.5
		Unidentified crustacean	9	9.0	1	6.7	0.0031		
		Carcharhinidae	1	1.0	1	6.7	0.0006	0.0811	3.6
		Sphyrna tiburo	1	1.0	1	6.7	0.0004	0.0572	2.6
		Megalops atlantica	2	2.0	1	6.7	0.0029	0.0699	3.1
		Serranidae	3	3.0	2	13.3	0.0066	0.1361	6.1
		Caranx sp.?	1	1.0	1	6.7	0.0009	0.0271	1.2
		Carangidae	6	6.0			0.0139	0.2488	11.2
		Lutjanus sp.	1	1.0	1	6.7	0.0021	0.0538	2.4
		Lutjanidae?	1	1.0			0.0006	0.0195	0.9
		Scarus sp.	1	1.0	1	6.7	0.0026	0.0640	2.9
		Unidentified teleost	32	32.0			0.0209	0.3462	15.6
		Caretta caretta/Lepidochelys kempi	1	1.0	1	6.7	0.0135	0.1659	7.5
		Kinosternidae	1	1.0	1	6.7	0.0010	0.0275	1.2
		Unidentified reptile?	1	1.0			0.0017	0.0397	1.8
		Unidentified bird?	2	2.0			0.0004	0.0089	0.4
		Canis familiaris	4	4.0	1	6.7	0.0218	0.4213	18.9
		Odocoileus virginianus	1	1.0	1	6.7	0.0042	0.0957	4.3
		Medium mammal	7	7.0			0.0077	0.1651	7.4
		Medium to large mammal	4	4.0			0.0053	0.1180	5.3
		Unidentified	13	13.0			0.0050		
			100	100.0	15	100.3	0.1217	2.2246	99.9
12	L5	Callinectes sp.	3	17.6	1	20.0	0.0040	0.0394	7.2
		Menippe sp.	3	17.6	1	20.0	0.0098	0.0735	13.3
		Scarus sp.	1	5.9	1	20.0	0.0014	0.0388	7.0
		Unidentified teleost	4	23.5			0.0037	0.0852	15.5
		Staurotypus triporcatus?	1	5.9	1	20.0	0.0007	0.0215	3.9
		Canis familiaris	1	5.9	1	20.0	0.0087	0.1843	33.5
		Medium to large mammal	4	23.5			0.0048	0.1079	19.6
			17	99.9	5	100.0	0.0331	0.5506	100.0
13	B15	Callinectes sp.	5	26.3	2	40.0	0.0056	0.0788	29.0
		Megalops atlantica	1	5.3	1	20.0	0.0031	0.0738	27.2

Table 9.1 conclusion

Lot	Level/Feature	Species	Fragments	%	MNI[1]	%	Bone Weight (kg)	Biomass (kg)[2]	%
(Lot 13 cont.)		Unidentified teleost	3	15.8			0.0017	0.0454	16.7
		Unidentified bird?	1	5.3			0.0006	0.0128	4.7
		Medium mammal	1	5.3	1	20.0	0.0005	0.0141	5.2
		Medium to large mammal	2	10.5	1	20.0	0.0019	0.0469	17.3
		Unidentified	6	31.6			0.0023		
			19	100.1	5	100.0	0.0157	0.2718	100.1
14	F9	*Callinectes* sp.	3	7.5	1	10.0	0.0017	0.0394	3.4
		Carcharhinidae	1	2.5	1	10.0	0.0003	0.0447	3.9
		Sphyraena sp.	1	2.5	1	10.0	0.0002	0.0080	0.7
		Serranidae	2	5.0	2	20.0	0.0138	0.2473	21.4
		Caranx sp.?	1	2.5	1	10.0	0.0021	0.0538	4.6
		Carangidae	8	20.0			0.0154	0.2703	23.3
		Diapterus plumieri	1	2.5	1	10.0	0.0007	0.0221	1.9
		Acanthurus sp.	2	5.0	1	10.0	0.0007	0.0221	1.9
		Unidentified teleost	11	27.5			0.0064	0.1327	11.5
		Unidentified bird?	2	5.0			0.0008	0.0167	1.4
		Canis familiaris	1	2.5	1	10.0	0.0079	0.1690	14.6
		Cervidae	1	2.5	1	10.0	0.0048	0.1079	9.3
		Medium to large mammal	1	2.5			0.0009	0.0239	2.1
		Unidentified	5	12.5			0.0030		
			40	100.0	10	100.0	0.0587	1.1579	100.0
16	L6	Unidentified teleost	4	36.4			0.0044	0.0980	6.2
		Kinosternidae	1	9.1	1	33.3	0.0016	0.0381	2.4
		Canis familiaris	1	9.1	1	33.3	0.0008	0.0215	1.4
		Odocoileus virginianus	1	9.1	1	33.3	0.0731	1.2518	79.2
		Large mammal	1	9.1			0.0062	0.1359	8.6
		Unidentified mammal	2	18.2			0.0014	0.0356	2.3
		Unidentified	1	9.1			0.0012		
			11	100.1	3	99.9	0.0887	1.5809	100.1
17	L6	Unidentified	2	100.0		(100.0)	0.0109		(100.0)

LATE PRECLASSIC MAYA AGRICULTURE, WILD PLANT UTILIZATION, AND LAND-USE PRACTICES

Cathy J. Crane

The main goals of the botanical research at Cerros are 1) to investigate Late Preclassic Maya agricultural practices and wild plant utilization, and 2) to examine Maya land-use practices by attempting to reconstruct the type(s) of vegetation present during the Late Preclassic. It is probable that the Maya extensively modified the composition of the vegetation on Lowry's Bight (Scarborough 1983). The botanical research includes analyses of pollen and macrobotanical remains recovered from Late Preclassic contexts, plus studies of the modern vegetation and its pollen rain.

METHODOLOGY

Extensive flotation of midden deposits was conducted during the excavation of the nucleated village at Cerros (Cliff, this volume). Approximately 325 flotation samples were collected, and a majority contained carbonized plant materials. These macrobotanical remains were examined with a dissecting microscope at 10X and 30X magnifications and identified by comparison with modern reference specimens. The tree species represented by the wood charcoal have not been determined, but eventually the charcoal will be thin sectioned and identified.

Pollen samples were collected from excavation profiles in the village midden, the raised fields, and the canals. The samples were taken in 5cm intervals and the stratigraphy noted. When an unconformity was present, samples were taken on each side of the junction. The samples were placed in whirl-pack bags and phenol was added to prevent destruction of the pollen by micro-organisms.

Approximately 50 pollen samples have been extracted by the modified Chevron method (Woosley 1978; Appendix A). Although the use of this extraction method resulted in the recovery of abundant, well-preserved pollen in all samples, the large amount of minerals and organic materials in the soils made it difficult to process the samples. Consequently, experimentation with other extraction methods is currently

underway to determine which method is most appropriate.

The identification of the pollen grains will be performed with a binocular microscope at 400X and 1000X (oil immersion) magnifications, and 200+ grain counts made. The pollen will be identified by comparison with modern reference materials. Quantitative studies of modern vegetation communities and their pollen rain as well as statistical techniques (e.g., principal component analysis and cluster analysis) will be used to facilitate interpretation of the fossil pollen data.

The pollen, seed and wood specimens needed to build the modern reference collections were obtained from several sources. A majority of the specimens came from plant collections made by the author during two field seasons at Cerros. Dr. Cyrus Lundell is in the process of determining the taxonomics of the Cerros plant specimens, and the plants identified by him to date are listed alphabetically by family in Table 1. Specimens of cultivated crops were collected from local markets, and from the *milpas* and kitchen gardens of the Maya farmers in Chunox. The reference collections were further supplemented by pollen and seeds collected from vouchered herbarium specimens housed at the SMU Herbarium and the Lundell Herbarium in Dallas.

LATE PRECLASSIC MAYA SUBSISTENCE PRACTICES

The macrobotanical remains indicate that the typical Mesoamerican triad of maize, beans and squash was cultivated during the Late Preclassic at Cerros. Maize cupules and/or kernels were present in approximately 75% of the samples, and consequently, it is probable that maize was a major staple of the community. More than one variety of maize is present in the samples, and eventually a more detailed analysis of the maize remains will be conducted to determine the types of maize grown. Six varieties of maize were grown at Cuello during the Late Preclassic (Miksicek *et al.* 1981), and it is likely that a similar situation existed at Cerros.

The remains of beans and squash were rare at Cerros, but this may be due, in part, to differential preservation and the methods used to prepare these foods for consumption (e.g., boiling). A few bean (*Phaseolus vulgaris*) cotyledons were recovered from Operation 41, and they appear to be quite similar to the small, black bean (called *samakbu'ul* or *frijole Veracruzano*) grown by the Maya *milperos* today. Although no squash seeds were found in the samples, the cultivation of squash at Cerros was confirmed by the recovery of squash (*Cucurbita pepo*) pollen from a midden deposit in Operation 41. In addition, several small fragments of possible squash rind were found in the same midden deposit.

The cultivation of cotton at Cerros during the Late Preclassic is suggested by the presence of *Gossypium* type pollen in the midden deposits of Operation 41. Since cotton is known to have been cultivated during the Late Preclassic at the nearby site of Cuello (Hammond and Miksicek 1981), it seems likely that it was also cultivated at Cerros. Furthermore, remains of textiles were found in a Postclassic cache in Structure 4A, and also in a Preclassic Burial in Op 33 (Cliff, personal communication 1985).

Several people have postulated that arboriculture was an important component of Maya subsistence. Lundell (1938) noted that there was a high correlation of several trees, including *ramon* (*Brosimum alicastrum*), *zapote* (*Achras zapota*), *mamey* (*Calocarpum mamosum*), avocado (*Persea americana*), *kinep* (*Talisia olivaeformis*), and persimmon (*Diospyros ebenaster*) with Maya ruins, and he suggested that they were relics of prehistoric orchards. Subsequently, Puleston (1974, 1978) postulated that the *ramon* nut was the primary staple of the Maya in the Peten. No *ramon* nuts have been recovered from an archaeological context, however, and it seems unlikely that the *ramon* nut was the primary staple since the sixteenth century Maya considered it to be a famine food (Marcus 1982:250). Furthermore, a more likely explanation for the distribution of *ramon* and other economically important tree species at Maya sites is that their requirements for growth and reproduction are optimal on the ruins (Lambert and Arnason 1982).

The macrobotanical remains from Cuello, Pulltrouser Swamp and Cerros indicate that the Late Preclassic Maya did utilize a number of tree species, but it is not known if they were actually cultivating any of these trees. This is because it is difficult, if not impossible in most cases, to determine whether a particular carbonized seed came from a wild or cultivated tree since the seeds of many cultivated trees do not differ morphologically from those of their wild relatives. Furthermore, the evidence for the utilization of several economic trees during the Late Preclassic consists solely of wood charcoal making the issue of cultivated versus wild even more problematical. At Cuello and Pulltrouser Swamp, for example, utilization of avocado, hogplum (*Spondias spp.*), zapote, guava (*Psidium guajava*), allspice (*Pimenta officinalis*), and *jicara* (*Crescentia cujete*) is represented only by fragments of wood charcoal (Turner and Miksicek 1981). Seeds from these trees have not been recovered from a Late Preclassic Maya context.

Further evidence for tree cultivation during the Late Preclassic is the presence of cacao beans at Cerros because neither *Theobroma cacao* nor *T. bicolor* grows in the wild in northern Belize. The extremely small number of cacao bean fragments found at Cerros, however, does not negate the possibility that the inhabitants obtained cacao beans through trade. Presently, the evidence needed to demonstrate that cacao was an important commercial and ritual crop as early as the Late Preclassic is lacking.

Also present in the Cerros flotation samples are seeds from two other trees which may have been cultivated, since they do not grow in the wild at Cerros today. These trees are nance (*Byrsonima crassifolia*) and the *cocoyol* palm (*Acrocomia mexicana*). *Nance* seeds are common at Cerros occurring in approximately 40% of the samples. Today *nance* trees are often grown in kitchen gardens for their fruits, which are sold in markets throughout the Yucatan (e.g., Smith and Cameron 1977). In the wild, the *nance* tree is a typical member of the pine savanna community southwest of Cerros. However, *nance* trees do grow today within 3 miles of Cerros, near Progresso lagoon. While it is tempting to speculate that the Maya at Cerros grew *nance* trees in kitchen gardens, it must be admitted that travel to the Progresso lagoon area and back could have been accomplished in one day, and *nance* may have grown in the bush at Cerros during the Late Preclassic. In addition, it has not yet been determined whether the Cerros seeds could actually be from the *nance blanco* tree (*Byrsonima bucidifolia*), which does grow in the high bush at Cerros. *Nance blanco* produces an edible fruit, but it is considered by the Maya to be inferior in taste to *B. crassifolia*.

Fragments of *cocoyol* palm seeds are common in the Cerros village midden. The *cocoyol* fruit is sweet and is commonly eaten by the present-day Maya. The fruit contains a large seed which is covered by a fibrous pulp. The fibers attached to the seed are so tenacious that the author still had difficulty in removing them after the fruits had been boiled for 3 days. Typically the Maya boil the fruit, and after chewing on it for several minutes the seed and masticated pulp are discarded. Today the *cocoyol* palm grows in the bush east of Lowry's Bight, and in general, it is best adapted to open areas with drier soils than those at Cerros (Standley and Record 1936:79).

Fruit seeds found at Cerros include *siricote* (*Cordia dodecandra*) and *huano* (*Sabal mayarum*). Both of these trees are common in the bush at Cerros, and the *siricote* fruits are considered particularly good to eat. The presence of seeds from the common swamp tree, *pucte* (*Bucida buceras*), and herbs such as *Jacquemontia pentantha* and *Euphorbia* sp. in the Cerros flotation samples are probably the result of prehistoric seed rain rather than human utilization of the plants.

VEGETATION RECONSTRUCTION AND LAND-USE PRACTICES

Reconstruction of past vegetation by means of palynology is based upon the assumption that the present-day relationships between the pollen spectra and the vegetation that produced them can be applied throughout the Quaternary. Therefore, the vegetation communities present at Cerros during the Late Pre-classic will be reconstructed from the fossil pollen record by using the modern pollen rain as an analog. The relationships between the modern vegetation and its pollen rain have to be documented, however, in order to calibrate the fossil pollen in terms of vegetation patterns (Markgraf *et al.* 1981:43). This calibration cannot be established theoretically, since studies have shown that the relative percentage of pollen grains and spores present in the sediments does not always correspond to the actual floristic composition of the vegetation (e.g., Webb 1974; Webb and Clark 1977). This is due, in part, to differential pollen production by plant species; and to differences in pollen dispersal mechanisms. For instance, where plant species are primarily insect-pollinated (e.g., in the tropical forest at Cerros), the pollen assemblage found in the sediments will give

an incomplete and essentially deceptive picture of the composition of the vegetation (Caratini *et al.* 1973:282). Consequently, quantitative studies of the modern vegetation at Cerros were conducted in order to document the relationship between the vegetation communities and their pollen spectra.

Seventeen line transects of contiguous 10×10 m quadrats (Lang *et al.* 1971) were placed in representative examples of identifiable community types. Within each quadrat the frequency of all tree species (dbh 2.5 cm or larger), shrubs, vines and epiphytes was recorded. Ground vegetation was sampled using five 1×1m units placed at the same points in each quadrat (Lambert and Arnason 1978:34). Representative samples of all species were collected for positive identification by Dr. Cyrus Lundell. By necessity, subjective sampling rather than stratified random sampling was used to avoid sampling the numerous areas that had been recently disturbed. Samples of the modern pollen rain were colleted from each quadrat using the method advocated by Adam and Mehringer (1975).

The frequencies of the plants identified to date in each transect are shown on Table 2. By placing transects in a number of localities (e.g., secondary bush, high bush, clearings, marsh, shoreline, mangrove swamp, aguada, *bajo*, ruins), it was possible not only to determine the plant compositions of the different vegetation associations, but also to observe the plant compositions of the different successional stages present at Cerros. This information is summarized below.

Successional Stages in the Tropical Dry Forest

A majority of the land surrounding the ceremonial center was cleared of vegetation about 20 years ago when an attempt was made to turn Cerros into a commercial ranch and plantation. Since that time small areas have been repeatedly cleared during the several seasons of archaeological fieldwork and also occasionally for *milpas*. As a result, various stages of succession are present within the settlement.

When the forest is cleared, the first pioneer species are small, herbaceous plants such as milkweed (*Asclepias curassavica*), *kuxubcan* (*Rivina humilis*), *sakpiche* (*Achyranthes indica*), *hobonkaax* (*Euphorbia heterophylla*), *pajilla* (*Commelina erecta*), *toplanxiw* (*Melanthera nivea*), various grasses, and numerous vines including morning glory

(*Ipomoea purpurea*), sombrerito azul (*Jacquemontia pentantha*), sorosee (*Momordica charantia*), xtulub (*Melothria trilobata*), chacmots (*Sicydium tamnifolium*), duck flower (*Centrosema plumieri*), ibuul (*Phaseolus lunatus*), passionflower (*Passiflora* spp.) and *tabkan* (*Cissus sicyoides*).

After a year or two a brambly, intertwined association of such species as xcanan (*Hamelia patens*), tulipan (*Malvaviscus arboreus*), pata de vaca (*Bauhinia divaricata*), tezak (*Byttneria aculeata*), palabra de caballero (*Lantana camara*), ochmul (*Triumfetta dumetorum*), latche (*Cornutia* sp.), and (*Solanum* spp.), become established in clearings. In abandoned *milpas*, papaya and guarumo (*Cecropia peltata*) become dominant. This shrub stage is replaced in 10 to 15 years by a low forest, 20–40 ft. high, with a broken canopy. Most of the Cerros settlement is currently covered by a forest of this type. In the area enclosed by the main canal, *pereskuch* (*Croton reflexifolius*) is the dominant tree, but caimito silvestre (*Chrysophyllum mexicanum*), moho (*Hampea trilobata*), chechem (*Metopium browneii*), boob (*Coccoloba belizensis* and *C. cozumelensis*), chacah (*Bursera simaruba*), pixoy (*Guazuma ulmifolia*), persimmon (*Diospyros* spp.), huano (*Sabal mayarum*), guarumo, tsulubmay (*Colubrina ferruginosa*), subin (*Acacia collinsii* and *A. glomerosa*), and several members of the Rubiaceae and Leguminosae families are common components.

On the western edge of the settlement approaching the New River the forest is more *bajo*-like in character. It differs from the area enclosed by the canal in that there is a dense understory composed of spine-covered species such as poknoboy (*Batris major*), katsim (*Mimosa hemiendyta*), una de gato (*Pisonia aculeata*), pinuela (*Bromelia karatas*), and xtub (*Aechmea bracteata*). The raised-field platforms located on the northeast terrace of the New River are covered with dense thickets composed of hulub (*Bravaisia tubiflora*), *pereskuch*, persimmon, and *huano*.

High bush (trees 50–70 ft. tall) exists on the southern periphery of the settlement where some areas have not been cleared for at least 35 years. Common trees in the high bush include negrito (*Simarouba glauca*), laurel (*Nectandra coriacea*), yaxnik (*Vitex gaumeri*), sapote (*Achras zapota*), chechem, ramon blanco (*Trophis racemosa*), chacah, chechem de caballo (*Cameraria latifolia*), boob, huano, caimito silvestre. Only a few specimens of mahogany (*Swietenia macrophylla*), cedar (*Cedrela mexicana*), and Santa Maria

(*Calophyllum brasiliense*) remain in the forest, since most of the trees have been culled by logging operations in this century. Plants present in the undergrowth of the high bush include a palm (*Desmoncus schippi*) and several species of xmakulan (*Piper*) and bakelak (*Psychotria*).

Marsh

Interspersed among the forest are small areas which hold standing water during most of the year and support large stands of cattails (*Typha domingensis*) and sedges. When the marsh dries out around February or March, the cattails are replaced by grasses and several species of *Solanum*. Surrounding the marshes are trees such as pucte (*Bucida buceras*), escabeche (*Pithecolobium dulce*), and pixoy (*Guazuma ulmifolia*) with a shrub understory of muc (*Dalbergia glabra*), hulub (*Bravaisia tubiflora*) and occasionally *Mimosa pigra*.

Vegetation on Ruins

Although the vegetation on the major Structures 3 and 6 has been partially cleared, it is obvious that the remaining vegetation forms a characteristic association that is readily distinguished from the surrounding forest. The *ramon* (*Brosimum alicastrum*) is the dominant tree. *Pixoy*, chacah (*Bursera simaruba*), salom (*Lysiloma latisitiqua*), chit (*Thrinax parviflora*) and guarumo (*Cecropia peltata*) occur less frequently. Common shrubs on the ruins include xmakulam (*Piper psilorachis*), palo de caja (*Allophyllus longeracemosus*) and *Chiococco alba*. The fern (*Adiantum tricholepis*), bobtun (*Anthurium schlechtendalii*), *Rhoeodiscolor*, and a tall grass (*Lasiacus papillosa*) form the ground cover. *Ramon*, palo de caja, bobtun and *Adiantum* are rarely found in non-ruin localities at Cerros because their requirements for growth and reproduction are probably optimal on the ruins.

Aguada Forest

The vegetation association found around the large aguada south of the center is distinct from the surrounding high bush. Botan palm (*Sabal mauritiiformis*), chit (*Thrinax parviflora*), tinta (*Haematoxylon campechianum*), *muc*, and *jicara* (*Crescentia cujete*) grow along the edge of the aguada. *Tinta* and *jicara* appear to be restricted to this locality at Cerros. Farther back from the water's edge are various components of the high bush including *negrito*, *chacah*, *chechem*, laurel, *yaxnik*, *boob*, and *sacpom* (*Cupania glabra*) with a shrub understory of *xcansik* (*Jaquinia auriantiaca*), *iximche* (*Casearia nitida*), *pechkitan* (*Randia aculeata*) and *bakelak* (*Psychotria nervosa*).

Shoreline and Mangrove Swamp

Trees growing along the shore, which are adapted to receiving a constant spraying of brackish water from Corozal Bay, include *uva* (*Coccoloba uvifera*), *butoncillo* (*Conocarpus erecta*), coconut (*Cocos nucifera*), *sapote* (*Achras zapota*), *chit* (*Thrinax parviflora*), and white mangrove (*Laguncularia racemosa*). Also common along the water are the shrub, *Bravaisia tubiflora*, and a fern called tiger bush (*Acrostichum aureum*). Pondweed (*Potamogeton pectinatus*) is abundant in the shallow water at the edge of Corozal Bay.

Along the west shore approaching the mouth of the New River, red mangrove trees (*Rhizophora mangle*) have colonized the fluvial sediments that accumulate along the shore. The red mangrove is conspicuous along the shore because of its stilt roots, which are usually exposed at high tide, and its large size (up to 60 ft. tall). Stands of *buttoncillo*, white mangrove, and *hulub* (*Bravaisia tubiflora*) are found in the beach behind the red mangrove trees. Another common plant of most mangrove swamps, *Avicennia mitida*, was not observed along the western shore of Cerros, but may exist in the more extensive area of mangrove swamp located on the south side of Lowry's Bight.

CONCLUSION

The botanical research at Cerros is still in its first stages since much of the lab work remains to be completed. The modern pollen rain samples from the various plant associations have not been extracted, and most of the archaeological pollen samples also await processing. As a result, little is known about late Preclassic land-use practices at this time. The small number of extracted pollen samples from 2 raised field localities did not contain pollen from any type of cultigen. Hence, it is not known what crop(s) were grown on the fields at Cerros. Pollen from several other field and canal localities will be extracted in order to determine the identity of the cultigens grown. Undoubtedly the completion of this research will provide more data on Late Preclassic Maya subsistence and land-use practices. These data, in turn, should aid in the investigation of several current issues in Maya prehistory such as the role of the intensive agricultural systems in the rise of Maya civilization and agriculture trade systems.

TABLE 10.1

List of Plant Specimens Collected at Cerros

Common Name(s)

ACANTHACEAE (Acanthus Family)

Aphelandra deppeana Schlecht. & Cham.	*chacanal*
Blechum brownei Juss.	*akabxiu*
Bravaisia grandiflora Donn. Sm.	
Bravaisia tubiflora Hemsl.	*hulub*
Carolwrightia costaricana Leonard	
Dicliptera assurgens (L.) Juss.	*nimiz*
Justicia sp.	*sulub*
Ruellia nudiflora (Engelm. & Gray) Urban	*kabalyaaxnik*

ADIANTACEAE

Adiantum tricholopis Fee

AIZOACAEAE (Carpetweed Family)

Sesuvium portulacastrum L.	verdolaga de playa
Sesuvium sp.	

AMARANTHACEAE (Pigweed Family)

Achyranthes aspera L.	*sakpiche*
Achyranthes indica (L.) Mill.	
Iresine celosia L.	hierba de gato

ANACARDIACEAE (Cashew Family)

Metopium brownei (Jacq.) Urban	chechem

ANNONACEAE (Custer Apple Family)

Guatteria ampliifolia Triana. & Planch

APOCYNACEAE (Dogbane Family)

Cameraria belizensis Standl.	chechem de caballo, white poisonwood
Cameraria latifolia	chechem blanco de sabana
Mesechites trifida (Jacq.) Muell.-Arg.	
Plumeria multiflora Standl.	*zopilote*
Rhabdadenia biflora (Jacq.) Muell.-Arg.	
Tabernaemontana chrysocarpa Blake	*chutsumpek*
Thevetia ahouai (L.) A. DC.	
Thevetia gaumeri Hemsl. in Hook Icon.	*akits*
Thevetia nitida (HBK) ADC	cojon de perro
Urechites andrieuxii Muell.-Arg.	

ARACEAE (Arum Family)

Anthurium schlechtendalii Kunth.	*bobtun*
Monstera sp.	pinanona
Syngonium podophyllum Schotl.	*ochil*

Table 10.1 continued

Common Name(s)

ASCLEPIADACEAE (Milkweed Family)

Asclepias curassavica L. cancerillo, milkweed
Sarcostemma bilobum Hook and Arn.
Sarcostemma clausum (Jacq.) R. & S.

BIGNONIACEAE (Bignonia Family)

Crescentia cujete L. jicara
Tabebuia rosea (Bertol.) DC. roble blanco

BORAGINACEAE (Borage Family)

Cordia dodecandra A. DC. *siricote*
Cordia sebastiana L. *siricote*
Cordia spinescens L.
Heliotropium angiospermum Murray *nemax*
Tournefortia glabra L. *boxak*

BROMELIACEAE (Pineapple Family)

Aechmea bracteata (SW.) Griseb. *xtub*
Bromelia karatas L. piñuela

BURSERACEAE (Torchwood Family)

Bursera simaruba (L.) Sarg. *chacah*

CAPPARIDACEAE (Caper Family)

Capparis cynophallophora L. *tayche*

CARICACEAE (Papaw Family)

Carica papaya L. papaya, *put*

COMBRETACEAE (Combretum Family)

Bucida buceras L. *pucte*, bullet tree
Conocarpus erecta L. *bottoncillo*
Laguncularia racemosa L. Gaertn. mangle blanco

COMMELINACEAE (Dayflower Family)

Aneilema geniculata (Jacq.) Woodson
Commelina erecta L. *pajilla*
Rhoeo discolor (L'Her.) Hance sancocho colorado

COMPOSITAE (Sunflower Family)

Conza canadensis (L.) Cronquist.
Delilea berterii Spreng.
Egletes liebmanii var. *yucatana*
Eupatorium alicaule Schultz B.P. *saktokaban*
Eupatorium odoratum L. *tokaban*

Table 10.1 continued

Common Name(s)

Lagascea mollis Cananilles
Melanthera nivea Small.   *toplanxiw*
Neurolaena lobata (L.) R. Br.   manao de lagarto
Pluchea symphytifolia (Miller) Gillis   Santa Maria
Synedralla nodiflora (L.) Gaertn.   *yaxxunil*
Vernonia cinerea L.   *tamanhub*
Wedelia hispida var. *ramossisma*

CONNARACEAE (Connarus Family)

Rourea glabra H.B.K.

COVOLVULACEAE (Morning-glory
    Family)

Ipomoea purpurea (L.) Roth   *ixhaail*, morning glory
Jacquemontia pentantha (Jacq.) Don.   sombrerito azul
Merremia tuberosa (L.) Rendle   *tsayuntsay*
Turbinia corymbosa (L.) Raf.   *tabentun*

CUCURBITACEAE (Gourd Family)

Cionosicyos excisus (Griseb.) C. Jeffrey
Melothria trilobata Cogn.   *xtulub*, sandia silvestre
Momordica charantia L.   *sorosee*
Sicydium tamnifolium (HBK) Cogn. in DC.   *chacmots*

CYPERACEAE (Sedge Family)

Cyperus mutisii (HBK) Griseb.
Cyperus ochraceus Vahl.   *maskabsuuk*
Cyperus odoratus L.
Dichromena ciliata Vahl.
Fimbrystilis spadicae (L.) Vahl.
Scleria lithosperma (L.) SW.

DENNSTAEDTIACEAE

Pteridium aquilinum var. *caudatum*   *heliche*

EBENACEAE (Ebony Family)

Diospyros sp.   *cylil*, persimmon

EUPHORBIACEAE (Spurge Family)

Cnidosculus souzae McVaugh.   *xchai*, bullnettle
Croton reflexifolius H.B.K.   *pereskuch*
Dalechampia tiliifolia Lam.   *moolkoh*
Euphorbia glomerifera (Millsp.) Wheeler   *tophanxiw*
Euphorbia heterophylla L.   *hobonkaax*
Euphorbia ocymoidea L.   *kambalsakchakah*
Phyllanthus micrandus Muell. Arg.   *kahyuk*
Tragia yucatenensis Millsp.   *popox*

Table 10.1 continued

Common Name(s)

FLACOURTIACEAE (Flacourtia Family)

Casearia nitida Jacq.   *iximche*
Xylosma celastrinum (HBK) Standl.   *nuumtsutsuy*

GENTIANACEAE (Gentian Family)

Eustoma excaltatum (L.) Salisb.

GRAMINEAE (Grass Family)

Cenchrus brownii   *guisaso*
Cynodon dactylon (L.) Pers.   bermuda grass
Lasiacis papillosa Swallen   *siit*
Olyra latifolia
Oplismensus hirtellus (L.) Beauv.   *hayalsitsuuk*
Panicum bartlettii Standl.
Panicum fasciculatum Swartz.   zacate de milpa
Panicum hirsutum Swartz.
Panicum maximum   zacate de guinea
Paspalum blodgetii Chapman   *ekchim*
Stenotaphrum secundatum (Walt.) Ktze.

GUTTIFERAE (Clusia Family)

Calophyllum brasiliense   Santa Maria

HIPPOCRATEACEAE (Hippocratea Family)

Nama jamaicense L.   *kutsbox*

IRIDACEAE (Iris Family)

Cipura paludosa Aubl.

LABIATAE (Mint Family)

Ocimum micranthum Willd.   *cacaltun*
Salvia hyptoides Mart. and Gal.   *chaktsits*
Salvia occidentalis SW.

LAURACEAE (Laurel Family)

Nectandra coriacea (SW.) Griseb.   laurel

LEGUMINOSAE (Bean Family)

Acacia collinsii Saford   *subin*
Acacia gentlei
Acacia glomerosa Benth.
Acacia pennatula (Schlecht. & Cham.)
Albizzia tomentosa (Micheli) Standl.   *xiahtsimin*
Bauhinia divaricata L.   pata de vaca
Bauhinia jenningsii P. Wilson   *tismin*

Table 10.1 continued
Common Name(s)

Caesalpinia yucatanensis Greenm.	*takinche*
Canavalia mexicana Piper	
Cassia anisopetala Donn. Smith	*kanchikinak*
Cassia petensis Britton and Rose	
Centrosema plumieri (Turp) Benth	*kantsin*
Clitoria ternatea L.	
Crotalaria pumila Ortega	tronadora
Dalbergia glabra (Mills). Standl.	*muc*
Desmanthus virgatus (L.) Willd.	*kabalpich*
Desmodium incanum	*kintah*
Diphysa carthagenensis Jacq.	*susuk*
Gliricidia sepium (Jacq.) Steud.	madre de cacao
Haematoxylon campechianum	tinta, logwood
Leucaena leucocephala (Lam.) DeWitt	*guaje*
Lonchocarpus hondurensis Benth.	*yaaxhabin*
Lysiloma latisiliqua (L.) Benth.	*salom*
Mimosa hemiendyta Rose and Robinson	*katsim*
Mimosa pigra L.	sensitive weed
Mimosa pudica L.	*xmuts*
Pachyrhizus erosus (l.) Urban	jicama
Pachyrhizus vernalis Clausen	
Phaseolus lunatus L.	*ibuul*, ratweed
Piscidia piscipula (L.) Sarg.	*habim*
Pithecolobium albicans (Kunth) Benth.	*chucum*
Pithecolobium donnell-smithii	
Pithecolobium dulce (Roxb.) Benth.	
Pithecolobium lanceolatum (Humb. & Bonpl.)	*siemche*
Pithecolobium pachypus Pittier	
Platymiscium dimorphandrum Donn. Sm.	*subinche*
Rynchosia minima (L.) DC.	*ibcho*
Senna bicapsularis (L.) Roxburgh	
Vigna candida	
Vigna linearis	
Vigna luteola (Jacqu.) Benth.	

LILIACEAE (Lily Family)

Dracaena americana Donn. Sm.	Candlewood, cerbatana
Sansevieria guianensis L. Willd.	

LOGANIACEAE (Strychnine Family)

Spigelia anthelmia L.	lombricera
Strychnos panamensis Seem.	*luch maax*

LOMARIOPSIDACEAE

Psittacanthus calyculatus (DC.) Don.	*chakxen*
Strutanthus cassythoides Millsp.	

MALPIGHIACEAE (Malpighia Family)

Bunchosia swartziana Gruseb.	*zipche*

Table 10.1 continued

Common Name(s)

Byrsonima bucidifolia Standl. — nance blanco
Malpighia glabra L. — *simche*

MALVACEAE (Mallow Family)

Hampea trilobata Standl. — *moho*
Hibiscus clypeatus L. — *hool*
Malachra alceifolia Jacq. — malva
Malachra fasciata Jacq. — wild okra
Malvaviscus arboreus var. *bihondus* Schery — tulipan
Malvaviscus arboreus var.
   mexicanus Schlecht.
Sida acuta Burm. — malva de caballo

MELIACEAE (Mahogany Family)

Cedrela mexicana Roem. — cedar, cedro
Swietenia macrophylla King. — mahogany

MENISPERMACEAE (Moonseed Family)

Cissampelos pareira L. — *peteltun*

MORACEAE (Mulberry Family)

Brosimum alicastrum SW. — ramon
Cecropia peltata L. — *guarumo*
Pseudolmedia spuria (Swartz) Griseb. — cherry
Trophis racemosa (L.) Urban — ramon blanco

MYRTACEAE (Myrtle Family)

Calyptranthes sp. — Ideio desnudo

NYCTAGINACEAE (Four-o'clock Family)

Boerhavia coccinea Mill. — *chacilxiu*
Pisonia aculeata L. — una de gato

NYMPHACEAE (Waterlily Family)

Nymphaea ampla (Salisb.) D.C. — waterlily

OCHNACEAE (Ochna Family)

Ouratea lucens (HBK) Engler — *xcanlol*

OLEANDRACEAE

Nephrolepis pandula (Raddi) J. Smith

PALMAE (Palm Family)

Acoelorrhaphe wrightii (Griseb.) Wendl. — Tasiste, pimenta palm
Bactris major Jacq. — poknoboy, *huiscoyol*

Table 10.1 continued

Common Name(s)

Chamaedorea erumpens H.E.Moore	*kabalxiat*
Desmoncus schippi Burret.	basket tie-tie, *ballal*
Sabal mayarum Bartlett.	huano
Thrinax parviflora Swartz.	*chit*

PASSILORACEAE
   (Passionflower Family)

Passiflora biflora Lam.	
Passiflora capsularis L.	
Passiflora foetida var. *mayarum* Killip.	melon de raton
Passiflora serratifolia L.	jujito amarillo

PHYTOLACCACEAE (Pokeberry Family)

Phytolacca icosandra L.	*telkox*, pokeberry
Rivinia humilis L.	*kuxubcan*

PIPERACEAE (Pepper Family)

Piper psilorachis C.D.C.	*xmakulam*
Piper yzabalanum C. DC. ex. Donn. Sm.	

POLYGONACEAE (Buckweat Family)

Coccoloba belizensis Standl.	*boob*
Coccoloba cozumelensis Hemsl.	*boob*
Coccoloba uvifera L.	uva, sea grape
Gymnopodium antigonoides (Rob.) Blake	cruceto

POLYPODIACEAE (Polypody Family)

Polypodium sp.

PONTEDERIACEAE
   (Pickerelweed Family)

Eichornia crassipes (Mart.) Solms.

POTAMOGETONACEAE
   (Pondweed Family)

Potamogeton pectinatus L.

PTERIDEACEAE

Acrostichum aureum L.	tiger bush

RANUNCULACEAE (Buckhorn Family)

Columbrina ferruginosa Brogn.	*tsulubmay*
Gouiana lupuloides (L.) Urb.	*xomak*

RHIZOPHORACEAE (Mangrove Family)

Rhizophora mangle L.	mangle colorado, mangrove

Table 10.1 continued

Common Name(s)

RUBIACEAE (Coffee Family)

Borreria verticillata (L.) G.F. Mey.
Chiococca alba (L.) Hitchc.   cainca
Guettarda sp.   kibche
Hamelia patens Jacq.   xcanan
Morinda rojoc L.   hoyok
Psychotria fruticetorum Standl.   bakelak
Psychotria nervosa
Psychotria oerstediana Standl.
Psychotria oerstediana Standl.
Psychotria pubescens Swartz.
Randia aculeata L.   pechkitam

RUTACEAE (Rue Family)

Casimiroa microcarpa Lundell   hyruy

SAPINDACEAE (Soapberry Family)

Allophylus kinlochii Standl.   palo de caja
Allophylus longeracemosus Standl.
Cupania glabra   sacpom
Paullina costaricensis Standl.
Paullina fuscescens HBK var. *glabrata*   kexak

SAPOTACEAE (Sapodilla Family)

Achras breviloba (Gilly) Lundell   sapote
Achras zapota L.   sapote
Chrysophyllum mexicanum Brandegee   caimito silvestre
Mastichodendron capiri (A. DC.)
Pouteria campechinana (H.B.K.)   zapote borracho

SCHIZAEACEAE

Lygodium venustum SW.

SCROPHULARIACEAE (Figwort Family)

Bacopa monnieri (L.) Wettst.   xaaxkach
Capraria biflora L.   claudiosa

SIMARUBACEAE (Simaruba Family)

Simarouba glauca DC.   negrito

SMILACACEAE (Sarsaparilla Family)

Smilax aristolochiaefolia Mill.   amakil
Smilax regelii Killip and Morton

SOLANACEAE (Potato Family)

Cestrum racemosum R. & P.   dama de noche

Table 10.1 conclusion

Common Name(s)

Lisianthus axillaris (Hemsl.) O. Ktze
Lycianthes lenta (Cav.) Bitter
Physalis pubescens L.   tomatillo, ground cherry
Solanum blodgetii Chapm.
Solanum campechiense L.
Solanum rovirosanum Donn. Sm.
Solanum tequilense Gray
Solanum torvum Swartz.

STERCULIACEAE (Cacao Family)

Byttneria aculeata Jacq.   *tezak*
Corchorus siliquosus L.   *chichibe*
Guazuma ulmifolia Lam.   *pixoy*
Melochia pyramidata L.

THEOPHRASTACEAE
    (Theophrasta Family)

Jacquinia auriantiaca Ait.   *xcansik*
Jacquinia pungens Gray

TILIACEAE (Linden Family)

Triumfetta dumetorum Schlecht.   *ochmul*

TYPHACEAE (Cattail Family)

Typha domingensis Pers.   cattail

ULMACEAE (Elm Family)

Trema floridana Britton ex. Small

VERBENACEAE (Teak Family)

Aegiphila monstrosa Moidenke   vara blanca
Callicarpa acuminata HBK   *pukin*
Cornutia sp.   *latche*
Lantana camara L.   palabra de caballero
Lantana glandulosissima Hayek.
Petrea volubilis L.   bejuco de caballo
Phyla stoechadifolia (L.) Small
Priva lappulacea (L.) Pers.   mozotillo
Stachytarpheta cayennesis (L. Rich.) Vahl.   *wanche*
Vitex gaumeri Greenm.   *yaxnik*

VITACEAE (Grape Family)

Cissus gossypiifolia Standl.
Cissus sicyoides L.   *tabkan*
Vitis Tilifolia Humb. & Bonpl.   grape

TABLE 10.2
Frequencies of Plants in the Transects

SPECIES	*Transects																
	1	2	3	4	5	6	7	8	9	10	11	12	13	14	15	16	17
Acacia collinsii																	
Acacia glomerosa			2	13	1							1	3	2	4		2
Acacia pennctula			17			1		8	10					1	1		3
Achras zapota										2	4					1	
Achyranthes indica																	
Acrostichum aureum												2					
Adiantum tricholepis	5																
Allophyllus longeracemosus	2																
Anthurium schlechtendalii	4					2											
Asclepias curassavica																	
Batris major				36											57		
Bauhinia divaricata								1									
Bravaisia tubiflora			12						48		38	85	18	2	5	77	
Bromelia karatas		5															
Brosimum alicastrum	13													1		2	
Bucida buceras								7	16								
Bursera simaruba	1		3						2		2	8	8	16	2		11
Cameraria latifolia									2								
Canavalia mexicana										1							
Capparis cynophallophora										2							
Carica papcya					8				2								
Casearia nitida										1		4					
Cecropia peltata	4	2	3		2				1								
Cenchrus brownii					6				2								
Centrosema plumieri					1				5								
Cestrum racemosum																	
Chamaedorea erumpens				4								1		6			
Chiococco alba	2																
Chrysophyllum mexicanum			6	5	2			7						8	6		6
Cionosicyos excisus					2												
Cissus gossypifolia	2	3			1								1				
Cissus sicyoides					4												
Cnidosculus souzae	1				1			18									
Coccoloba belizensis												6	6	6	1		15
Coccoloba cozumelensis																	1
Coccoloba uvifera											1	4					
Cocos nucifera											5	16				1	2
Colubrina ferruginosa	1		7									1					

Table 10.2 continued

Transects*

SPECIES	1	2	3	4	5	6	7	8	9	10	11	12	13	14	15	16	17
Commelina erecta										10							
Conocarpus erecta																	
Corchorus siliquosus					10						5	32				2	
Corunutia sp.					3												
Crescentia cujete										4					3		
Croton reflexidolius			62	30	4			32	8				6				
Cupania glabra			2	9	4			6					9	10	5		
Cyperus mutisii															6		
Dalbergia glabra						56	91		17				58				
Dalechampia tillifolia					4												
Desmanthus virgatu					1												
Desmoncus schippi																	
Diospyros sp.				1				5						2			4
Diphysa carthagenensis								2							1		4
Euphorbia glomerifera						3											
Euphorbia heterophylla																	
Gliricidia sepium									3	34							
Guazuma ulmifolia	4		5	7	7						5				8		
Guettarda sp.						3			4				2				1
Gymnopodium antigonoides								17									
Haematoxylon campechianum												7					
Hamelia patens										21							
Hampea trilobata			3	2					6		1	4		6	2	2	3
Heliotropium angiospermum										1							
Hibiscus clypeatus	3																
Hippocratea volubilis											2					1	
Ipomoea purpurea					2	2				14							
Jacquinia auriantiaca								5	2								
Jacquemontia pentantha					15								9				1
Justicia sp.										12							
Lagascea mollis										2							
Laguncularia racemosa		3															
Lantana gladulosissima											3	8					
Lasiacus papillosa	6															10	
Leucaena leucocephala	1	4	1					8					4	1			3
Lygodium venustum	1								2	11							
Lysiloma latisiliqua	1			2				15				2	2		1		3
Malachra alcefolia									3						1		
Malpighia glabra				1		3											
Malvaviscus arboreus			2										2	3			
Melanthera angustifolia	1	2			18			1	1					3			

Table 10.2 continued

SPECIES	1	2	3	4	5	6	7	8	9	10	11	12	13	14	15	16	17
Melanthera nivea										6							
Melothria trilobata										3							
Metopium browneii			1	2		1		4	3		7	3	6	7			3
Mimosa hemiendyta								3									1
Mimosa pigra							56										
Mimosa pudica					1												
Momordica charantia	1									4							
Monstera sp.																	
Morinda roioc			1	4				8									
Nectandra coriacea													7	3	1		
Nephrolepis pendula													1	1			
Pachyrhizus erosus				72	2					12							
Panicum maximum													1				
Passiflora capsularis				1													
Paullina fuscescens		2	2												4		
Petrea volubilis			2														1
Phaseolus lunatus					1					8							
Phytolacca icosandra					2												
Piper psilorachis	6		3	3	2							3	9	1	1		1
Piscidia piscipula			3	8				4				2	1	2	2		2
Pithecolobium dulce			1	7		2		7	2		1		4		1	1	
Platymiscium dimorphandrum									9	8							
Priva lappula																	
Psychotria fruticetorum														1			
Psychotria nervosa													1	5	1		
Psychotria oerstediana																	
Pteridium aquilinum				10	5												11
Randia aculeata								22					4	10	10	31	
Rhizophora mangle	4																
Rhoeo discolor												2					
Rhynchosia minima										2							
Rivinia humilis										30					2		
Rourea glabra			3	13									2				
Sabal mayarum		1	3	13		18		17	1	6	6	3	27	18	7		20
Sarcostemma bilobum							5										
Sarcostemma clausum							2										
Scleria lithosperma					7												
Sicydium tamnifolium										1							
Sida acuta										4							
Simarouba glauca													4	1			
Smilax aristolochiaefolia															2		2

Table 10.2 conclusion

SPECIES	Transects*																
	1	2	3	4	5	6	7	8	9	10	11	12	13	14	15	16	17
Smilax regelii					3												
Solanum blodgettii						60	57		46								
Solanum campechiense						37	25						7				
Stenotaphrum secundatum																	
Strychnos panamensis										3							
Tabernaemontana chrysocarpa		1	2											1			8
Talisia oliviformis															3		
Thevetia gaumeri	1		12	3					1			4	11	1		2	
Thrinax parviflora	2	1	1	4					1			1	19	6		5	
Trophis racemosa								2			12				1		4
Typha domingensis						275	146										
Vigna luteola								2		1							
Vitex gaumeri													7	2	2		
Xylosma celastrinum													2				1

* Vegetation on ruins = transects 1, 2
Secondary growth - transects 3, 8
Marsh - transects 6, 7
Shoreline = transects 11, 12
Mangrove swamp = transect 16
High bush = transects 14, 17
Aguada forest = transect 13
Pioneer vegetation = transect 13
Bajo = transects 4, 15
Canal edge = transect 9
Abandoned milpa = transect 5

APPENDIX A

MODIFIED CHEVRON TECHNIQUE FOR POLLEN EXTRACTION
(Woosley 1978)

1. Add concentrated HCL (hydrochloric acid) to 50g. of sample.
2. Add distilled water, centrifuge and decant to remove acid. Repeat until pH is neutral.
3. Add concentrate HF (hydrofluoric acid) and heat for one hour.
4. Add distilled water, centrifuge and decant to remove acid. Repeat until pH is neutral.
5. If sample is too "hunky" or crystals have formed, put sample back in HCL and heat for no more than 5 minutes. Then add distilled water, centrifuge and decant to remove acid.
6. Dissolve calgon in hot distilled water and add to residue of sample. Centrifuge and decant sample.
7. Stain in safranine.
8. Sieve sample successively in 100ü, 60ü, 40ü, 20ü, and 10ü micron mesh nylon screens.
9. Pan in watch glass to concentrate pollen.
10. Prepare slides.

Basically, the HCL dissolves the carbonates in the sample, and the HF dissolves the silicates. The calgon removes the organic residues from the sample.

BIBLIOGRAPHY

Adam, David P., and Peter J. Mehringer, Jr., 1975, Modern pollen surface samples: An analysis of subsamples. *Journal of Research of the U. S. Geological Survey* 3:733–736.

Adams, Richard E. W., 1971, The ceramics of Altar de Sacrificios. *Papers of the Peabody Museum of Archaeology and Ethnology,* Harvard University, Vol. 63(1).

———, 1977, Rio Bec archaeology and the rise of Maya civilization. In *The origins of Maya civilization,* edited by R. E. W. Adams, pp. 77–99. University of New Mexico Press, Albuquerque.

Adams, Richard E. W., and T. Patrick Culbert, 1977, The origins of civilization in the Maya lowlands. In *The origins of Maya civilization,* edited by R. E. W. Adams, pp. 3–24. University of New Mexico Press, Albuquerque.

Ahler, Stanley A., 1979, Functional analysis of nonobsidian chipped stone artifacts: terms, variables, and quantification. In *Lithic use-wear analysis,* edited by B. Hayden, pp. 301–328. Academic Press, New York.

Andresen, John M., 1976, Notes on the Pre-Columbian chert industry of Northern Belize. In *Maya lithic studies: Papers from the 1976 Belize Field Symposium,* edited by T. R. Hester and N. Hammond, pp. 51–176. Center for Archaeological Research, University of Texas at San Antonio, Special Report No. 4.

Andrews, E. Wyllys, IV, 1959, Dzibilchaltun: lost city of the Maya. *National Geographic* 115(1): 90–109.

———, 1965, *Progress report on the 1960–1964 field seasons, National Geographic Society–Tulane University Dzibilchaltun Program.* Middle American Research Institute, Tulane University, Publication 31: 23–68.

———, 1969, *The archaeological use and distribution of Mollusca in the Maya Lowlands.* Middle American Research Institute, Tulane University, Publication 34.

Andrews, E. Wyllys, IV, and Irwin Rovner, 1973, *Archaeological evidence on social stratification and commerce in the Northern Maya Lowlands: two mason's tool kits from Muna and Dzibilchaltun, Yucatan.* Middle American Research Institute, Tulane University, Publication 31: 81–102.

Andrews, E. Wyllys, V, 1981, Dzibilchaltun. In *Archaeology,* edited by J. A. Sabloff, Supplement to the *Handbook of Middle American Indians,* Vol. 1, edited by V. R. Bricker, pp. 313–341. University of Texas Press, Austin.

Ball, Joseph W., 1977, *The archaeological ceramics of Becan, Campeche, Mexico.* Middle American Research Institute, Tulane University, Publication 43.

———, 1978, Archaeological pottery of the Yucatan-Campeche Coast. In *Studies in the Archaeology of Coastal Yucatan and Campeche,* by J. W. Ball and J. D. Eaton. Middle American Research Institute, Tulane University, Publication 46:69–146.

Ball, Joseph W., and E. Wyllys Andrews V, 1978, *Preclassic architecture at Becan, Campeche, Mexico.* Middle American Research Institute, Tulane University, Occasional Papers No. 3.

Becker, Marshall J., 1973, Archaeological evidence for occupational specialization among the Classic Period Maya at Tikal, Guatemala. *American Antiquity* 38:396–406.

Bender, Edward Samuel, 1971, *Studies of the life history of the stone crab,* Menippe Mercenaria (Say), *in the Cedar Key Area.* Unpublished Master's thesis, Department of Zoology, University of Florida.

Birney, Elmer C., John B. Bowles, Robert M. Timm, and Stephen L. Williams, 1974, *Mammalian distributional records in Yucatan and Quintana Roo, with comments on reproduction, structure, and status of peninsula populations.* Bell Museum of Natural History, University of Minnesota, Occasional Papers No. 13.

Bullard, William R., Jr., 1973, Postclassic culture in Central Peten and adjacent British Honduras. In *The Classic Maya collapse,* edited by T. P. Culbert, pp. 221–241. University of New Mexico Press, Albuquerque.

Burt, William Henry, and Richard Philip Grossenheider, 1976, *A Field Guide to the Mammals* (third). Houghton Mifflin, Boston.

Caratini, C., F. Blasco, and G. Thanikaimoni, 1973, Relation between the pollen spectra and the vegetation of a South Indian mangrove. *Pollen et Spore* 15:281–292.

Carr, Robert F., and James E. Hazard, 1961, *Tikal report No. 11; map of the ruins of Tikal, El Peten, Guatemala.* Museum Monographs, The University Museum, University of Pennsylvania.

Casteel, Richard W., 1977, Characterization of faunal assemblages and the minimum number of individuals determined from paired elements: continuing problems in archaeology. *Journal of Archaeological Science* 4:125–134.

———, 1978, Faunal assemblages and the "Wiegemethode" or weight method. *Journal of Field Archaeology* 5:71–77.

Clark, John E., 1980, *An approach to the study of chipped stone function in Mesoamerica: a program for Chiapas, Mexico.* Paper presented at the 45th Annual Meeting of the Society for American Archaeology, Philadelphia.

Cliff, Maynard B., 1977, *Late Preclassic burial patterning at the Site of Cerros, Northern Belize: preliminary results.* Paper presented at the 42nd Annual Meeting of Society for American Archaeology, New Orleans.

———, 1982, *Lowland Maya nucleation: a case study from*

Northern Belize. Ph.D. dissertation, Southern Methodist University. University Microfilms, Ann Arbor.

——, 1983, Domestic architecture and origins of complex society at Cerros, paper presented at the 48th Annual Meeting of the Society for American Archaeology, Pittsburgh.

Coe, William R., 1959, *Piedras Negras archaeology: artifacts, caches, and burials.* Museum Monographs, The University Museum, University of Pennsylvania.

——, 1965, Tikal, Guatemala, and emergent Maya civilization. *Science* 147:1401–1419.

——, 1967, *Tikal: A handbook of the ancient Maya ruins.* The University Museum, University of Pennsylvania.

Crabtree, Don E., 1972, *An introduction to flintworking.* Idaho State University Museum, Pocatello, Occasional Papers No. 28.

Crabtree, Don E., and E. L. Davis, 1968, Experimental manufacture of wooden implements with tools of flaked stone. *Science* 159:426–428.

Culbert, T. Patrick, 1977, Early Maya development at Tikal, Guatemala. In *The origins of Maya civilization*, edited by R. E. W. Adams, pp. 27–43. University of New Mexico Press, Albuquerque.

Digby, Adrian, 1964, *Maya jade.* British Museum, London.

Eaton, Jack D., 1976, Ancient fishing technology on the Gulf Coast of Yucatan, Mexico. *Bulletin of the Texas Archaeological Society* 47:231–243.

Feldman, Lawrence H., 1971, *A tumpline economy: production and distribution systems of early Central-East Guatemala.* Ph.D. dissertation, Pennsylvania State University. University Microfilms, Ann Arbor.

Flannery, Kent V., and Marcus C. Winter, 1976, Analyzing household activities. In *The early Mesoamerican village*, edited by K. V. Flannery, pp. 34–47. Academic Press, New York.

Freidel, David. A., 1976, Cerro Maya: a Late Preclassic center in Corozal District. In *Recent Archaeology in Belize*, edited by R. Buhler, SJ, pp. 73–99. Belize Institute for Social Research and Action, Belize City, Belize, Occasional Paper No. 3.

——, 1977, A Late Preclassic monumental mask at Cerros, Northern Belize. *Journal of Field Archaeology* 4:488–491.

——, 1978, Maritime adaptation and the rise of Maya civilization: the view from Cerros, Belize. In *Prehistoric Coastal Adaptations*, edited by B. L. Stark and B. Voorhies, pp. 239–265. Academic Press, New York.

——, 1979, Culture areas and interaction spheres: contrasting approaches to the emergence of civilization in the Maya Lowlands. *American Antiquity* 44:36–54.

——, In press, Polychrome facades of the Maya Preclassic, in *Painted Architecture and Polychromed Monumental Sculpture in Mesoamerica*, edited by E. Boone, Dumbarton Oaks, Washington, D. C.

Freidel, David A., and Vernon Scarborough, 1982, Subsis-

tence, trade, and development of the coastal Maya. In *Maya Subsistence: studies in memory of Dennis E. Puleston*, edited by K. V. Flannery, pp. 131–151. Academic Press, New York.

Freidel, David A., and Linda Schele, 1982, Symbol and power a history of the Lowland Maya cosmogram, Paper presented at the Princeton Conference on the Origins of Maya Iconography, Princeton University.

Frison, George, 1979, Observations on the use of stone tools: dulling of working edges of some chipped stone tools in bison butchering. In *Lithic use-wear analysis*, edited by B. Hayden, pp. 259–268. Academic Press, New York.

Fry, Robert E., 1969, *Ceramics and settlement in the periphery of Tikal, Guatemala.* Ph.D. dissertation, University of Arizona. University Microfilms, Ann Arbor.

Gann, Thomas W. F., 1918, *The Maya Indians of Southern Yucatan and Northern British Honduras. Bureau of American Ethnology*, Smithsonian Institution, Bulletin 64.

Gann, Thomas W. F., and Mary Gann, 1939, *Archaeological investigations in the Corozal District of British Honduras.* Bureau of American Ethnology, Smithsonian Institution, Bulletin 123.

Garber, James F., 1981, *Material culture and patterns of artifact consumption and disposal at the Maya site of Cerros in Northern Belize.* Ph.D. dissertation, Southern Methodist University. University Microfilms, Ann Arbor.

Gifford, James. C., 1976, Prehistoric pottery analysis and the ceramics of Barton Ramie in the Belize Valley. *Memoirs of the Peabody Museum of Archaeology and Ethnology*, Harvard University, Vol. 18.

Gould, Richard A., 1980, *Living archaeology.* Cambridge University Press, Cambridge, England.

Grayson, Donald K., 1979, On the quantification of vertebrate archaeofaunas. In *Advances in archaeological method and theory* (Vol. 2), edited by M. B. Schiffer, pp. 199–237. Academic Press, New York.

Hammond, Norman, 1974, Preclassic to Postclassic in Northern Belize. *Antiquity* 48:177–189.

Hammond, Norman (editor), 1973, *British Museum-Cambridge University Corozal Project, 1973 Interim Report.* Centre of Latin American Studies, Cambridge University, Cambridge.

——, 1975, *Archaeology in Northern Belize: British Museum-Cambridge Univrsity Corozal Project 1974–75 Interim Report.* Centre of Latin American Studies, Cambridge University, Cambridge.

——, 1979, *Cuello Project 1978 Interim Report.* Archaeological Research Program, Douglas College, Rutgers University, New Brunswick, New Jersey, Publication 1.

Hammond, Norman, and Charles J. Miksicek, 1981, Ecology and economy of a Formative Maya site at Cuello, Belize. *Journal of Field Archaeology* 8:259–269.

Hammond, Norman, Duncan Pring, Richard Wilk, Sara Donaghey, Frank P. Saul, Elizabeth S. Wing, Arlene V. Miller, and Lawrence H. Feldman, 1979, The earliest Maya? Definition of the Swasey Phase. *American Antiquity* 44: 92–110.

Harrison, Peter, 1970, *The central acropolis, Tikal, Guatemala: a preliminary study of the functions of its structural components during the Late Classic Period*. Ph.D. dissertation, University of Pennsylvania. University Microfilms, Ann Arbor.

Haury, Emil W., 1976, *The Hohokam, desert farmers and craftsmen: excavations at Snaketown*. University of Arizona Press, Tucson.

Haviland, William A., 1963, *Excavation of small structures in the northeast quadrant of Tikal, Guatemala*. Ph.D. dissertation, University of Pennsylvania. University Microfilms, Ann Arbor.

———, 1969, A new population estimate for Tikal, Guatemala. *American Antiquity* 34:429–433.

———, 1970, Tikal, Guatemala and Mesoamerican urbanism. *World Archaeology* 2:186–198.

———, 1981, Dower houses and minor centers at Tikal, Guatemala: an investigation into the identification of valid units in settlement hierarchies. In *Lowland Maya Settlement Patterns*, edited by W. Ashmore, pp. 89–117. University of New Mexico Press, Albuquerque.

Hay, Conran A., 1978, *Kaminaljuyu obsidian: lithic analysis and the economic organization of a prehistoric Mayan chiefdom*. Ph.D. dissertation, Pennsylvania State University. University Microfilms, Ann Arbor.

Hayden, Brian, 1979, Snap, shatter, and superfractures: use-wear of stone skin scrapers. In *Lithic use-wear analysis*, edited by B. Hayden, pp. 207–229. Academic Press, New York.

Hester, Thomas R., and Norman Hammond (editors), 1976, *Maya lithic studies: papers from the 1976 Belize Field Symposium*. Center for Archaeological Research, University of Texas at San Antonio, Special Report No. 4.

Hester, Thomas R., and Robert F. Heizer, 1971, Problems in the functional interpretation of artifacts: scraper planes from Mitla and Yagul, Oaxaca. *Contributions of the California Archaeological Research Facility* 14:107–123.

Hurley, William M., 1979, *Prehistoric cordage*. Aldine Manuals in Archaeology, Taraxacum, Washington, D.C.

Ingle, Robert M., and F. G. Walton Smith, 1949, *Sea turtles and the turtle industry of the West Indies, Florida, and the Gulf of Mexico, with annotated bibliography*. University of Miami Press, Miami, Florida.

Keeley, Lawrence H., 1980, *Experimental determination of stone tool uses: a microwear analysis*. University of Chicago Press, Chicago.

Kidder, Alfred Vincent, 1947, *The artifacts of Uaxactun, Guatemala*. Carnegie Institution of Washington, Washington, D.C., Publication 576.

Kidder, Alfred V., J. D. Jennings, and E. M. Shook, 1946, *Excavations at Kaminaljuyu, Guatemala*. Carnegie Institution of Washington, Washington, D.C., Publication 561.

Kurjack, Edward B., 1974, *Prehistoric Lowland Maya community patterning and social organization: a case study at Dzibilchaltun, Yucatan, Mexico*. Middle American Research Institute, Tulane University, Publication 38.

———, 1976, *Pre-Columbian polities and communities in Northwest Yucatan, Mexico*. Paper presented at the 41st Annual Meeting of the Society for American Archaeology, St. Louis.

Lamberg-Karlovsky, C. C., 1975, Third millenium modes of exchange and modes of production. In *Ancient Civilization and Trade*, edited by J. A. Sabloff and C. C. Lamberg-Karlovsky, pp. 341–368. University of New Mexico Press, Albuquerque.

Lambert, John D. H., and Thor Arnason, 1978, Distribution of vegetation on Maya ruins and its relationship to ancient land-use at Lamanai, Belize. *Turrialba* 28:33–41.

———, 1982, Ramon and Maya ruins: an ecological, not an economic relation. *Science* 216: 298–299.

Lang, Gerald E., Dennis H. Knight, and Donald A. Anderson, 1971, Sampling the density of tree species with quadrats in a species-rich tropical forest. *Forest Science* 17:395–400.

Large, E. G., 1975, *Cotton: a basic resource for the Classic Maya of the Southern Lowlands?* Paper presented at the 74th Annual Meeting of the American Anthropological Association, San Francisco.

Lee, Thomas A., Jr., 1969, *The artifacts of Chiapa de Corzo, Chiapas, Mexico*. Papers of the New World Archaeological Foundation, Brigham Young University, Provo, Utah, No. 26.

Lewenstein, Suzanne M., 1981, Mesoamerican obsidian blades: an experimental approach to function. *Journal of Field Archaeology* 8:175–188.

Littman, Edwin R., 1972, A study of Altar de Sacrificios floors. In *Excavations at Altar de Sacrificios: architecture, settlement, burials, and caches*, by A. L. Smith, pp. 270–277. Papers of the Peabody Museum of Archaeology and Ethnology, Harvard University, Vol. 62(2).

Lundell, Cyrus L., 1938, Plants probably utilized by the Old Empire Maya of Peten and adjacent lowlands. *Papers of the Michigan Academy of Sciences, Arts and Letters* 24:37–59.

Marcus, Joyce, 1982, The plant world of the Sixteenth and Seventeenth-Century Lowland Maya. In *Maya subsistence: studies in memory of Dennis E. Puleston*, edited by K. V. Flannery, pp. 239–274. Academic Press, New York.

Markgraf, Vera, H. L. D'Antoni, and Thomas A. Ager, 1981, Modern pollen dispersal in Argentina. *Palynology* 5:43–63.

Masucci, Maria, n.d., *Beyond the "assemble-it-yourself" censer: a sense of Preclassic incensarios at Cerros, Belize*. Unpublished paper on file, Department of Anthropology, Southern Methodist University.

Matheny, Ray T., 1970, *The Ceramics of Aguacatel, Campeche, Mexico*. Papers of the New World Archaeological Foundation, Brigham Young University, Provo, Utah, No. 27.

Michels, Joseph W., 1976, Some sociological observations on obsidian production at Kaminaljuyu, Guatemala. In *Maya lithic studies: papers from the 1976 Belize Field Symposium*, edited by T. R. Hester and N. Hammond, pp. 109–118. Center for Archaeological Research, University of Texas at San Antonio, Special Report No. 4.

——, 1979, *The Kaminaljuyu chiefdom*. Pennsylvania State University Press, University Park, Pennsylvania.

Miksicek, Charles H., Robert McK. Bird, Barbara Pickersgill, Sara Donaghey, Juliette Cartwright, and Norman Hammond, 1981, Preclassic Lowland maize from Cuello, Belize. *Nature* 289:50–59.

Murie, Adolph, 1935, *Mammals from Guatemala and British Honduras*. University of Michigan Museum of Zoology, Ann Arbor, Miscellaneous Publication 26.

Neill, Wilfred T., 1965, *New and noteworthy amphibians and reptiles from British Honduras*. Bulletin of the Florida State Museum, University of Florida, Gainesville, Biological Sciences Vol. 9(3).

Neill, Wilfred T., and Ross Allen, 1959, *Studies on the amphibians and reptiles of British Honduras*. Ross Allen's Reptile Institute, Silver Springs, Florida, Publications of the Research Division Vol. 2(1).

Odell, George H., 1980, Toward a more behavioral approach to archaeological lithic concentrations. *American Antiquity* 45:404–431.

Parsons, Mary H., 1972, Spindle whorls from the Teotihuacan Valley, Mexico. In *Miscellaneous studies in Mexican Prehistory*, by M. W. Spence, J. R. Parsons, and M. H. Parsons, pp. 45–80. Museum of Anthropology, University of Michigan, Anthropological Papers No. 45.

Pendergast, David M., 1976, *Altun Ha: a guidebook to the ancient Maya ruins* (2nd rev. ed). University of Toronto Press, Toronto.

——, 1979, *Excavations at Altun Ha, Belize, 1964–1970* (Vol. 1). Royal Ontario Museum, Toronto, Canada.

——, 1981, Lamanai, Belize: summary of excavation results, 1974–1980. *Journal of Field Archaeology* 8:29–53.

Phillips, David A., Jr., 1978, *Adddditional notes on the fishing technology of the Yucatan Peninsula, Mexico*. Bulletin of the Texas Archaeological Society 49:349–353.

——, 1979, *Material culture and trade of the Post-classic Maya*. Ph.D. dissertation, University of Arizona. University Microfilms, Ann Arbor.

Pires-Ferreira, Jane W., 1975, *Formative Mesoamerican exchange networks with special reference to the Valley of Oaxaca*. Museum of Anthropology, University of Michigan, Memoir 7.

Pohl, Mary E. D., 1976, *Ethnozoology of the Maya: an analysis of fauna from five sites in the Peten, Guatemala*. Unpublished Ph.D. dissertation, Department of Anthropology, Harvard University.

Prange, Henry D., 1977, The scaling and mechanics of arthropod exoskeletons. In *Scale effects in animal locomotion*, edited by T. J. Pedley, pp. 169–181. Academic Press, London.

Prange, Henry D., John F. Anderson, and Herman Rahn, 1979, Scaling of skeletal mass to body mass in birds and mammals. *American Naturalist* 113:103–122.

Pring, Duncan, 1976, Corozal Project 1975. In *Recent archaeology in Belize*, edited by R. Buhler, SJ, pp. 46–52. Belize Institute for Social Research and Action, Belize City, Belize, Occasional Paper No. 3.

——, 1977, *The Preclassic ceramics of Northern Belize*. Ph.D. dissertation, University of London. University Microfilms, Ann Arbor.

Pring, Duncan, and Norman Hammond, 1975, Investigation of a possible port installation at Nohmul. In *Archaeology in Northern Belize: British Museum-Cambridge University Corozal Project 1974–75 Interim Report*, edited by N. Hammond, pp. 116–127. Centre of Latin American Studies, Cambridge University, Cambridge, England.

Prouskouriakoff, Tatiana, 1962, The artifacts of Mayapan. In *Mayapan, Yucatan, Mexico*, by H. E. D. Pollack, R. L. Roys, T. Prouskouriakoff, and A. L. Smith, pp. 321–442. Carnegie Institution of Washington, Washington, D.C., Publication 619.

Puleston, Dennis E., 1973, *Ancient Maya settlement patterns and environment at Tikal, Guatemala: implications for subsistence models*. Ph.D. dissertation, University of Pennsylvania. University Microfilms, Ann Arbor.

——, 1974, Intersite areas in the vicinity of Tikal and Uaxactun. In *Mesoamerican Archaeology: new approaches*, edited by Norman Hammond, pp. 303–311. University of Texas Press, Austin.

——, 1977, The art and archaeology of hydraulic agriculture in the Maya Lowlands. In *Social process in Maya Prehistory*, edited by N. Hammond, pp. 449–467. Academic Press, New York.

——, 1978, Terracing, raised fields and tree cropping in the Maya Lowlands: A new perspective on the geography of power. In *Pre-Hispanic Maya agriculture*, edited by Peter D. Harrison and B. L. Turner II, pp. 225–246. University of New Mexico Press, Albuquerque.

Puleston, Olga Stavrakis, 1969, *Functional analysis of a workshop tool kit from Tikal*. Unpublished Master's thesis, Department of Anthropology, University of Pennsylvania.

Randall, John E., 1968, *Caribbean reef fishes*. T. H. F. Publications, Hong Kong.

Rathje, William L., 1971, The origin and development of Lowland Classic Maya civilization. *American Antiquity* 36:275–285.

——, 1972, Praise the Gods and pass the metates: a hypothesis of the development of Lowland rain-forest civilizations in Mesoamerica. In *Contemporary archaeology: a guide to theory and contributions*, edited by M. Leone, pp. 365–392. Southern Illinois University Press, Carbondale.

Record, Samuel J., and Clayton D. Mell, 1924, *Timbers of tropical America*. Yale University Press, New Haven.

Rice, Don S., 1976, Middle Preclassic Maya settlement in the Central Maya Lowlands. *Journal of Field Archaeology* 3:423–445.

Rice, Don S., and Prudence M. Rice, 1980, The Northeast Peten revisited. *American Antiquity* 45:432–454.

Ricketson, Oliver G., Jr., and Edith Bayles Ricketson, 1937, *Uaxactun, Guatemala: Group E—1926–1931*. Carnegie Institution of Washington, Washington, D.C., Publication 477.

Robertson, Robin, 1980, *Late Preclassic ceramics from Cerros, Belize: their importance for interpreting the Protoclassic*. Paper presented at the 79th Annual Meeting of the American Anthropological Association, Washington, D.C.

——, 1983, Functional analysis and social process in ceramics: the pottery from Cerros, Belize. In *Civilization in the ancient americas: essays in honor of Gordon R. Willey*, edited by R. M. Leventhal and A. L. Kolata, pp. 105–142. University of New Mexico Press, Albuquerque.

Robertson-Freidel, Robin A., 1980, *The ceramics from Cerros: a late Preclassic site in Northern Belize*. Unpublished Ph.D. dissertation, Department of Anthropology, Harvard University.

Rovner, Irwin, 1975, *Lithic sequences from the Maya Lowlands*. Ph.D. dissertation, University of Wisconsin. University Microfilms, Ann Arbor.

——, 1976, Pre-Columbian Maya development of utilitarian lithic industries: the broad perspective from Yucatan. In *Maya lithic studies: papers from the 1976 Belize Field Symposium*, edited by T. R. Hester and N. Hammond, pp. 41–53. Center for Archaeological Research, University of Texas at San Antonio, Special Report No. 4.

Sabloff, Jeremy A., 1975, *Excavations at Seibal, Department of Peten, Guatemala: ceramics*. Memoirs of the Peabody Museum of Archaeology and Ethnology, Harvard University, Vol. 13(2).

Sanders, William T., 1973, The cultural ecology of the Lowland Maya: a reevaluation. In *The Classic Maya collapse*, edited by T. P. Culbert, pp. 325–365. University of New Mexico Press, Albuquerque.

Sanders, William T., and Barbara J. Price, 1968, *Mesoamerica: the evolution of a civilization*. Random House, New York.

Santley, Robert S., 1977, *Intra-site settlement patterns at Loma Torremote and their relationship to Formative Prehistory in the Cuautitlan Region, State of Mexico*. Ph.D. dissertation, Pennsylvania State University. University Microfilms, Ann Arbor.

Scarborough, Vernon, 1980, *The settlement system in a Late Preclassic Maya community: Cerros, Northern Belize*. Ph.D. dissertation, Southern Methodist University. University Microfilms, Ann Arbor.

——, 1983, A Preclassic Maya water system. *American Antiquity* 48:720–744.

Scarborough, Vernon, Beverly Mitchum, Sorayya Carr, and David Freidel, 1982, Two Late Preclassic ballcourts at the Lowland Maya center of Cerros, Northern Belize. *Journal of Field Archaeology* 9:21–34.

Scarborough, Vernon, and Robin Robertson, In press, Civic and residential settlement at a Late Preclassic Maya center. *Journal of Field Archaeology*.

Schele, Linda, 1985, The Hauberg stela: bloodletting and the mythos of Maya rulership, *Fifth Palenque Roundtable, 1983*, Vol. VII. General Editor, Merle Greene Robertson, Volume Editor, Virginia M. Fields, pp. 135–149. Pre-Columbian Art Research Institute, San Francisco.

Semenov, S. A., 1964, *Prehistoric technology*. Translated by M. W. Thompson. Adams & Dart, Bath, England.

——, 1970, The forms and funktions of the oldest tools (a reply to Prof. F. Bordes). *Quartar* 21:1–20.

Shafer, Harry J., 1976, Belize lithics: orange peel flakes and adze manufacture. In *Maya lithic studies: papers from the 1976 Belize Field Symposium*, edited by T. R. Hester and N. Hammond, pp. 21–34. Center for Archaeological Research, University of Texas at San Antonio, Special Report No. 4.

——, 1983, The lithic artifacts of the Pulltrouser area: settlements and fields. In *Pulltrouser Swamp: ancient Maya habitat, agriculture, and settlement in Northern Belize*, edited by B. L. Turner II and Peter D. Harrison, pp. 212–245. University of Texas Press, Austin.

Sheets, Payson D., 1978, Part one: artifacts. In *The prehistory of Chalchuapa, El Salvador* (Vol. 2), edited by R. J. Sharer, pp. 1–131. University Monographs, The University Museum, University of Pennsylvania.

——, 1979, Maya recovery from volcanic disasters: Ilopango and Ceren. *Archaeology* 32(3):32–42.

Sidrys, Raymond V., and John M. Andresen, 1976, Metate import in Northern Belize. In *Maya lithic studies: papers from the 1976 Belize Field Symposium*, edited by T. R. Hester and N. Hammond, pp. 177–190. Center for Archaeological Research, University of Texas at San Antonio, Special Report No. 4.

——, 1978, A second round structure from Northern Belize, Central America. *Man* 13:638–650.

Smith, A. Ledyard, 1972, *Excavations at Altar de Sacrificios: architecture, settlement, burials, and caches*.

Papers of the Peabody Museum of Archaeology and Ethnology, Harvard University, Vol. 62(2).

Smith, A. Ledyard, and Alfred V. Kidder, 1951, *Excavations at Nebaj, Guatemala*. Carnegie Institution of Washington, Washington, D.C., Publication 594.

Smith, C. Earle, Jr., and Marguerita L. Cameron, 1977, Ethnobotany in the Puuc, Yucatan. *Economic Botany* 31:93–110.

Smith, Robert E., 1955, *Ceramic sequence at Uaxactun, Guatemala*. Middle American Research Institute, Tulane University, Publication 20.

Smith, Robert E., and James C. Gifford, 1966, Maya ceramic varieties, types, and wares at Uaxactun: supplement to "Ceramic sequence at Uaxactun, Guatemala." *Middle American Research Institute Publication* 28(3):125–174, Tulane University.

Spence, Michael, 1979, *Obsidian production and the state in Teotihuacan, Mexico*. Paper presented at the 44th Annual Meeting of the Society for American Archaeology, Vancouver, B.C.

Standley, Paul C., and Samuel J. Record, 1936, *The forests and flora of British Honduras*. Field Museum of Natural History, Chicago, Publication 350, Botanical Series Vol. 12.

Stark, Barbara, and Lynette Heller, 1981, Economia Preclasica en El Balsamo, Guatemala: ideas y evidencia. *Publicaciones del Centro de Investigaciones Regionales de Mesoamerica* 1:(2):189–219.

Stenholm, Nancy A., 1979, Identification of house structures in Mayan archaeology: a case study at Kaminaljuyu. In *Settlement pattern excavations at Kaminaljuyu, Guatemala*, edited by J. W. Michels, pp. 31–182. Pennsylvania State University Press, University Park, Pennsylvania.

Suarez Diez, Lourdes, 1977, *Tipologia de los objectos Prehispanicos de concha*. I.N.A.H. Coleccion Cientifica No. 54, Mexico, D.F.

Stuart, David, 1982, The iconography of blood in the symbolism of Maya rulership. Paper presented at the Princeton Conference on the Origins of Maya Iconography, Princeton University.

Terzuola, Robert, 1975, The greenstone. In *Jade workers in the Motagua Valley: the Late Classic Terzuola Site*, by L. Feldman, R. Terzuola, P. Sheets, and C. Cameron, pp. 5–7. Museum of Anthropology, University of Missouri, Columbia, Museum Brief No. 17.

Thomas, David H., 1969, Great basin hunting patterns: a quantitative method for treating faunal remains. *American Antiquity* 34:392–401.

Thompson, J. Eric, 1931, *Archaeological investigation in the Southern Cayo District, British Honduras*. Field Museum of Natural History, Publication 301, Anthropological Series Vol. 17(3).

———, 1938, Sixteenth and seventeenth century reports on the Chol Mayas. *American Anthropologist* 40:584–604.

———, 1939, *Excavations at San Jose, British Honduras*.

Carnegie Institution of Washington, Washington, D.C., Publication 506.

———, 1964, *Trade relations between the Maya Highlands and Lowlands. Estudios de Cultura Maya* 4:13–49.

Tourtellot, Gair, and Jeremy A. Sabloff, 1972, Exchange systems among the ancient Maya. *American Antiquity* 37:126–135.

Tozzer, Alfred M., 1907, *A comparative study of the Mayas and the Lacandones*. Macmillan, New York.

Tozzer, Alfred M. (editor), 1941, *Landa's Relacion de las Cosas de Yucatan: A Translation*. Papers of the Peabody Museum of Archaeology and Ethnology, Harvard University, Vol. 18.

Turner, B. L., II, 1983, The excavations of raised and channelized fields at Pulltrouser Swamp. In *Pulltrouser Swamp: ancient Maya habitat, agriculture, and settlement in Northern Belize*, edited by B. L. Turner II and Peter D. Harrison, pp. 30–51. University of Texas Press, Austin.

Turner, B. L., II, and Charles H. Miksicek, 1981, *Economic species associated with prehistoric agriculture in the Maya Lowlands*. Paper presented at the Symposium on History and Ecology of Crops and Cropping Systems in the Americas, 13th International Botanical Congress, Sydney, Australia.

Wauchope, Robert, 1938, *Modern Maya houses: a study of their archaeological significance*. Carnegie Institution of Washington, Washington, D.C., Publication 502.

Webb, Thompson, III, 1974, Corresponding patterns of pollen and vegetation in Lower Michigan: a comparison of quantitative data. *Ecology* 55:17–28.

Webb, Thompson, III, and D. R. Clark, 1977, Calibrating micropaleontological data in climatic terms: a critical review. *Annals of the New York Academy of Science* 288:93–118.

White, Theodore H., 1953, A method of calculating the dietary percentage of various food animals utilized by aboriginal peoples. *American Antiquity* 18:396–398.

Wilk, Richard, 1975, Superficial examination of Structure 100, Colha, 1975. In *Archaeology in Northern Belize: British Museum-Cambridge University Corozal Project 1974–75 Interim Report*, edited by N. Hammond, pp. 152–173. Centre of Latin American Studies, Cambridge University, Cambridge, England.

Wilkens, G. C., 1969, Drained-field agriculture: an intensive farming system in Tlaxcala, Mexico. *Geographical Review* 59:215–241.

Willey, Gordon R., 1972, *The artifacts of Altar de Sacrificios*. Papers of the Peabody Museum of Archaeology and Ethnology, Harvard University, Vol. 64(1).

———, 1978, *Excavations at Seibal, Department of Peten, Guatemala: Artifacts*. Memoirs of the Peabody Museum of Archaeology and Ethnology, Harvard University, Vol. 14(1).

Willey, Gordon R., William Bullard, Jr., John B. Glass, and

James C. Gifford, 1965, *Prehistoric Maya settlements in the Belize Valley*. Papers of the Peabody Museum of Archaeology and Ethnology, Harvard University, Vol. 54

Willey, Gordon R., T. Patrick Culbert, and Richard E. W. Adams (editors), 1967, Maya Lowland ceramics: a report from the 1965 Guatemala City Conference. *American Antiquity* 32:289–315.

Wing, Elizabeth S., 1981, A comparison of Olmec and Maya foodways. In *The Olmec and Their neighbors: essays in memory of Matthew W. Stirling*, edited by E. P. Benson, pp. 20–28. Dumbarton Oaks, Washington, D.C.

Woosley, Anne I., 1978, Pollen extraction for arid-land sediments. *Journal of Field Archaeology* 7:65–74.

Wright, A. C. S., D. H. Romney, R. H. Arbuckle, and V. E. Vial, 1959, *Land in British Honduras: report of the British Honduras land use Survey Team*. Her Majesty's Stationary Office, London.

Zier, Christian J., 1980, A Classical-Period Maya agricultural field in Western El Salvador. *Journal of Field Archaeology* 7:65–74.